PROCESS PLANNING AND COST ESTIMATION

PROCESS PLANNING AND COST ESTIMATION

SECOND EDITION

R. KESAVAN
Assistant Professor
Department of Production Technology
M.I.T. Campus, Anna University
Chennai

C. ELANCHEZHIAN
Assistant Professor
Department of Mechanical Engineering
Sri Sai Ram Engineering College
Chennai

B. VIJAYA RAMNATH
Senior Faculty
Department of Mechanical Engineering
Sri Sai Ram Engineering College
Chennai

Publishing Globally

NEW AGE INTERNATIONAL (P) LIMITED, PUBLISHERS

New Delhi • Bangalore • Chennai • Cochin • Guwahati
Hyderabad • Kolkata • Lucknow • Mumbai
Visit us at **www.newagepublishers.com**

Published by New Age International (P) Ltd., Publishers
First Edition: 2005
Second Edition: 2009
Reprint: 2015

BRANCHES

- **Bangalore** 37/10, 8th Cross (Near Hanuman Temple), Azad Nagar, Chamarajpet, Bangalore-560 018 Tel.: (080) 26756823, Telefax: 26756820, **E-mail: bangalore@newagepublishers.com**
- **Chennai** 26, Damodaran Street, T. Nagar, Chennai-600 017, Tel.: (044) 24353401 Telefax: 24351463, **E-mail: chennai@newagepublishers.com**
- **Cochin** CC-39/1016, Carrier Station Road, Ernakulam South, Cochin-682 016 Tel.: (0484) 2377303, Telefax: 4051303, **E-mail: cochin@newagepublishers.com**
- **Guwahati** Hemsen Complex, Mohd. Shah Road, Paltan Bazar, Near Starline Hotel, Guwahati-781 008 Tel.: (0361) 2513881, Telefax: 2543669, **E-mail: guwahati@newagepublishers.com**
- **Hyderabad** 105, 1st Floor, Madhiray Kaveri Tower, 3-2-19, Azam Jahi Road, Near Kumar Theater Nimboliadda, Kachiguda, Hyderabad-500 027, Tel.: (040) 24652456, Telefax: 24652457 **E-mail: hyderabad@newagepublishers.com**
- **Kolkata** RDB Chambers (Formerly Lotus Cinema) 106A, 1st Floor, S.N. Banerjee Road, Kolkata-700 014 Tel.: (033) 22273773, Telefax: 22275247, **E-mail: kolkata@newagepublishers.com**
- **Lucknow** 16-A, Jopling Road, Lucknow-226 001, Tel.: (0522) 2209578, 4045297, Telefax: 2204098 **E-mail:lucknow@newagepublishers.com**
- **Mumbai** 142C, Victor House, Ground Floor, N.M. Joshi Marg, Lower Parel, Mumbai-400 013 Tel.: (022) 24927869, Telefax: 24915415, **E-mail: mumbai@newagepublishers.com**
- **New Delhi** 22, Golden House, Daryaganj, New Delhi-110 002, Tel.: (011) 23262368, 23262370 Telefax: 43551305, **E-mail: sales@newagepublishers.com**

ISBN: 978-81-224-2605-2

M R P: ₹ 199.00
(No Tax on books)

C-15-07-8598

Printed in India at Kanishik Printing Press, Delhi.
Typeset at In-house, Delhi.

PUBLISHING GLOBALLY
NEW AGE INTERNATIONAL (P) LIMITED, PUBLISHERS
7/30 A, Daryaganj, New Delhi-110002
Visit us at **www.newagepublishers.com**

Dedicated to Our

Beloved Parents

and

Future Engineers

FOREWORD

The book on **"PROCESS PLANNING AND COST ESTIMATION"** by Dr. R. Kesavan et al. is a good attempt towards making a textbook for the students of Engineering and Technology. The book is written in five chapters in simple language, which will help the students immensely. The authors have taken pains in explaining in detail the concepts and the nuances of Cost Estimation and the steps involved in Process Planning. A number of illustrations make the book eminently readable.

I congratulate the authors for attempting to write a book on such an important subject.

S. NATARAJAN
Professor and Head
Department of Mechanical Engineering
College of Engineering, Guindy
Anna University, Chennai - 600 025.

PREFACE TO THE SECOND EDITION

This edition of "Process Planning and Cost Estimation" is based on the latest syllabus of B.E., B.Tech.— Mechanical, Production, Metallurgy and Industrial Engineering courses of Anna University as well as other Universities. It is also a valuable asset for entrepreneurs, training managers of various mechanical workshops and diploma students.

Valuable suggestions and constructive criticism from number of colleagues at various institutions and the feedback from the students as well as our friends motivate us to write this second edition.

The second edition of this book has been presented in a simple and systematic way with numerous diagrams and number of solved problems and review questions. This edition provides all necessary information about process planning and cost estimation for various products, work study, ergonomics and production cost estimation.

We are grateful to our management for their continuous support in bringing out this book successfully. Suggestions for improvement are most welcomed and would be incorporated in the next edition to make this book more useful.

Dr. R. KESAVAN
C. ELANCHEZHIAN
B. VIJAYA RAMNATH

PREFACE TO THE FIRST EDITION

This edition of "Process Planning and Cost Estimation" is based on the latest syllabus of B.E., B.Tech.— Mechanical and Production Engineering for Anna University as well as other Universities. It is a valuable asset for entrepreneurs, training managers of various mechanical workshops, and diploma students.

This book is an attempt to provide all necessary information about process planning and cost estimation. The subject matter has been presented in a simple and systematic way with numerous diagrams and illustrations so as to make thorough understanding of the topics.

We have put our best efforts to provide solved problems and excellent exercise problems at the end of each chapter. Various complex topics have been discussed pointwise and supported by practical example problems wherever possible. To apprise the student about expected type of questions which can be asked in the examinations, important review questions have been provided at the end of each chapter.

We thank the publishers who have come forward to publish this book.

Suggestions for improvement of this book are welcomed and would be incorporated in the next edition to make it more useful.

Dr. R. KESAVAN
C. ELANCHEZHIAN
B. VIJAYA RAMNATH

SYLLABUS

ME1007 PROCESS PLANNING AND COST ESTIMATION

(Common to Mechanical, Metallurgy and Production-core)

1. Work Study and Ergonomics

Method study – Definition – Objectives – Motion economy – Principles – Tools and techniques – Applications – Work measurements – Purpose – Use – Procedure – Tools and techniques – Standard time – Ergonomics – Principles – Applications.

2. Process Planning

Definition – Objective – Scope – Approaches to process planning – Process planning activities – Finished part requirements – Operating sequences – Machine selection – Material selection parameters – Set of documents for process planning – Developing manufacturing logic and knowledge – Production time calculation – Selection of cost optimal process.

3. Introduction to Cost Estimation

Objective of cost estimation – Costing – Cost accounting – Classification of cost – Elements of cost.

4. Cost Estimation

Types of estimates – Methods of estimates – Data requirements and sources – Collection of cost– Allowances in estimation.

5. Production Cost Estimation

Estimation of material cost, Labour cost and overheads, Allocation of overheads – Estimation for different types of jobs.

CONTENTS

UNIT–2 PROCESS PLANNING 35–76

Unit–1

WORK STUDY

1.0 WORK STUDY

The main problem in our country is poor standard of living of most of our population. More than 70% of our people live in very poor living conditions. They are not in a position to satisfy their basic needs like food, cloth and shelter.

If we want to raise the standard of living of our people we must produce goods at a lesser cost. This can be done only by increasing the efficiency of production. Efficiency in production is known as productivity. There are many techniques used for increasing productivity. Work study is one of the technique for improving productivity and hence raise the standard of living.

Definition: Work study is a generic term for the techniques of method study and work measurement. These techniques are used in the examination of human work in all its contexts. They lead systematically to the investigation of all the factors which affect the efficiency and economy at the work place in order to affect improvement.

Work study was previously known as time and motion study. This was developed by F.W.Taylor and Frank B.Gilberth.

1.1 IMPROVING PLANT LAYOUT

Work study consists of method study and work measurement. Work study is considered as an important tool in increasing productivity because of the following reasons.

1. By method study,
   Working condition is improved.
   Work content is reduced.
   Worker's efficiency is increased.
   Plant layout is improved.
2. By work measurement,
   Ineffective time is reduced.
   Production time is standardized.
   It helps in planning and controlling.

Work study can be applied to any field of activity. The increase in productivity can be achieved immediately. It needs very less investment. Work study finds out the defects in the organization. Work study is always the first technique applied for increasing productivity.

Hence, work study is considered as a valuable tool in increasing productivity.

1.2 IMPORTANCE OF WORKING CONDITIONS

Working conditions mean the physical conditions and facilities available in the working place. They are

1. Lighting and ventilation.
2. Temperature and humidity.
3. Safety and healthy.
4. Layout and house keeping.
5. Noise and vibration.
6. Ergonomics.

Bad working conditions will affect the performance of the workers. The worker will not be able to work efficiently. So, production is affected. Workers will not be regular in their duty. Because of the bad working conditions, the workers may even resign their job. If work study is done in bad working condition, it will give inaccurate results. Only in good working conditions, the workers will give their normal performance. The different working conditions are explained here.

1. Lighting and Ventilation

Lighting: For doing any work, proper lighting is essential. Proper lighting will lead to the increased production and hence increased productivity. Improper lighting will cause headache, visual fatigue and avoidable accidents.

Level of lighting required will depend upon the type of works viz., casual work, rough work, fine work, inspection work etc. As a general rule, lighting should be uniformly spread. Natural light should be used wherever possible. Artificial light should add to natural light to give uniform light. Glare should be avoided. Fluorescent light with anti-glare fitting is ideal for industrial applications.

Ventilation: Ventilation means free and fresh supply of air. Insufficient air circulation will affect the health of workers. It leads to fatigue of workers. It reduces productivity. Therefore, good ventilation must be provided. Recommended minimum air flow is 50 cubic metres per hour. Fumes, smokes and dusts should be driven out using exhaust fans. Main function of ventilation are

Dispersal of atmospheric contaminations.

Dispersal of heat generated by men and machines.

Maintaining correct level or oxygen, carbon dioxide and carbon monoxide.

2. Temperature and Humidity

High temperature and humidity in the shop floor will cause fatigue to workers. In deep mines, textile mills and sugar mills, ventilation will be poor and relative humidity will be high. So working condition will be very poor. Humidity must be controlled by proper means. More rest during work must be provided.

Similarly, workers working at low temperature must be provided with suitable clothing and footwear. They must be given periodic exposure to normal temperature. They must be provided with not drinks at regular intervals. The air temperature normally recommended is 20° to 22°C for light physical work and 14° to 16°C heavy work in standing position.

3. Safety and Health

Safety of workers in the work place is very important. Management must provide safe environment to the workers and prevent occurrence of accidents. Only when the workers feel that they are in an accident free environment, they can give maximum output.

Safe workplace layout should be provided with safe material handling methods. Personal protective devices for protecting head, face, eyes, lungs and other body parts like hand, foot and legs should be provided.

Clean workplace with healthy environment must be provided to protect workers against infection and occupational diseases.

4. Layout and Housekeeping

Good workplace layout and housekeeping play important roles in providing better working condition. Workplace should have

1. Sufficient window area—at least 20% of floor area.
2. Ceiling height should be at least 3 metres.
3. Every workers should be provided with at least 10 cubic metres of air and a free floor area of 2 square metres.
4. Traffic aisles should be wide enough to allow free movement of material handling equipment and workers.
5. Floor should be non-slip, non-dust forming and easy to clean.

A good house keeping should be ensured in the plant. There should be a place reserved for every material and every material should be stored in its place. Tools and other production aids must be stored systematically in their own locations. In process materials should be kept in such a way that they do not obstruct the free movement of men and material.

5. Noise and Vibration

Noise: Noise is defined as unwanted sound to which an individual is exposed. In industries, almost all machines generate noise and this must be reduced to the lowest level. The effects of noise are

1. Disturbs concentration and causes annoyance.
2. Interferes with speech communication.
3. Causes hearing losses to workers.
4. Increases fatigue and blood pressure.

Exposure to continuous noise above 90 dB is dangerous for hearing. Noise level can be controlled in the following ways:

1. Replacing noisy machine and equipment.
2. Dynamically balancing rotating parts.
3. Using rubber and plastic components wherever possible.
4. Separating the noise sources with brick walls.
5. Using ear plugs and protecting the ears.

Vibration: Vibration is created by

1. Rotating components.

2. Machines during hand grinding.
3. When using pneumatic chipping and riveting hammers.

When one's body is in contact with vibration source continuously, it may lead to

1. Loss of sense of touch and temperature in fingers.
2. Muscular weakness.
3. Loss of mental alertness.
4. Pain and stiffness in joints.

Vibrations can be controlled by the following means.

1. Control at source by balancing all revolving parts.
2. Reducing speed of rotating parts.
3. Maintaining machineries and tools regularly.
4. Protecting the workers by minimizing the exposure and providing rest breaks.

6. Ergonomics

Ergonomics can be defined as human engineering which studies the relationship between man and his working environment. Ergonomic process attempts to fit the job to the worker. It aims at

1. Designing the workplace to fit the requirement of the worker.
2. Designing the equipment, machines and controls to minimize physical and mental strain to the workers.
3. Providing a favourable environment for working.

The workplace should be designed for the use of the specific worker whose dimensions are known. It may be designed to suit a group of persons. It can be adjusted to suit the individuals.

Workplace layout, design of seat and arrangement of different equipment should not cause discomfort to workers. Proper foot rest, arm rest and leg room must be provided. Design and location of various manual controls, knobs, wheels and levers should not cause excessive strain to workers.

1.3 METHOD STUDY

Method study is the technique of systematic recording and critical examination of existing and proposed ways of doing work and developing an easier and economical method.

1.3.1 Objectives of Method Study

1. Improvement of manufacturing processes and procedures.
2. Improvement of working conditions.
3. Improvement of plant layout and work place layout.
4. Reducing the human effort and fatigue.
5. Reducing material handling
6. Improvement of plant and equipment design.
7. Improvement in the utility of material, machines and manpower.
8. Standardisation of method.
9. Improvement in safety standard.

1.4 BASIC PROCEDURE FOR METHOD STUDY

The basic procedure for conducting method study is as follows:

1. Select the work to be studied.

2. Record all facts about the method by direct observation.
3. Examine the above facts critically.
4. Develop the most efficient and economic method.
5. Define the new method.
6. Install the new method
7. Maintain the new method by regular checking.

1. Select

While selecting a job for doing method study, the following factors are considered:

(a) Economical factors.
(b) Human factors.
(c) Technical factors.

(a) Economical Factors

The money saved as a result of method study should be sufficiently more. Then only the study will be worthwhile. Based on the economical factors, generally the following jobs are selected.

(a) Operations having bottlenecks (which holds up other production activities).
(b) Operations done repetitively.
(c) Operations having a great amount of manual work.
(d) Operations where materials are moved for a long distance.

(b) Human Factors

The method study will be successful only with the co-operation of all people concerned *viz.,* workers, supervisor, trade unions etc.

Workers may resist method study due to

1. The fear of unemployment.
2. The fear of reduction in wages.
3. The fear of increased work load.

The supervisors may resist because of the feeling that their prestige may be lost.

So, the workers and supervisors must be educated about the benefits of method study. Even then if they do not accept method study, the study should be postponed.

(c) Technical Factors

To improve the method of work all the technical details about the job should be available. Every machine tool will have its own capacity. Beyond this, it cannot be improved. For example, a work study man feels that speed of the machine tool may be increased and HSS tool may be used. But the capacity of the machine may not permit increased speed. In this case, the suggestion of the work study man cannot be implemented. These types of technical factors should be considered.

2. Record

All the details about the existing method are recorded. This is done by directly observing the work. Symbols are used to represent the activities like operation, inspection, transport, storage and delay.

Different charts and diagrams are used in recording. They are:

Sl. No.	Type of chart	Purpose
1.	Operation process chart	All the operations and inspections are recorded.
2.	Flow process chart	
	(a) Man type	All the activities of man are recorded
	(b) Material type	All the activities of the material are recorded
	(c) Equipment type	All the activities of equipment or machine are recorded.
3.	Two-handed process chart or Right hand-Left hand chart	Motions of both lands of worker are recorded independently.
4.	Multiple activity chart	Activities of a group of workers doing a single job or the activities of a single worker operating a number of machines are recorded.
5.	Flow diagram	This is drawn to suitable scale. Path of flow of material in the shop is recorded.
6.	String diagram	The movements of workers are recorded using a string in a diagram drawn to scale.

Note: The different charts and diagrams are explained in detail at the end of this chapter.

3. Examine

Critical examination is done by questioning technique. This step comes after the method is recorded by suitable charts and diagrams.

The individual activity is examined by putting a number of questions.

The following factors are questioned

1. Purpose – To eliminate the activity, if possible.
2. Place – To combine or re-arrange the activities.
3. Sequence – -do-
4. Person – -do-
5. Means – To simplify the activity.

The following sequence of questions is used:

1. Purpose – What is actually done?
   Why is it done?
   What else could be done?
   What should be done?
2. Place – Where is it being done?
   Why is it done there?
   Where else could it be done?
   Where should it be done?
3. Sequence – When is it done?
   Why is it done then?
   When could it be done?
   When should it be done?
4. Person – Who is doing it?

Why does that person do it?
Who else could do it?
Who should do it?

5. Means – How is it done?
Why is it done that way?
How else could it be done?
How should it be done?

By doing this questioning unwanted activities can be eliminated. A number of activities can be combined or re-arranged. The method can be simplified. All these will reduce production time.

4. Develop

The answer to the questions given below will result in the development of a better method.

1. Purpose – What should be done?
2. Place – Where should it be done?
3. Sequence – When should it be done?
4. Person – Who should do it?
5. Means – How should it be done?

Development of a better method is explained in the following example.

In sending letters to the customers it was found that the address of the customer was typed twice. The address was typed in the letter and also over the cover. By the questioning technique, typing on the cover was eliminated. A window cover was devised and used.

5. Define

Once a complete study of a job has been made and a new method is developed, it is necessary to obtain the approval of the management before installing it. The work study man should prepare a report giving details of the existing and proposed methods. He should give his reasons for the changes suggested. The report should show

(a) Brief description of the old method.
(b) Brief description of the new method.
(c) Reasons for change.
(d) Advantages and limitations of the new method.
(e) Savings expected in material, labour and overheads.
(f) Tools and equipment required for the new method.
(g) The cost of installing the new method including.

1. Cost of new tools and equipment.
2. Cost of re-layout of the shop.
3. Cost of training the workers in the new method.
4. Cost of improving the working conditions.

Written standard practice: Before installing the new method, an operator's instructions sheet called written standard practice is prepared. It serves the following purposes:

1. It records the improved method for future reference in as much detail as may be necessary.
2. It is used to explain the new method to the management foreman and operators.
3. It gives the details of changes required in the layout of machine and work places.
4. It is used as an aid to training or retraining operators.
5. It forms the basis for time studies.

The written standard practice will contain the following information:

(*a*) Tools and equipment to be used in the new method.
(*b*) General operating conditions.
(*c*) Description of the new method in detail.
(*d*) Diagram of the workplace layout and sketches of special tools, jigs or fixtures required.

6. Install

This step is the most difficult stage in method study. Here the active support of both management and trade union is required. Here the work study man requires skill in getting along with other people and winning their trust. Instal stage consists of

(*a*) Gaining acceptance of the change by supervisor.
(*b*) Getting approval of management.
(*c*) Gaining the acceptance of change by workers and trade unions.
(*d*) Giving training to operators in the new method.
(*e*) To be in close contact with the progress of the job until it is satisfactorily executed.

Rearrangement of layout etc: The machines are rearranged as per the layout suggested in the new method. New tools and devices are introduced as per the new method. The working conditions like lighting, ventilation etc. are improved as required in the new method.

Training of workers and rehearsal: The workers are given training in the new method; i.e., in the new tools and devices. The trial run (rehearsal) of the new method is done. This is done to check the success of the new method. If there is any problem, modifications are made. Meeting with the supervisor is held daily to discuss the progress.

7. Maintain

The work study man must see that the new method introduced is followed. The workers after sometime may slip back to the old methods. This should not be allowed. The new method may have defects. There may be difficulties also. This should be rectified in time by the work study man.

Periodical review is made. The reactions and suggestions from workers and supervisors are noted. This may lead to further improvement. The differences between the new written standard practice and the actual practice are found out. Reasons for variations are analysed. Changes due to valid reasons are accepted. The instructions are suitably modified.

1.5 CHARTS AND DIAGRAMS USED IN METHOD STUDY (TOOLS AND TECHNIQUES)

As explained earlier, the following charts and diagrams are used in method study.

1. Operation process chart (or) Outline process chart.
2. Flow process chart.
   (*a*) Material type
   (*b*) Operator type
   (*c*) Equipment type
3. Two-handed process chart. (or) Left hand-Right hand chart
4. Multiple activity chart.
5. Flow diagram.
6. String diagram.

1.5.1 Process Chart Symbols

The recording of the facts about the job in a process chart is done by using standard symbols. Using of symbols in recording the activities is much easier than writing down the facts about the job. Symbols are very convenient and widely understood type of short hand. They save a lot of writing and indicate clearly what is happening.

1. Operation

A large circle indicates operation. An operation takes place when there is a change in physical or chemical characteristics of an object. An assembly or disassembly is also an operation.

When information is given or received or when planning or calculating takes place it is also called operation.

Example 1.1

Reducing the diameter of an object in a lathe. Hardening the surface of an object by heat treatment.

2. Inspection

A square indicates inspection. Inspection is checking an object for its quality, quantity or identifications.

Example 1.2

Checking the diameter of a rod. Counting the number of products produced.

3. Transport

An arrow indicates transport. This refers to the movement of an object or operator or equipment from one place to another. When the movement takes place during an operation, it is not called transport.

Example 1.3

Moving the material by a trolley
Operator going to the stores to get some tool.

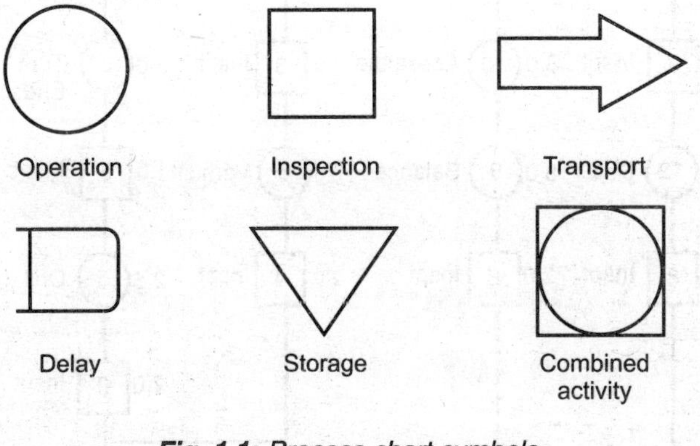

Fig. 1.1: Process chart symbols

4. Delay or temporary storage

A large capital letter D indicates delay. This is also called as temporary storage. Delay occurs when an object or operator is waiting for the next activity.

Example 1.4

An operator waiting to get a tool in the stores. Work pieces stocked near the machine before the next operation.

5. Permanent storage

An equilateral triangle standing on its vertex represents storage. Storage takes place when an object is stored and protected against unauthorized removal.

Example 1.5

Raw material in the store room.

6. Combined activity

When two activities take place at the same time or done by the same operator or at the same place, the two symbols of activities are combined.

Example 1.6

Reading and recording a pressure gauge. Here a circle inside a square represents the combined activity of operation and inspection.

1.5.2 Operation Process Chart

An operation process chart is a graphic representation of the sequence of all operations and inspections taking place in a process. It is also known as outline process chart. It gives a bird's eye view of the overall activities. Entry points of all material are noted in the chart.

An example of operation process chart is shown in the figure 1.2. Here the process of manufacture of electric motor is shown.

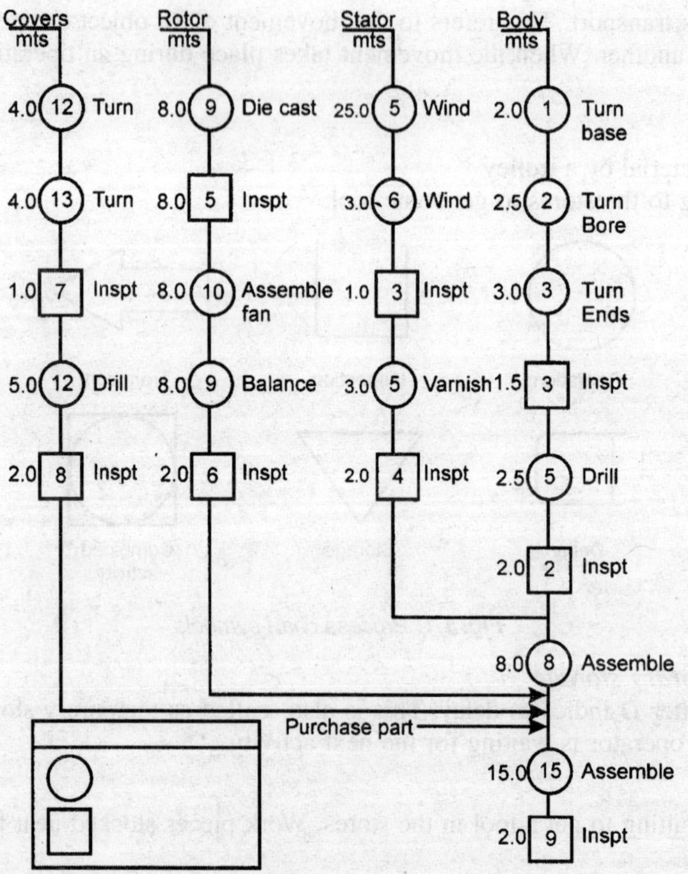

Fig. 1.2: Operation process chart

The conventions followed in preparing the chart are

1. Write title at the top of the chart.
2. Begin the chart from the right hand side top corner.
3. Represent the main component at the right extreme.
4. Represent the sequence of operations and inspections by their symbols. Connect them by vertical flow lines.
5. Record the brief description of the activity to the right side of the symbols.
6. Note down the time for each activity to the left of the symbol.
7. Number all operations in one serial order. Start from the right hand top (from number 1).
8. Similarly number all inspections in another serial order (starting from 1).
9. Continue numbering, till the entry of the second component.
10. Show the entry of purchased parts by horizontal lines.

1.5.3 Flow Process Chart

A flow process chart is a graphical representation of the sequence of all the activities (operation, inspection, transport, delay and storage) taking place in a process. Process chart symbols are used here to represent the activities. There are three types of flow process charts. They are

1. Man type flow process chart

This flow process chart records what the worker does.

2. Material type flow process chart

This flow process chart records how the material is handled or treated.

3. Equipment type flow process chart

This flow process chart records how the equipment or machine is used.

Example 1.7

The activities of a stenographer in preparation of a letter are recorded in the operator type flow process chart shown in figure 1.3.

Chart No.	: 001	Date :	
Job	: Typing A letter	Charted by:	....
Chart begins	: Steno in her seat	Chart ends-putting the typed letter in the way	
Method	: Present/Proposed		

Sl. No.	*Description of the activities*	*Distance*	*Time in Sec.*	*Symbols*	*Remarks*
				O □ ⇒ D ∇	
1.	Steno in her seat	-	-		
2.	Hears the bell	-	3		
3.	Goes to manager's room	6m	10		
4.	Takes down dictation	-	120		
5.	Returns to her seat	6m	10		
6.	Prepares typewriter	-	15		
7.	Types the letter	-	150		
8.	Checks the matter	-	40		
9.	Goes to manager's room	6m	10		
10.	Waits till the manager signs	-	20		
11.	Returns to her seat	6m	10		
12.	Types envelope	-	20		
13.	Puts the letter inside envelope	-	5		
14.	Puts the envelope in dispatch tray	-	5		

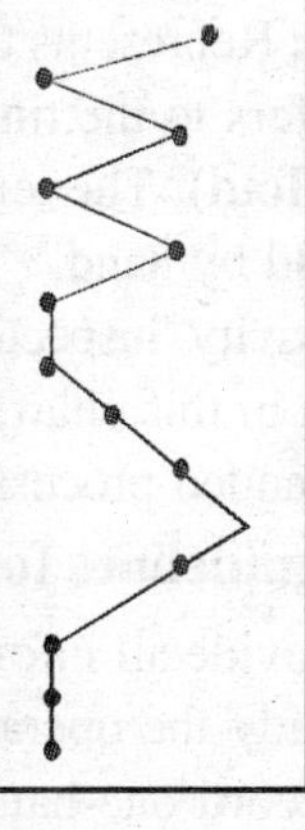

Fig. 1.3: Flow process chart—operator type

The chart records the activities of the steno. Here, the manager calls the steno and dictates a letter. The steno takes notes of the letter, types it, gets the signature of the manager and sends it for dispatching. These activities are shown in the chart. This is operator type flow process chart.

Considering the message in the letter as material, we can prepare the material type flow process chart.

Similarly, considering the type writer as the equipment, we can prepare the equipment type flow process chart.

General guidelines for making a flow process chart

1. The details must be obtained by direct observation—charts must not be based on memory.
2. All the facts must be correctly recorded.
3. No assumptions should be made.
4. Make it easy for future reference.
5. All charts must have the following details:
   (a) Name of the product, material or equipment that is observed.
   (b) Starting point and ending point.
   (c) The location where the activities take place.
   (d) The chart reference number, sheet number and number of total sheets.
   (e) Key to the symbols used must be stated.

1.5.4 Two-Handed Process Chart (or) Right Hand, Left Hand Chart

It is the process chart in which the activities of two hands of the operator are recorded.

It shows whether the two hands of the operator are idle or moving in relation to one another, in a timescale. That is, we know from the chart what the two hands are doing at any given moment of time.

The two-handed process chart is generally used for repetitive operations. Here one complete cycle of work activities is recorded. Recording is done in more detail than ordinary flow process chart. What is shown as a single activity in a flow process chart is broken into small elemental activities and recorded.

Two-handed process chart generally use the same symbols as other process charts. But the definitions of symbols are slightly different. This is because we record the activities of hands only.

Operation: Represents the activities grasp, position, use, release etc. of a tool, component or material.

Transport: Represents the movement of the hand or limb to or from the work or a tool or material.

Delay: Refers to the time when the hand or limb is idle.

Storage (Hold): The term 'hold' is used here instead of storage. This refers to the time when the work is held by hand.

The activity 'inspection' by hand is considered as an operation. Hence, the symbol for inspection is not used in this chart.

Two-handed process chart can be used for assembly, machining and clerical jobs.

General guidelines for preparing the chart

1. Provide all information about the job in the chart.
2. Study the operation cycle a few times before starting to record.
3. Record one hand at a time.

4. First record the activities of the hand which starts the work first.
5. Do not combine the different activities like operations, transport etc.

Example 1.8

Example of a two-handed process chart is shown in figure 1.4. Here the assembly of a nut and washer over a bolt is recorded.

The work place layout is shown in the right hand corner. The activities of left hand are recorded at left half of the chart. The activities of the right hand are recorded at the right half of the chart.

Job : Assembly of washer and nut to a bolt
Chart begins : Both hands free before assembly
Chart ends : Both hands free after assembly
Chart : Existing method/Proposed method
Operator :

Assembly Bolt Washer Nut
Date : Operator
Chart No :

Left hand			Right hand		
Sl. No.	*Description of the activities*	*Symbols* O ⇒ ∇	*Sl. No.*	*Description of the activities*	*Symbols* O ⇒ ∇
1.	To the bolt tray		1.	To the washer tray	
2.	Picks up one bolt		2.	Picks up one washer	
3.	Returns to original position		3.	Returns to the initial position	
4.	Holding the bolt		4.	Assembles washer over bolt	
5.	Idle		5.	To the nut tray	
6.	Idle		6.	Picks up one nut	
7.	Idle		7.	Returns to initial position	
8.	Idle		8.	Assemble nut to the bolt	
9.	To the assembly tray		9.	Idle	
10.	Puts the bolt in the tray		10.	Idle	
11.	Returns to the original position		11.	Idle	

Fig. 1.4: Two-handed process chart

The horizontal lines represent the time scale. Activities of left hand and right hand shown in the same line occur at the same moment.

Summary of the number of each activity can be tabulated at the bottom of the chart.

The chart is first drawn for the existing method. This chart is analysed and if it is found that one hand is over loaded than the other, modification are done in the layout of the workplace or in the sequence of activities. Then a new chart is made for the proposed cycle.

1.5.5 Man-Machine Chart

A man-machine chart is a chart in which the activities of more than one worker or machine are recorded. Activities are recorded on a common time scale to show the inter-relationship. It is also known as multiple activity chart.

It is used when a worker operates a number of machines at a time. It is also used when a number of workers jointly do a job.

Activities of workers or machines are recorded in separate vertical columns (bars) with a horizontal time scale. The chart shows the idle time of the worker or machine during the process.

By carefully analyzing the chart, we can rearrange the activities. Work load is evenly distributed among the workers or machines by this the idle time of worker or machine is reduced.

Multiple activity chart is very useful in planning team work in production or maintenance. Using the chart we can find out the correct number of machines that a worker can operate at a time. We can also find out the exact number of workers needed to do a job jointly.

To record the time, ordinary wrist watch or stop watch is used. High accuracy is not needed.

Man-machine chart is a type of multiple activity chart. Here, the activities of a number of machines are recorded.

An example of man-machine chart is shown in figure 1.5. Here one operator two semi-automatic machines simultaneously. The activities of the operator is recorded in a separate vertical column. The activities of the two machines are recorded in two separate vertical columns. The different activities like loading, machining and unloading are represented by different symbols. Blank space shows the idle time.

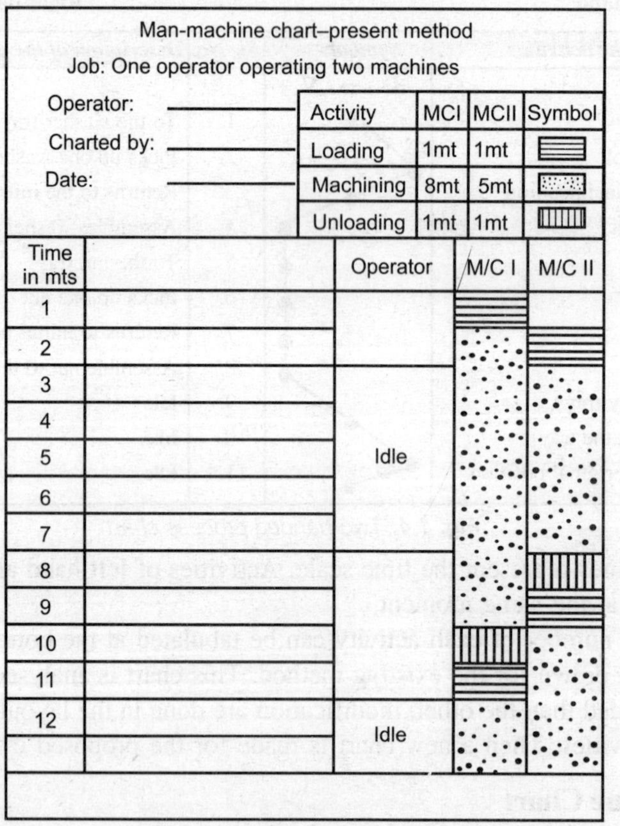

Fig. 1.5: Man-machine chart

1.5.6 Flow Diagram

In any production shop, repair shop or any other department, there are movements of men and material from one place to another. Process charts indicate the sequence of activities. They do not show the frequent movements of men and material. If these movement are minimized, a lot of savings can be achieved in cost and effort. If the path of movement of material is not frequent and simple, a flow diagram is used for recording the movement.

A flow diagram is a diagram which is drawn to scale. The relative position of machineries, gang ways, material handling equipment etc. are drawn first. Then the path followed by men or material is marked on the diagram. Different movements can be marked in different colours. Process symbols are added to the diagram to identify the different activities at different work centres.

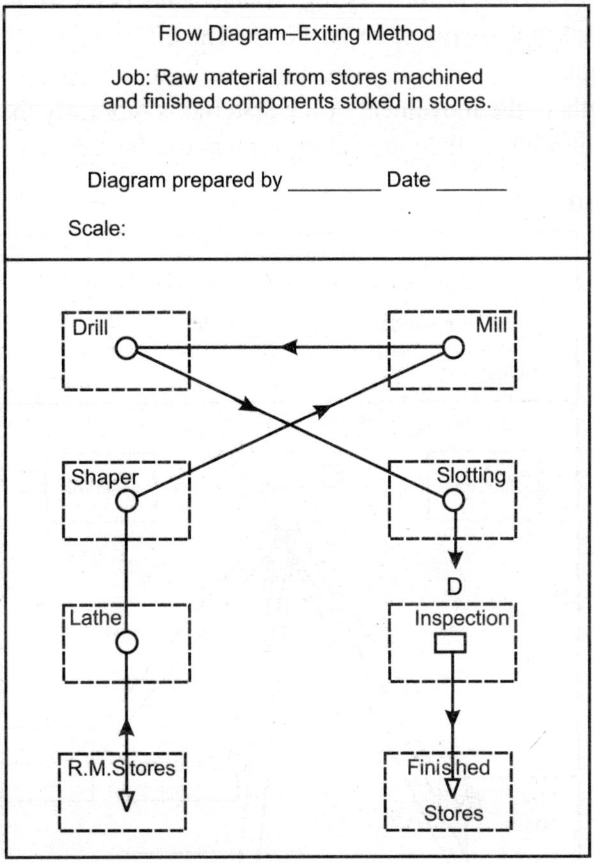

Fig. 1.6: Flow diagram

The flow diagram are used for the following purposes:

1. To remove unwanted material movement.
2. To remove back tracking.
3. To avoid traffic congestion.
4. To improve the plant layout.

Conventions adopted are

1. Heading and description of the process should be given at the top of the diagram.
2. Other informations like location, name of the shop, name of the person drawing the diagram are also given.

3. The path followed by the material is shown by a flow line.
4. Direction of movement is shown by small arrows along the flow lines.
5. The different activities are represented by the symbols on the flow lines. (Same symbols used in flow process chart are used here).
6. If more than one product is to be shown in the diagram different colours are used for each path.

Examples of a flow diagram of the existing arrangements is shown in the figure 1.6. The path of movement of material in the work floor is shown. The different activities done on the material are shown using symbols.

In this existing method, the movement of the material is more. By interchanging the positions of drilling and milling machines, the material movement can be reduced.

1.5.7 String Diagram

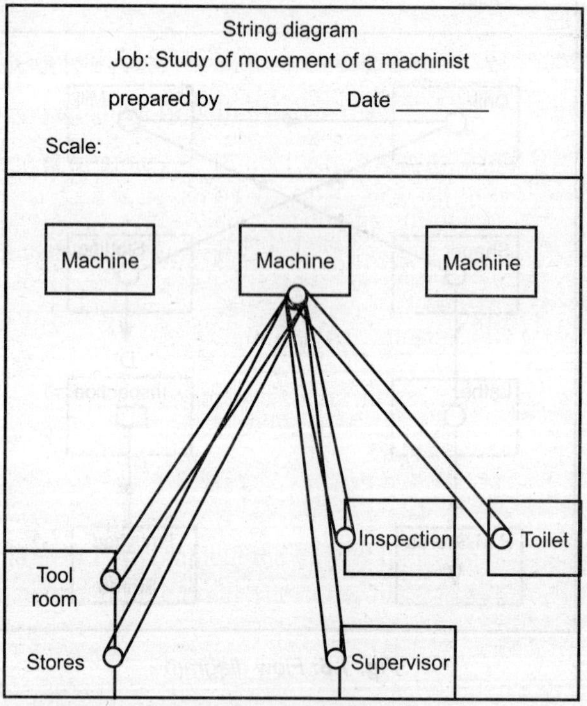

Fig. 1.7: String diagram

We make use of flow diagram for recording the movement of men or material when the movement is simple and the path is almost fixed. But when the paths are many and are repetitive, it may not be possible to record them in a flow diagram. Here a string diagram is used.

String diagram is a scaled plan of the shop. Location of machines and various facilities are drawn to scale in a drawing sheet. Pins are fixed at the various work centres in the drawing sheet. A continuous coloured thread or string is taken round the pins where the material or worker moves during the process.

Constructions

1. Draw the layout of the shop to scale in a drawing sheet.

2. Mark the various work centres like machines, stores, work bench etc. in the diagram.
3. Hold the drawing sheet on a soft board and fix pins at the work centres.
4. Tie one end of a coloured string to the work centre from which the movement starts.
5. Follow the path of the worker to different work centre and accordingly take the thread to different points on the drawing board.
6. At the end of the session note down the number of movements from one work centre to another.
7. Remove the string and measure the total length of the string. Multiply by the scale and get the actual distance of movement.

Applications

1. It is used for recording the complex movements of material or men.
2. Back tracking, congestion, bottlenecks, under utilized paths are easily found out.
3. It is used to check whether the work station is correctly located.
4. Used to record irregular movements.
5. Used to find out the most economical route.

1.6 WORK MEASUREMENT

Work measurement is a technique to establish the time required for a qualified worker to carry out a specified job at a defined level of performance.

Objectives of work measurement

1. To reduce or eliminate non-productive time.
2. To fix the standard time for doing a job.
3. To develop standard data for future reference.
4. To improve methods.

Uses of work measurements

1. To compare the efficiency of alternate methods. When two or more methods are available for doing the same job, the time for each method is found out by work measurement. The method which takes minimum time is selected.
2. Standard time is used as a basis for wage incentive schemes.
3. It helps for the estimation of cost. Knowing the time standards, it is possible to work out the cost of the product. This helps to quote rates for tenders.
4. It helps to plan the workload of man and machine.
5. It helps to determine the requirement of men and machine. When we know the time to produce one piece and also the quantity to be produced, it is easy to calculate the total requirement of men and machines.
6. It helps in better production control. Time standards help accurate scheduling. So the production control can be done efficiently.
7. It helps to control the cost of production. With the help of time standards, the cost of production can be worked out. This cost is used as a basis for control.
8. It helps to fix the delivery date to the customer. By knowing the standard time we will be able to calculate the time required for manufacturing the required quantity of products.

1.7 TECHNIQUES OF WORK MEASUREMENT

The different techniques used in work measurement are

1. Stop watch time study.
2. Production study.
3. Work sampling or Ratio delay study.
4. Synthesis from standard data.
5. Analytical estimating.
6. Predetermined motion time system.

1.7.1 Stop Watch Time Study

Stop watch time study is one of the techniques of work measurement commonly used. Here we make use of a stop watch for measuring the time.

Procedure for conducting stop watch time study

The following procedure is followed in conducting stop watch time study:

1. Selecting the job.
2. Recording the specifications.
3. Breaking operation into elements.
4. Examining each element.
5. Measuring using stop watch.
6. Assessing the rating factor.
7. Calculating the basic time.
8. Determining the allowances.
9. Compiling the standard time.

1. Selection of job

Time study is always done after method study. Under the following situations, a job is selected for time study:

1. A new job, new component or a new operation.
2. When new time standard is required.
3. To check the correctness of the existing time standard.
4. When the cost of operation is found to be high.
5. Before introducing an incentive scheme.
6. When two methods are to be compared.

2. Record

The following informations are recorded

1. About the product-name, product-number, specification.
2. About the machine, equipment and tools.
3. About the working condition-temperature-humidity-lighting etc. These informations are used when deciding about the allowances.
4. About the operator name-experience-age etc. This is needed for rating the operator.

3. Break down operation into elements

Each operation is divided into a number of elements. This is done for easy observation and accurate measurement. The elements are grouped as constant element, variable element, occasional element, man element, machine element etc.

4. *Examine each element*

The elements are examined to find out whether they are effective or wasteful. Elements are also examined whether they are done in the correct method.

5. *Measure using a stop watch*

The time taken for each element is measured using a stop watch. There are two methods of measuring. *viz.*, Fly back method and Cumulative method. Cumulative method is preferable.

The time measured from the stop watch is known as observed time. Time for various groups of elements should be recorded separately.

This measurement has to be done for a number of times. The number of observations depend upon the type of operation, the accuracy required and time for one cycle.

6. *Assess the rating factor*

Rating is the measure of efficiency of a worker. The operator's rating is found out by comparing his speed of work with standard performance. The rating of an operator is decided by the work study man in consultation with the supervisor. The standard rating is taken as 100. If the operator is found to be slow, his rating is less than 100 say 90. If the operator is above average, his rating is more than 100, say 120.

7. *Calculate the basic time*

Basic time is calculated as follows by applying rating factor

$$\text{Basic time} = \text{Observed time} \times \frac{\text{Operator rating}}{\text{Standard rating}}$$

$$BT = OT \times \frac{OR}{SR}$$

8. *Determine the allowance*

A worker cannot work all the day continuously. He will require time for rest going for toilet, drinking water etc. Unavoidable delays may occur because of tool breakage etc. So some extra time is added to the basic time. The extra time is known as allowance.

9. *Compile the standard time*

The standard time is the sum of basic time and allowances. The standard time is also known as allowed time.

1.7.1.1 Breaking a Job into Elements

It is necessary to break down a task (job) into elements for the following reasons:

1. To separate productive time and unproductive time.
2. To assess the rating of the worker more accurately.
3. To identify the different types of elements and to measure their timings separately.
4. To determine the fatigue allowance accurately.
5. To prepare a detailed work specification.
6. To fix standard time for repetitive elements (such as switch on or switch off of machine).

Classification of elements

1. Repetitive elements

It is an element which occurs in every work cycle of the job.

Example 1.9

Loading the machine, locating a job in a fixture.

2. Constant element

It is an element for which the basic time remains constant whenever it is performed.

Example 1.10

Switching on the machine, switching off the machine.

3. Variable element

It is an element for which the basic time varies depending on the characteristics of the product, equipment or process.

Example 1.11

Saving a log of wood-time changes with diameter or the work.

4. Occasional element

It is an element which does not occur in every work cycle of the job. It may occur at regular or irregular intervals.

Example 1.12

Regrinding of tools, re-setting of tools.

5. Foreign element

It is an element which is not a part of the job.

Example 1.13

Cleaning a job that is to be machined.

6. Manual element

It is an element performed by the worker.

Example 1.14

Cleaning the machine, loading the machine.

7. Machine element

It is the element automatically performed by a power driven machine.

Example 1.15

Turning in a lathe using automatic feed.

General rules to be followed in breaking down a task into elements

1. Element should have a definite beginning and ending.
2. An element should be as short as possible so that it can be conveniently timed. The shortest element that can be timed using a stop watch is 0.04 mt.
3. Manual elements and machine elements should be separately timed.
4. Constant element should be separated from variable elements.
5. Occasional and foreign elements should be timed separately.

1.7.1.2 Measuring Time with a Stop Watch

There are two methods of timing using a stop watch. They are

1. Fly back or Snap back method.
2. Continuous or Cumulative method.

1. Fly back method

Here the stop watch is started at the beginning of the first element. At the end of the element the reading is noted in the study sheet (in the WR column). At the same time, the stop watch hand is snapped back to zero. This is done by pressing down the knob, immediately the knob is released. The hand starts moving from zero for timing the next element. In this way the timing for each element is found out. This is called observed time (O.T.)

2. Continuous method

Here the stop watch is started at the beginning of the first element. The watch runs continuously throughout the study. At the end of each element the watch readings are recorded on the study sheet. The time for each element is calculated by successive subtraction. The final reading of the stop watch gives the total time. This is the observed time (O.T.).

Comparison of fly back and continuous method

Sl. No.	*Fly back*	*Continuous*
1.	Element times are obtained directly. No successive subtraction needed.	Elemental times obtained only by successive subtractions.
2.	Time is lost in snapping back of watch.	No time is lost in snapping back.
3.	So error is introduced.	No such error and hence study is accurate.
4.	Short elements may be missed.	Even if a short element is missed, its time will get included in the total time.

Note: As we find that the continuous method is accurate, it is preferable.

1.8 RATING FACTOR

Rating is the assessment of the rate of working of the operator by the work study man. The work study man does this rating based upon his idea of standard performance.

Standard performance is the rate of output which a qualified worker will give on an average. The worker gives this output willingly without much strain.

Bench mark for standard rating. The motion of the operator with standard rating will be equivalent to the speed of motion of the limbs of a man of average physique when

1. Walking without a load in a straight line on a level ground at a speed of 6.4 km per hour.
2. Distributing a pack of 52 playing cards at the four corners of a square table of 1 foot side in 0.375 mts.

Rating scales

The different rating scale universally adapted are

1. 60–80 scale.
2. 75–100 scale.
3. 100–133 scale.

In the above scales, the lower figures 60,75 and 100 correspond to standard performance of the workers, when the worker is given a time rate of pay. No incentives are given. The higher figures 80,100 and 133 correspond to the standard performance of the workers, when they are motivated by incentives. Among the above scales 75–100 scale is universally adopted.

Applying rating factor

Here, normally we adopt the scale of 75–100. When the performance of the operator is above average, he is given a rating of more than 100, say 110, 115 etc.

If the performance of the operator is below average, he is given a rating of less than 100, say 85, 90 etc.

If the performance of the operator is average, he is given a rating of 100

The rating number should be always rounded of to the nearest multiples of five on the scale.

1.9 CALCULATION OF BASIC TIME

Basic time is the time taken by an operator of standard performance (rating of 100).

A man whose work is observed, may be a slow worker or a fast worker. His rating may be less than 100 or above 100. The observed time cannot be taken as the basic time. Here the rating factor is applied and basic time is calculated as follows.

$$\text{Basic time} = \text{Observed time} \times \frac{\text{Operator rating}}{\text{Standard rating}}$$

For example, assume that observed time for an operation is 0.7 mts. The rating of the operator is found to be 120.

$$\text{The Basic Time or Normal Time} = 0.7 \times \frac{120}{100} = 0.84 \text{ mts.}$$

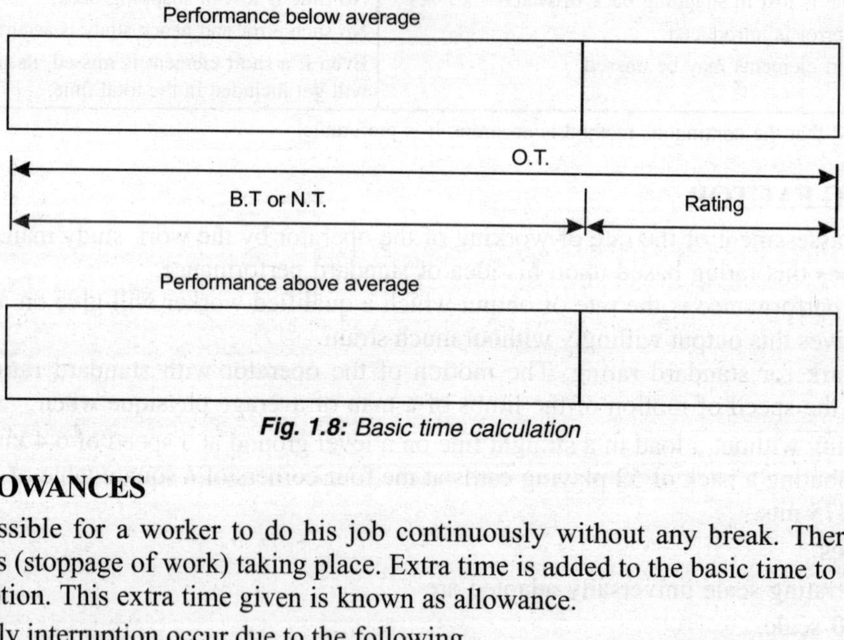

Fig. 1.8: Basic time calculation

1.10 ALLOWANCES

It is not possible for a worker to do his job continuously without any break. There are many interruptions (stoppage of work) taking place. Extra time is added to the basic time to compensate this interruption. This extra time given is known as allowance.

Generally interruption occur due to the following

1. Personal factors.
   Going for drinking water, toilet etc.
2. Nature of work.
   Taking rest after hard work
3. Other factors.
   Tool breakage, listening to supervisor etc.

Various types of allowance are

1. Rest and personal allowance.
2. Process allowance.
3. Contingency allowance.
4. Special allowance.
5. Policy allowance.

1. Rest and personal allowance

This is the allowance given for the personal needs of the worker *viz*., going to toilet, drinking water, taking rest etc. Personal allowance given, depends upon the working condition and nature of work. For example heavy work at high temperature (working near furnace) needs more allowance. This allowance is also known as relaxation allowance.

2. Process allowance

This is also known as unavoidable delay allowance. A worker working in an incentive system may have to be idle due to unavoidable delays. This delay may be due to process, machine operation, waiting for work, waiting for material etc. To compensate this delay, process allowance is given.

3. Contingency allowance

In a shop, there may be small delays due to

1. Waiting for the inspector.
2. Consulting the supervisor.
3. Obtaining special tools etc.

These delays are of very short duration. The allowance given to compensate these delays is called contingency allowance. Generally 5% of basic time is given as contingency allowance.

4. Special allowance

In a shop, some activities take place occasionally. These activities will not be part of the production cycle. But these are necessary for production work. Example of these activities are

1. Tool re-setting.
2. Cleaning.
3. Tool maintenance.
4. Shut down.

For these activities an allowances known as special allowance is given.

5. Policy allowance

This is an allowance given according to the policy of the management. It is not included for calculating the standard time. This is an extra benefit given by the management to the workers. This allowance is given to increase the workers, earnings.

1.11 CALCULATION OF STANDARD TIME

Standard time or allowed time is the total time in which a job should be completed at standard performance. It is the sum of normal time (basic time) and allowances. Policy allowance is not included.

Standard time is worked out in a stop watch time study in the following manner.

Observed time

This is the actual time observed by using a stop watch. The observed time of an operation is the total of the elemental times.

The time study for the same job is conducted for a number of times. The average of the observed times is calculated.

Basic or normal time

Basic time is the time taken by a worker with standard performance. Basic time is calculated from the observed time by applying the rating factor.

Basic time or

$$\text{Normal time} = \text{Observed time} \times \frac{\text{Rating of the operator}}{\text{Standard rating (100)}}$$

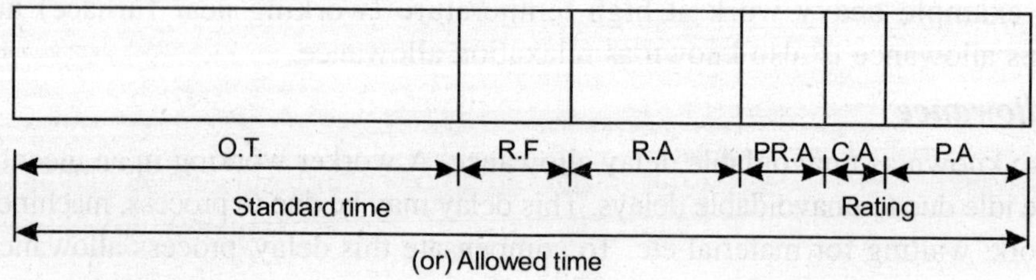

OT	–	Observed time
RF	–	Rating factor
RA	–	Rest allowance
PRA	–	Process allowance
CA	–	Contingency allowance
PA	–	Policy allowance

Fig. 1.9

Allowed time or standard time

The standard time is obtained by adding the following allowances with the basic or normal time.

1. Rest and personal allowance or relaxation allowance.
2. Process allowance or unavoidable delay allowance.
3. Contingency allowance.
4. Special allowance.

Policy allowance may be added to the standard time if the management wants.

1.12 PRODUCTION STUDY

By stop watch time, study time standards are set. But there may be complaints from the operator that the time given for a job is not sufficient. So it is necessary to check the original time study production study is a technique of work measurement to check accuracy of the original time study. This study is done to find the time delay due to occasional elements. These elements may occur at irregular intervals. Example: Tool grinding, setting tools etc. There are chances of missing these elements in the stop watch time study. Production study is conducted for a longer period—at least for half a day or one shift.

Uses of production study

1. To check the accuracy of time standards.
2. To make sure that all the ineffective elements are included in the time study.
3. To observe the waiting time and other delays of operator.
4. To get the data for working out the contingency allowance.
5. When the output goes down, this study is conducted to find out the reasons for it.

Procedure for production study

Production study is conducted just like ordinary stop watch time study. But here the time for occasional elements alone are observed. This is done for a long period, say for 1 shift. Repetitive or routine activities are not timed. The timings for occasional elements are compared with the allowance already included in the standard time.

1. Error in the original time study.
2. Changes in conditions of material, tools and equipments.
3. Inexperienced operator.
4. Changes in the method of doing work.
5. Changes in the working condition.
6. Changes in the layout.
7. Incorrect machine speed.

The exact reasons for the error are found out and rectified.

1.13 RATIO DELAY STUDY

This study is also known as work sampling or activity sampling. Here the ratio of the delay time and working time to the total time of an activity is found out. This is done by random (irregular) observations. This study is applied to

1. Long cycle operations.
2. Activities where time study is not possible.

Example 1.16

Office work, supervising work, activities in stores and warehouses etc.

3. Estimate the percentage utilization of machine tools, cranes, trucks etc.,
4. Estimate the percentage idle time of men in group activities.
5. Estimate the standard time for manual task.

Procedure

1. Define the objectives

Decide the element to be studied. State whether idle time of men or machine is to be studied. Decide the shop floor. Decide the nature of activity—Indicate the location of men and machine.

2. Select the sampling technique

Decide the number of observations to be made—Decide the length of time of observations—Referring to the random number tables, decide the schedule of observations i.e., at what time each observation has to be made.

3. Prepare the forms for recording

Prepare the form as shown in the figure 1.10.

Date	*Observer*	*Study No.:*	
Number of observation : 150		**Total**	**Percentage**
Machine Running	𝍸 𝍸	120	80-0
Repairs	IIII	3	2-0
Machine Supplies	𝍸 𝍸 𝍸 II	12	8-0
Idle Personal	𝍸 I	6	4-0
Idle	𝍸 IIII	9	6-0

Fig. 1.10

4. Make observations

Visit the work spot as per this timing noted in the form. Note down whether men or machine is working or idle in the form.

5. Process the data

Analyse the observed data and calculate the percentage utilization or idle time for men or machine.

Example 1.17

Number of observations made – 150

Number of times m/c found working – 120

Number of times m/c found idle – 30

% utilization of machine – $(120 \div 150) \times 100 = 80\%$

% idle time of machine – $(30 \div 150) \times 100 = 20\%$

Advantages

1. Activities which cannot be studied by stop watch time study can be observed.
2. Cost of the study is less. A single study man can observe several machines and operations.
3. This study is not a continuous study. So lesser time is spend on the study.
4. The study will not interrupt the production.
5. The operators do not feel that they are closely watched by study man. So they work freely.
6. Trained study man is not required.
7. Calculation is easy.
8. No equipment—Stop watch or other devices are not needed.

Limitations

1. This is economical only when the study is made in a wide area. *i.e.*, group of machines or group of operators.
2. This is not suitable for short cycle repetitive operations.
3. This is not a detailed study.

1.14 SYNTHESIS FROM STANDARD DATA

Synthesis is a work measurement technique to work out standard time for a job by totaling the elemental times already obtained from previous time studies.

Many operators in an industry have several common elements. Example: starting the machine, stopping the machine etc. Whenever these activities occur, they take the same duration of time. These elements are called constant elements. Time for some elements vary proportionately with the speed, feed, length of cut etc. in machining operation. These elements are known as variable elements.

Time for all these constant elements and variable elements are collected from the time studies previously made. These are stored in a file. This is called time standard data bank. Data bank contains data in the form of

1. Tabulated standard time for constant elements.
2. Charts and graphs.
3. Formulae etc.

So, the time for any operation can be worked out without actually making the time study.

Procedure

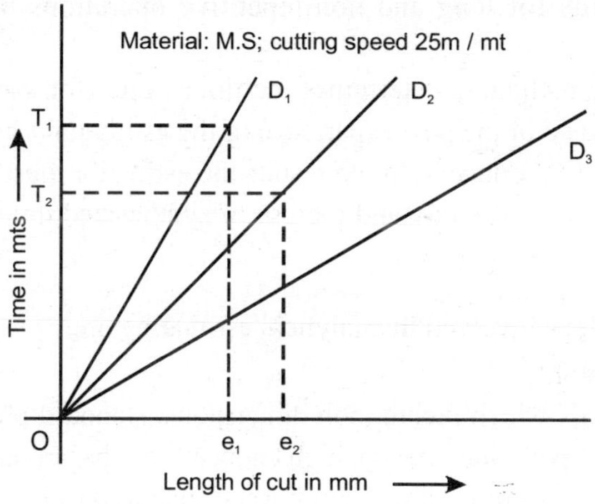

Fig. 1.11

1. Break the operation into elements.

The operations are broken into a number of elements. Variable elements and constant are separated.

2. Collect the elemental time for constant elements from the standard data bank.
3. For variable elements, the elemental time can be found out by using the charts and graphs.

An example of graph taken from a data bank is given in figure 1.11. In the graph, time for machining is plotted in Y axis. The length of cut is plotted in X axis. The graph, the time for machining various lengths of cut for different diameters for example, for the job with a diameter D1, the machining time for a length of cut I1 is T1. Similarly, for a job with a diameter D2, the machining time for a length of cut I2 is T2.

4. Add all the elemental times for constant and variable elements. With this, add the allowances such as rest allowance, interference allowance, process allowance, special allowance, contingency allowance etc. to get the standard time. The time for various allowance are also available in the standard data bank.

Advantages

1. The time calculated using standard data is more accurate than the stop watch time study.
2. The process is very quick.
3. It is a cheaper method.
4. It is used for estimating the cost of production before actually producing. It is used to offer quotation.
5. It is useful for planning team work such as assembly work.

Limitations

1. Collection of data bank is a costly affair.
2. It is applied only in larger industries.
3. The data bank should be updated periodically.

1.15 ANALYTICAL ESTIMATING

Setting the time standards for long and non-repetitive operations by stop watch method are uneconomical.

Analytical estimating technique determines the time values for such jobs either by using the synthetic data or on the basic of the past experience of the estimator when no synthetic or standard data is available. In order to produce accurate results the estimator must have sufficient experience of estimating, motion study, time study and the use of synthesized time standards.

1.15.1 Procedure

The various procedural steps involved in analytical estimating are:

1. Select the estimator.
2. Find out job details which include job dimensions, standard procedure and especially the job conditions, *i.e.*, poor illumination, high temperatures, hazardous environments, availability of special jigs, fixtures or toolings, condition of materials, etc.
3. Break the job into constituent elements.
4. Select the time values for as many elements possible from the data bank (i.e., synthetic data).
5. To the remaining elements for which no synthetic data is available, usually the estimator gives suitable time values from his past knowledge and experience.
6. Add 4 and 5 and this is the total basic time at a 100% rating.
7. Add to 6 appropriate Blanket Relaxation allowance. In analytical estimating, relaxation allowance is not added to individual elements, rather a blanket R.A. depending upon the type of job and job conditions. This is calculated as a percentage (10 to 20%) of the total basic time and is added to the total basic time.
8. Any additional allowances if applicable may be added to 7 in order to arrive standard time for the given job.

1.15.2 Advantages

1. It possesses almost the same advantages as enjoyed by synthesis from standard data.
2. It aids in planning and scheduling.
3. It provides a basis for rate fixing for non-repetitive works in industries.
4. It improves labour control.

1.15.3 Limitations

The estimate will not be accurate.

1.15.4 Application

Analytical estimating is used.

1. For non-repetitive jobs, jobs involved long cycle times and the jobs having elements of variable nature.
2. In repair work,
   - Tool rooms.
   - Job production.

- Maintenance work.
- Inspection work.
- Erection work.
- Engineering construction.
- One time large projects, and
- Office routines etc.

1.16 PREDETERMINED MOTION TIME SYSTEM (PMTS)

1.16.1 Definition

PMTS is a work measurement technique where by times, established for basic human motions (classified according to the nature of the motion and the conditions under which it is made) are used to build up the time for a job at a defined level of performance. Few well-known systems using this concept are

1. M.T.M. : Method Time Measurement.
2. W.F.S. : Work Factor System.
3. M.T.A. : Motion Time Analysis.
4. D.M.T. : Dimensional Motion Times.
5. B.M.T. : Basic Motion Times.

Out of these, MTM technique is widely used.

1.16.2 Method Time Measurement (M.T.M.)

M.T.M. analyses an industrial job into the basic human movements required to do the same. From the tables of these basic motions, depending upon the kind of motion, and conditions under which it is made, predetermined time values are given to each motion. When all such times are added up, it provides the normal time for the job. Standard time can be found by adding suitable allowances.

According to M.T.M. the various classification of motions are

1. Reach – R.
2. Move – M.
3. Turn and Apply Pressure – T and AP.
4. Grasp – G.
5. Position – P.
6. Release – RL.
7. Disengage – D.
8. Eye travel time and eye focus – ET and EF.
9. Body, leg and foot motions and,
10. Simultaneous motions.

A table is provided for each motion. Depending upon different characteristics of a motion, the time can be read from the table.

1.16.3 Table Preparation

Groups of average workmen (by age, physical attributes, temperament) were selected and placed under laboratory conditions (average heat, light atmospheric conditions etc.). These work men were made to perform a wide variety of motions which were filmed with a cine camera at 16 frames per sec. These films were later exhibited using a constant speed projector to a group of highly qualified industrial engineers who rated the films.

The net result of these experiments were the development of MTM tables for the time values for all the basic motions performed by a human body. There are 10 MTM tables, 9 of which provide time for various types of motions.

Unit time in the tables is one hundred, thousandth of an hour (0.00001 hr) and is referred to one time measurement unit (TMU)

$$1.\ \text{T.M.U.} = \frac{1}{100 \times 1000} = 1 \times 10^{-5}\ \text{hr}$$

$$= 0.00001\ \text{hr} = 0.0006\ \text{minutes.}$$

The conversion system of TMU's into hours, minutes or seconds is as under

1 hour = 1,00,000 TMU's
1 minute = 1,667 TMU's
1 second = 28 TMU's
1 TMU = 0.00001 hrs.
= 0.00006 minutes.

1.16.4 Advantages of MTM

1. Time standard for a job can be arrived at without going to the place of work.
2. Alternative methods are compared easily.
3. It helps in tool and product design.
4. It eliminates in accuracies associated with stop watch time study.

1.16.5 Limitations

MTM can deal only with manual motions of an operation.

1.17 ERGONOMICS

Ergons means 'work' and Nomos means 'Natural laws'. Ergonomics or its American equivalent 'Human Engineering may be defined as the scientific study of the relationship between man and his working environments.

Ergonomics implies 'Fitting the job to the worker'. Ergonomics combines the knowledge of a psychologist, physiologist, anatomist, engineer, anthropologist and a biometrician.

1.17.1 Objectives

The objectives of the study of ergonomics is to optimize the integration of man and machine in order to increase work rate and accuracy. It involves

1. The design of a work place befitting the needs and requirements of the worker.
2. The design of equipment, machinery and controls in such a manner so as to minimize mental and physical strain on the worker thereby increasing the efficiency, and
3. The design of a conductive environment for executing the task most effectively.

Both work study and Ergonomics are complementary and try to fit the job to the workers; however Ergonomics adequately takes care of factors governing physical and mental strains.

1.17.2 Applications

In practice, ergonomics has been applied to a number of areas as discussed below

1. Working environments 2. The work place, and 3. Other areas.

1. Working environments

(a) The environment aspect includes considerations regarding light, climatic conditions (i.e., temperature, humidity and fresh air circulation), noise, bad odour, smokes, fumes, etc., which affect the health and efficiency of a worker.
(b) Day light should be reinforced with artificial lights, depending upon the nature of work.
(c) The environment should be well-ventilated and comfortable.
(d) Dust and fume collectors should preferably be attached with the equipments giving rise to them.
(e) Glares and reflections coming from glazed and polished surfaces should be avoided.
(f) For better perception, different parts or sub-systems of equipment should be coloured suitably. Colours also add to the sense of pleasure.
(g) Excessive contrast, owing of colour or badly located windows, etc., should be eluded.
(h) Noise, no doubt distracts the attention (thoughts, mind) but if it is slow and continuous, workers become habituated to it. When the noise is high pitched, intermittent or sudden, it is more dangerous and needs to be dampened by isolating the place of noise and through the use of sound absorbing materials.

2. Work place layout

Design considerations

(a) Materials and tools should be available at their predetermined places and close to the worker.
(b) Tools and materials should preferably be located in the order in which they will be used.
(c) The supply of materials or parts, if similar work is to be done by each hand, should be duplicated. That is materials or parts to be assembled by right hand should be kept on right hand side and those to be assembled by the left hand should be kept on left hand side.
(d) Gravity should be employed, wherever possible, to make raw materials reach the operator and to deliver material at its destination (e.g., dropping material through a chute).
(e) Height of the chair and work bench should be arranged in a way that permits comfortable work posture. To ensure this
    - Height of the chair should be such that top of the work table is about 50 mm below the elbow level of the operator.
    - Height of the table should be such that worker can work in both standing and sitting positions.
    - Flat foot rests should be provided for sitting workers.
    - Figure 1.12 shows the situation with respect to bench heights and seat heights.
    - The height and back of the chair should be adjustable.
    - Display panel should be at right angles to the line or sight of the operator.
(f) An instrument with a pointer should be employed for check readings where as for quantitative readings, digital type of instrument should be preferred.
(g) Hand tools should be possible to be picked up with least disturbance or rhythm and symmetry of movements.

(h) Foot pedals should be used, wherever possible, for clamping declamping and for disposal of finished work.

(i) Handles, levers and foot pedals should be possible to be operated without changing body position.

(j) Work place must be properly illuminated and should be free from glare to avoid eye strain.

(k) Work place should be free from the presence of disagreeable elements like heat, smoke, dust, noise, excess humidity, vibrations etc.

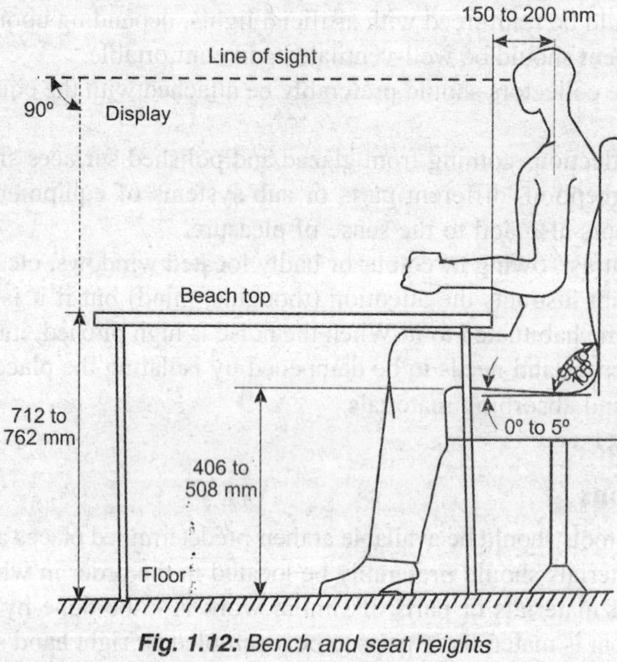

Fig. 1.12: Bench and seat heights

Suggested work place layout

Figure 1.13 shows a work place layout with different areas and typical dimensions. It shows the left hand covering the maximum working area and the right hand covering the normal working area.

Normal working area

It is within the easy reach of the operator.

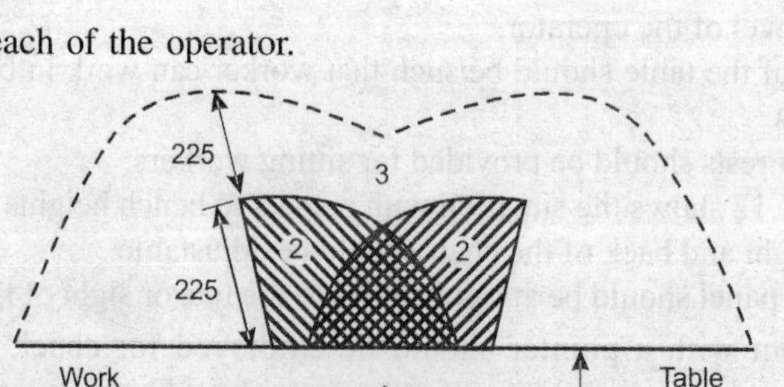

Fig. 1.13: Work place layout showing different areas and typical dimensions (mm)

Maximum working area

It is accessible with full arm stretch.

Figure 1.14 shows work place layout for assembling small component parts. A-1 is the actual working area and the place of assembly (POA) where four component parts P-1, P-2, P-3, and P-4 are assembled together. Bins containing P-1, P-2, P-3, and P-4 and commonly employed tools (CET) (like screw driver, plier, etc.) lie in the normal working area A-2.

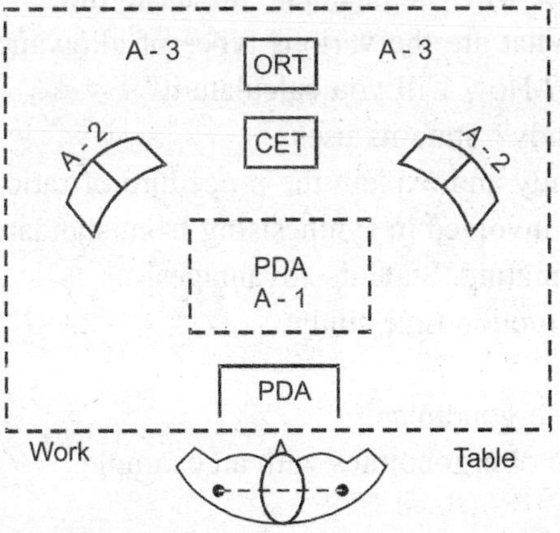

Fig. 1.14: Work place layout for an assembly job

Occasionally required Tools (ORT) (hammers etc.) lie in the maximum working area A-3. After the assembly has been made at POA, it is dropped into the cut portion in the work table – PDA (Place for dropping assemblies) from where the assembly is delivered at its destination with the help of a conveyer. This work place arrangement satisfies most of the principles of motion economy.

3. Other areas

Other areas include studies related to fatigue, losses caused due to fatigue, rest pauses, amount of energy consumed, shift work and age considerations.

REVIEW QUESTIONS

1. Define work study.
2. Explain the importance of working condition.
3. What do you mean by Ergonomics?
4. Define method study. What are the objectives of method study?
5. Explain the basic procedure for method study.
6. What are the types of charts used in method study?
7. Draw the symbols used in process chart.
8. Explain the operation process chart with an example.
9. What are types of flow process chart?
10. Explain main type flow process chart with an example.
11. Explain two-handed process chart with an example.
12. Explain man-machine chart.

13. Explain flow diagram and string diagram.
14. What is work measurement?
15. What are the techniques used for work measurement?
16. Describe the procedure for conducting stop watch time study.
17. Define rating factor.
18. Compare flyhack and continuous method of stop watch measurement.
19. Define basic time. How will you calculate the basic time?
20. What is allowance? What are the various types of allowances.
21. What is standard time? How will you calculate it?
22. What is production study? State its uses.
23. What is ratio delay study and explain the procedure of ratio delay study?
24. Explain the procedure involved in synthesising from standard data.
25. Explain analytical estimating. State its advantages.
26. Define predetermined motion time study.
27. Define Ergonomics.
28. State the objectives of ergonomics.
29. Explain the application of ergonomics with an example.

Unit–2

PROCESS PLANNING

2.0 INTRODUCTION

A process is defined as any group of actions instrumental to the achievement of the output of an operation's system in accordance with a specified measure of effectiveness.

When the product of the enterprise is designed, certain specifications are established; physical dimensions, tolerances, standards, and quality are set forth. Then it becomes a matter of deciding the specific details of how to achieve the desired output. This decision is the essence of process planning.

2.1 PROCESS PLANNING—DEFINITION

Process planning has been defined as the sub-system responsible for the conversion of design data to work instruction.

Process planning can also be defined as the systematic determination of the methods by which a product is to be manufactured economically and competitively. It consists of devising, selecting and specifying processes, machine tools and other equipment to convert raw material into finished and assembled products.

2.1.1 Purpose of Process Planning

The purpose of process planning is to determine and describe the best process for each job so that,

1. Specific requirements are established for which machines, tools and others equipment can be designed or selected.
2. The efforts of all engaged in manufacturing the product are coordinated.
3. A guide is furnished to show the best way to use the existing or the providing facilities.

Process planning is an intermediate stage between designing the product and manufacturing it (figure 2.1).

Where the product design ends, the process planning begins. However, the basic process planning must begin during the product design stages where the selection of materials and initial forms, such as casting, forging and die casting take place. The accepted end point for production design is manifested by the drawing release, which summarizes the exact specifications of what is

2.1.2 Concept of Process Planning

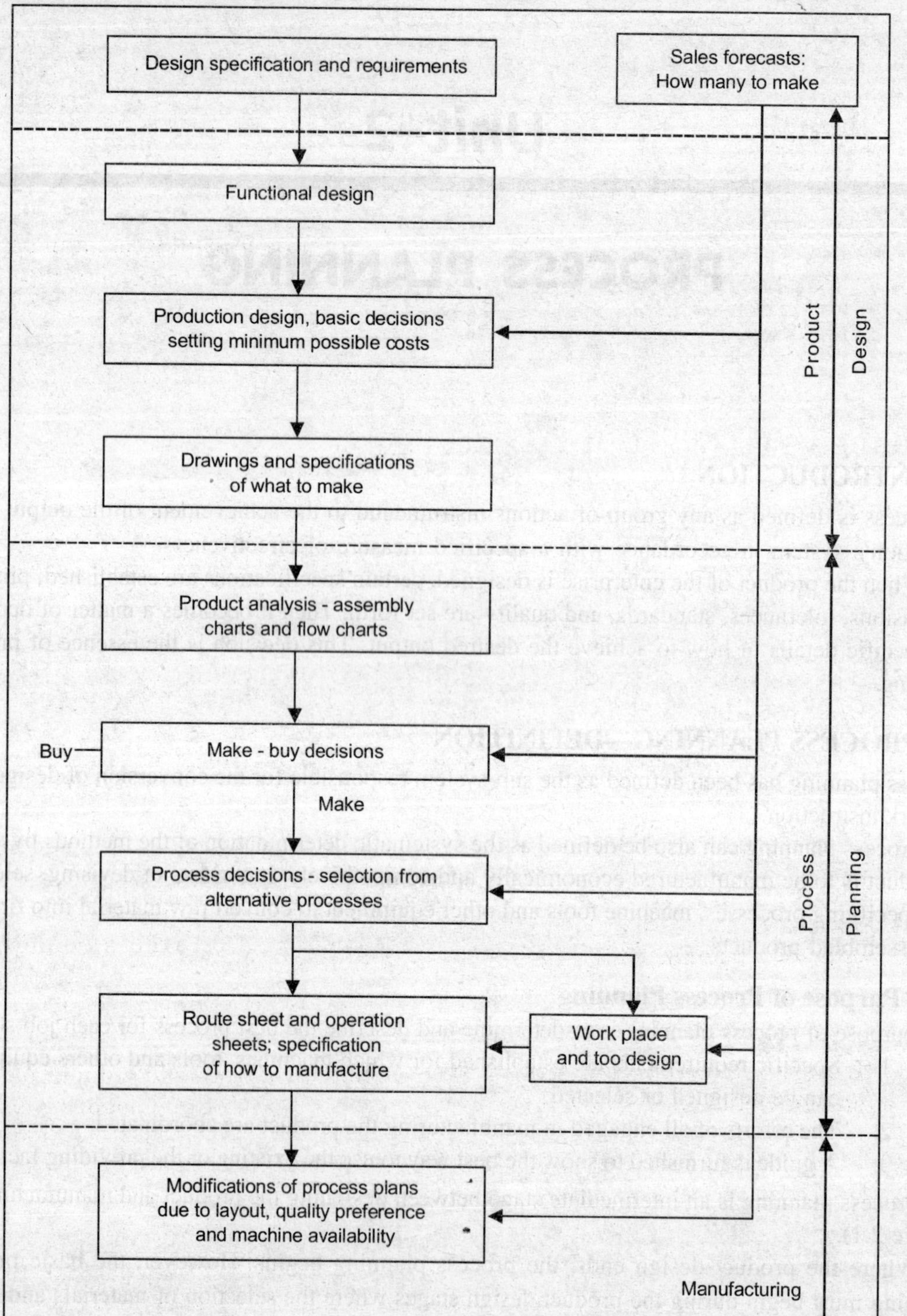

Fig. 2.1: Overall development of processing plans

to be made. Process planning takes over from this point and develops the broad plan of manufacture for the part of product.

Process planning takes as its inputs the drawings or other specifications which indicate what is to be made and how many are to be made.

The drawings are then analysed to determine the overall scope of the project. If it is a complex assembled product, considerable effort may go into exploding the product into its components and subassemblies.

Preliminary decisions about subassembly groupings to determine which parts to make and which to buy, as well as to determine the general level of tooling expenditure, may be made at this point.

Then, for each part, a detailed routing is developed. Here technical knowledge of processes, machines, and their capabilities is required, but of almost equal importance is a knowledge of production economics.

In brief, the engineering drawing of the component is interpreted in terms of the manufacturing process to be used. This step is referred to as process planning and it is concerned with the preparation of a route sheet.

The route sheet is a listing of the sequence of operations which must be performed on the component. It is called a route sheet because it also lists the machines through which the part must be routed in order to accomplish the sequence of operations.

2.2 OBJECTIVES OF PROCESS PLANNING

The systematic determination of the engineering processes and systems to manufacture a product competitively and economically is called operations planning. It is the stage between design and production. The plan of manufacture considers functional requirements of the product, quantity, tools and equipment, and eventually the costs for manufacture.

2.3 SCOPE OF PROCESS PLANNING

A process is defined as any group of actions instrumental to the achievement of the output of an operations system in accordance with specified measure of effectiveness. When the product designed, certain specifications are established; physical dimensions, tolerance, standards and quality are set forth. Then it becomes a matter of deciding over the specific details of how to achieve the desired output. This decision is the essence of process planning. The production function essentially is a transformation process that accepts the inputs and gives the outputs after adding value to the inputs. Process selection is a major strategic decision as it involves allocation of men and material resources as well as financial commitments for a long period.

Operation planning is a responsibility of the manufacturing organization. A number of functional staff arrangements are possible. This process leads to the same output despite organizational differences. The following are business objectives for operations planning:

1. New product manufacture

A new design may have not been produced before or, alternatively, new manufacturing operations may be introduced for the product. Unless there is planning, the product introduction will be helter-skelter.

2. Sales

Opportunity for greater saleability of an existing or new product can develop from different colours, materials, finish, or functional and non-functional features. Sales and marketing departments provide advice to help manufacturing planning.

3. Quantity

Changes in quantity require different sequences, tools, and equipment. The OP planner differentiates for these fluctuations. If volume increases, the chance is for lower cost. In contrast, if volume decreases, the cost should not increase out of reason. There may be a fortuitous opportunity for reduced cost, if economics and technology will allow substitution of new process, training, and resources even if quantities are reduced. If quantity reduces too much, however, it is appropriate for the OP planner to recommend that production may no longer be economical, perhaps, a supplier may be the appropriate lower cost alternative.

4. Effective use of facilities

Operation planning often can find alternate opportunities for the plant's production facilities to take up any slack that may develop. Seasonal products, which might be popular in the summer, need an alternative product for the winter season. For example, companies that produce sporting equipment may use the same facilities to produce tennis rackets and skis.

5. Cost reduction

Various opportunities become available if the company has an ongoing cost reduction effort. Suggestion plans, value analysis, design for manufacturing (DFM), and directed and systematic effort involve operations planning.

2.4 INFORMATIONS REQUIRED TO DO PROCESS PLANNING

1. Quantity of work to be done along with product specifications.
2. Quality of work to be completed.
3. Availability of equipments, tools and personnels.
4. Sequence in which operations will be performed on the raw material.
5. Names of equipment on which the operations will be performed.
6. Standard time for each operation.
7. When the operations will be performed?

2.5 PROCESS PLANNING ACTIVITIES

2.5.1 Concept of Process Planning

The concept of process planning is to determine

1. The operations involved in the manufacture of each product.
2. The machines on which operations are to be done.
3. The tools, jigs and fixtures required.
4. The material requirements including scrap.
5. The speeds and feeds that are to be used.
6. The type of labour required.
7. The time required for each operation.

The above informations are made available on process sheet. The main objective of process planning is to find the most economic method of performing an activity.

The following informations are necessary to carry out this function effectively:

1. Product data.
2. Volume of production.
3. Quality requirements.
4. Equipments and personnel available.
5. Time available to perform the work or delivery date.

2.5.2 Preparing Operation Planning Sheet

The following informations are required to do the process planning effectively:

1. Quantity of work to be done along with product specifications.
2. Quality of work to be completed.
3. Availability of equipment, tools and personnel.
4. Sequence in which operations will be performed on the raw material.
5. Names of equipments on which the operations will be performed.
6. Standard time for each operation.
7. When the operations will be performed?
8. Cutting speed
9. Feed
10. Material specification.
11. Job rating of labours.

Operation planning sheet

Part Name:		Material:		Part No.:		
Material Specification:						
Operation No.	Description of Operation	Machine	Tools	Jigs	Gauges	Time Analysis

2.5.3 Process Planning Procedure

1. Preparation of working drawings.
2. Deciding to make or buy.
3. Selecting manufacturing process.
4. Machine capacity and machine selection.
5. Selection of material and bill of materials.
6. Selection of jigs, fixtures and other attachments.
7. Operation planning and tooling requirement.
8. Preparation of documents such as operation sheet and route sheet etc.

(a) Make or buy decision

Recommendations should be made whether to make or buy the material, part or assembly informations should be sufficiently detailed to take intelligent decisions. Cost and availability of the production capacity are the two important factors in arriving to make or buy decision.

Make

It requires appropriate production equipment, suitable personnel, material, adequate space, supervisions, design standards and overheads maintenance, taxes, insurances, management attention and other indirect and hidden costs.

Buy

It permits lower investments, small labour force, less handling, lower plant cost for building and up keep, less overhead or taxes, insurance and supervision and less problems of man-management relations.

A company has a choice of three alternatives before starting for a new product.

1. Purchase the product from a contracted manufacturer.
2. Purchase some components and materials and manufacture and assemble the balance in its own plant.
3. Manufacture the product completely, starting with the extraction of basic raw materials.

(b) Determination of material requirements

The materials required are worked out and arrangements to procure them are made. The procedure for examining the material requirements are given below.

1. Existing requirements for works on hand.
2. The new or extra material required. It is to be calculated from bill of materials.
3. Total material required.
4. Existing stock of materials.
5. Additional materials to be produced.

(c) Selection of material, jigs, fixtures etc.

The selection of material has become complicated by the great increase not only in the kinds of materials but also in the various forms. The material should be of right quality and chemical composition as per the product specifications. The shape and size of material should restrict the scrap.

(i) Bill of material

The most common method of analyzing a product into component parts is through the use of bills of material or specification sheets. Bill of material is a means of determining, purchasing and production order requirements. It should indicate if the part is to be manufactured or purchased. The production control department uses the bill of material to determine manufacturing and scheduling dates.

Process engineering uses it as a check list to complete their work. Methods engineering uses it in the preparation of time allowances for assembling operations. Accumulations are made by the stores department according to the bills of materials. The releases by assembly units are made by the finished stores department in accordance with the bills of material.

The design of the bill of material varies slightly in minor details. It depends upon the various uses made of it by individual companies. The information usually required on the bill of material form includes:

1. The product name.
2. Product code identification
3. Sheet number.
4. Use.
5. Date of preparation.
6. Name of preparer.
7. Name of checker.
8. Item numbers.
9. Make/purchase designations.
10. Sub assembly part numbers and names.
11. Quantity requirements and,
12. Material used in each part.

Note: Bill of materials is also known as parts list.

Table 2.1: *Bill of materials*

Item Switch: S25			Sheet No: 2 of 5			
Drawing: A8			Assembly: 3 kW motor			
					Date:	
Part No.	***Part Name***	***No. Item***	***Material***	***Quantity per item***	***Cost per item***	***Remarks***
SJ-64	Drive Spring	3	Spring steel	-	Rs.100/-	Purchase
-	-	-	-	-	-	-
-	-	-	-	-	-	-
-	-	-	-	-	-	-
-	-	-	-	-	-	-
-	-	-	-	-	-	-
-	-	-	-	-	-	-
Prepared by…………………				Checked by ……………..		

(ii) Selection of jigs, fixture and other special attachments

These supporting devices are necessary

1. To give higher production rate, and
2. To reduce the cost of production per piece.

(d) Selection of machinery

The selection of the correct machinery is closely related to the selected process of manufacturing. But it is difficult to separate one from the other. However, there is a major difference between the selection of a process and the selection of a machine.

Machines generally, represent long terms capital commitments. But process may be designed for relatively short duration. The following factors must be taken into account while selecting a correct equipment:

- The size and shape of the workpiece.
- The work material.

- The accuracy and surface quality required.
- The quantity of parts.
- The sizes of lots required and,
- Personal preferences.

1. If a number of surfaces are to be machines on a part, the choice is offered of machining them separately, all together or in various combinations. If surfaces on a part are similar in shape and size, they are better suited to being treated in one operation than if they are different from one another.
2. More powerful machines may be needed to work hard material than soft material.
3. Work piece size and dimensions may dictate particular features that a machine tool must have.
4. Small work pieces are handled on equipment different from that used for large parts. As an example, small and medium size parts are turned on horizontal lathes, but short pieces of large diameters are commonly machines on vertical lathes.
5. Small tolerance call for certain types of machine, whereas large tolerance does not call for specific machine.

In general, very large parts must be produced by slower methods. As a result, they must be produced on the larger and slower machines, mainly on a tool room basis. Smaller parts whose shape is contributing to ease of handling can be produced on faster machines. They are more readily adapted to mass production. They are exceptions in the pressed metal industry.

The size and shape of the workpiece associates itself closely with the size and type of machine required to produce it. Choice may be made between general purpose machines (centre lathes, planners, shapers, drill pressers etc.) and special purpose machines.

The general purpose machines have the following characteristics:

1. Usually less initial investment in machines.
2. Greater machine flexibility.
3. Fewer machines may be required.
4. Less maintenance cost.
5. Less set up and debugging time.
6. Less danger of obsolescence.

The special purpose machines have the following characteristics:

1. Uniform product flow.
2. Reduced in process inventory.
3. Reduced man power requirements.
4. Reduced factory floor space.
5. Higher output.
6. Higher product quality.
7. Reduced inspection cost.
8. Reduced operator skill requirements.

The machines and equipment that will do a job at the lowest total cost are the ones that should be selected. Direct, overhead and fixed costs should be considered. Generally, more items put into one operation. The lesser the handling time, the more the chance for simulation and the lower the direct costs. But the operation is likely to become more complex, calling for more expensive machine. As a rule, a high rate of production justifies a largest investment in machine to reduce direct costs.

To select machine tools, an investigation must be made to ascertain the aptitude, range and capacity required for the job. Each type of machine is best suited for certain kind of work. Lathes for turning, drilling machines for holes. A machine must have adequate range and capacity for the work it is to do.

The factors determining the range and capacity may be the size of the work piece, the working area, length of stroke, speeds, feed, forces and power required.

Personal preference or specific conditions may influence the selection of a machine tool. A particular type of make of machine may be favoured, because a person in the past found it dependable, easy to operate, safe and accurate. Often a new machine is not purchased if one almost as good is already in the plant and not fully loaded.

(e) Operation planning sheet

A process plan is a complete concept of a process. It is recorded and transmitted in a number of ways to suit various conditions. In a small plant or where skilled workers may be relied upon to perform without detailed instructions, process plans may be recorded quite incompletely. In a large organization with a complex product and highly refined procedures, process plans may be recorded in minute details.

Process sheet and its necessity

***Table 2.2:** Process sheet*

Part description .... | Part No. ....
Drawing number .... | Assembly No. ....
Material specification .... | Material size .... | Lot size ....
Quantity required per unit .... (Inclusive of scrap) | Issued by ....

Sl. No.	Dept.	Operation	Machine Code	Tools	Labour Code	Speed	Feed	Set-up Time	Standard Time

A process planning medium almost universally used is the routing also known as route sheet, process sheet and operation planning sheet. It lists and describes the operations of a process. Routings are written as briefly as possible to save time. They completely designate departments, machines, tools, etc. The operation sheet form will vary for different companies. However, the description of the operation special instructions is usually similar.

A process sheet is a manufacturing engineering document. It should be sufficiently explicit so that operational personnel (example: workers) can perform every operation/function necessary to produce the finished component and that operations can establish staffing and piece cost from which to judge operation efficiency during and after physically launching the operation.

The process sheet contains columns for recording operations, tools, types of machine used, speed, feed, times etc.

Shop floor personnels i.e., supervisors and workers will follow the informations/instructions given in the process sheet to carry out the necessary operations to make a finished part. The process sheet gives an estimate of time required to manufacture the finished part and the requirements men, machines, materials and tools required for the said purpose. It also indicates through which departments and machines, the raw material has to route before being converted into finished goods.

A process sheet is required to be made for every component to be manufacturer.

A process sheet is necessary in order to

(*i*) Check the progress of component parts through the cycle of production operations.

(*ii*) Make sure that the delivery dates (of the finished goods) will be met.

(*iii*) Control and expedite the work if required.

2.6 APPROACHES OF PROCESS PLANNING

2.6.1 Manual Process Planning

This type of planning is known as non-variant process planning. It is the commonest type of planning used for production today. Planning the operations to be used to produce a part requires knowledge of two groups of variables.

(*a*) The part requirements, and

(*b*) The available machines and processes and the capabilities of each process.

Given these variables, the planner selects the combination of processes required to produce a finished part. In selecting this combination of processes, a number of criteria are employed.

Production cost and time are usually the dominant criteria in process selection. However, machine utilization and routing affect the plans chosen. In general, the process planner tries to select the best set of process and machines to produce a whole family of parts rather than just a single part.

There are variations in the level of detail found in route sheets among different companies and industries. Process planning is accomplished by releasing the drawing to the production shop with the instructions 'make to drawing'. More firms provide a more detailed list of steps describing each operation and identifying each work center. The process planning procedure is very much dependent on the experience and judgments of the planner.

The manual approach to process planning begins when a detailed engineering drawing and data on batch size are issued to a production engineer. This information is used to determine the following:

- The manufacturing processes involved.
- The machine tools required to execute these processes.
- The tools required at each stage of processing.
- The fixtures required at each stage of processing.
- The number and depth of passes in a machining operation.
- The feeds and speeds appropriate to each operation.
- The type of finishing process necessary to achieve the specified tolerances and surface quality.

As a first step, the production engineer examines the part drawing to identify similarities with previously produced parts. If similarities are recognized, a process plan is manually retrieved for the similar item. The process plan is either used without modifications for identical parts or modified to meet the manufacturing requirements of the new part. Although old process plans are used as references for similar parts, there is still significant duplication of effort due to the lack of efficient information retrieval, comparison, and editing techniques. The manual method may also lead to inconsistency in the final plans because it is unlikely that two process planners will generate identical process plans.

As a part design changes during the product development cycle, the process plan must also change, to incorporate new features in the part. As equipment, processes and batch sizes changes, the optimum method for manufacturing the part also changes and these changes must be reflecting in current process plans. However, the lack of consistency and the labour intensity of the manual method make rapid incorporation of process changes extremely difficult.

The experience of the process planner plays a significant role in modifying or creating process plans, since the planner selects processes and process variable settings which have been successfully implemented in similar situations in the past. Since manual process planning is largely subjective, the quality of the process plan is directly related to the skill and experience of the planner.

For these reasons, it is difficult or impossible to achieve consistent, optimized process plans with the conventional manual method. As a consequence planning and manufacturing costs are increased because of the duplication of effort in the process planning function as well as specification of excessive tooling and material requirements. Production lead times also increase due to redundancies in the planning function.

2.6.2 Computer Aided Process Planning

Computer Aided Process Planning (CAPP) has been investigated for more than 20 years; it can be categorized in two major areas; variant planning, where library retrieval procedures are applied to find standard plans for similar components, and generative process planning, where plans are generated automatically for new components without reference to existing plans. The latter system is most desirable but also the most difficult way of performing CAPP.

The process planning function bridges the gap between engineering design and manufacturing and is thus a critical element in integrating activities within manufacturing organizations. Current CAPP systems range from simple editors for manual planning to fully-automated systems for planning a range of products. Some of the specific benefits of CAPP are:

1. Improved productivity

More efficient use of machines, tooling, material and labour. "Best practice" (in the form of optimized process plans) is documented for consistent application throughout the organization rather than captured mentally by the process planner.

2. Lower production cost

Cost reduction are realized through productive improvements. Also, the skill level required to produce process plans is less than that required for manual methods.

3. Consistency

Computerized methodologies assure consistent application of planning criteria. Also the number of errors generated during process planning is reduced.

4. Time savings

Time savings can range from days to minutes. Lead times are reduced and flexibility is increased due to the ability to react quickly to new or changing requirements. The amount of paper work and clerical effort involved with design changes is also reduced.

5. Rapid integration of new production capabilities

With the rapid changes in production capabilities, maintaining a competitive advantage requires fast integration of new processes. CAPP allows process plans to be quickly updated to include new process technologies.

There are also several problems, associated with automation of the planning process.

1. The designer's intention may not always be obvious to the process planner who must act on the designer's intentions. Differences in terminology and perspectives separate these two functions.
2. In order to fully automate process planning, the features of a part must be extracted from the product model without human intervention; however, engineering drawings sometimes do not convey all the information about a part. Information may be inaccessible or in a form incompatible with CAPP.
3. One problem source for all CAPP systems is the interface between CAD and CAPP, where features are translated into a form recognizable by CAPP. Different CAD systems have different methods of representing dimensions. Translation from CAD to CAPP is difficult and often requires a human interface. In the future, this problem will diminish both as CAPP develops improved methods for translating geometric representation and as CAD systems become more standardized.
4. The designer is often unaware of the potential manufacturing constraints and may produce a design that is either infeasible or costly to produce.
5. The generation and execution of a production plan may take a long time and involve several organizations in different geographical locations. Plan-monitoring and improvement may be complex and difficult to automate.

Of the various CAPP methods, variant process planning is the easiest to implement. Variant systems allow rapid generation of process plans through comparison of features with other known features in a database. However in order to implement variant process planning, products must first be grouped into part families based on feature commonality. If a new part cannot be easily placed into an existing family, then a feasible process plan cannot be generated. Also as the complexity of feature classification increase, the number of part families also increases, causing excessive search times during process plan generation. When there are only a few part families with little feature deviation for new designs, variant process planning can be a fast and efficient method for generating new process plans.

Generative process planning (GCAPP) relies on a knowledge base to generate process plans for a new design independent of existing plans. The knowledge base is a set of rules derived from the experience of human process planner. With generative methods; process plans can be generated for a wide variety of designs with dissimilar features. However, generative methods are difficult to implement in terms of constructing a set of rules which can encompass all anticipated design features likely to be encountered. GCAPP systems are difficult to implement due to the large quantity of data and knowledge required to provide even simple manufacturing feedback. Countless scenarios must be represented, and the required memory space comes at a cost of computing ability. The largest single limitation of many current GCAPP systems is their inability to accurately and completely represent the product or part model. Technicians are often called upon to do the dimensioning and tolerancing because CAPP is either not able to do it in a reasonable time frame or simply not able to do it at all commercially, generative process planning has been limited to a few specialized applications.

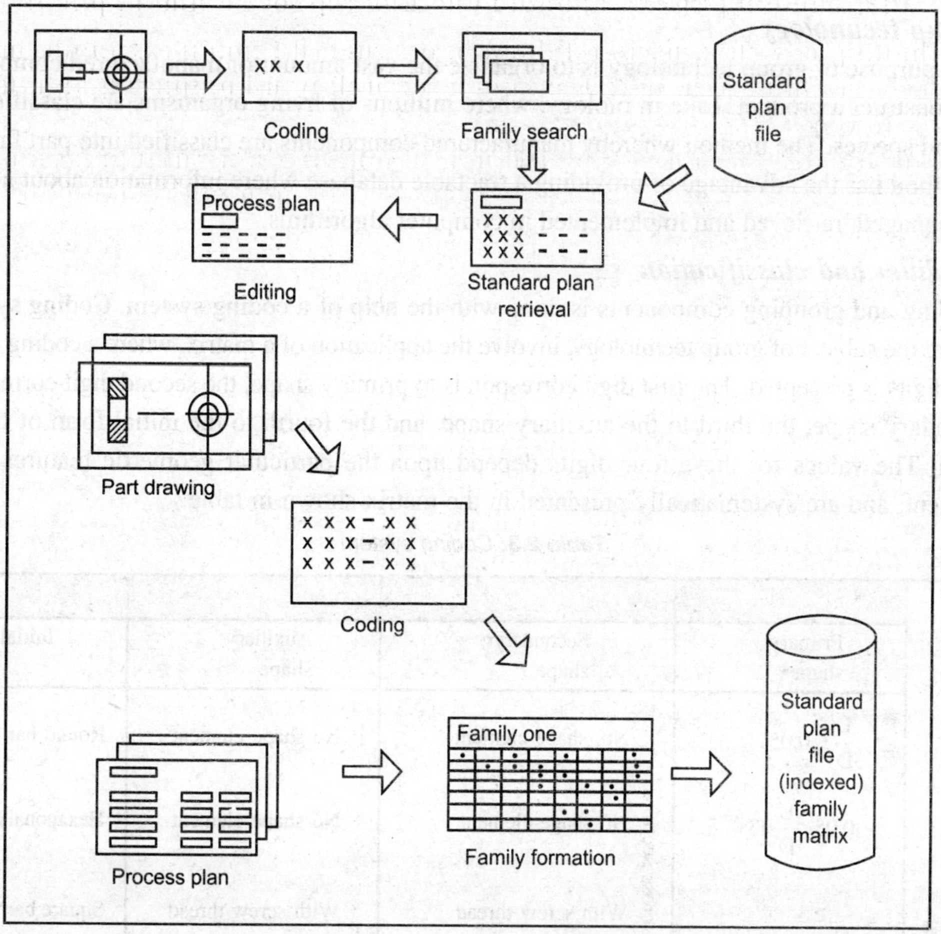

Fig. 2.2: Variant process planning procedures

2.6.2.1 Retrieval Type Approach

Variant process planning explores the similarities among components and searches through a database to retrieve the standard process plan for the part family in which the component belongs. A standard process plan is a process plan that applies to an entire part family when a standard plan is retrieved; a certain degree of modification follows in order to accommodate the details of the design. In general, variant process planning has two operational stages, a preparatory stage and a production stage.

I. Stages in retrieval type

(a) The preparatory type stage involves coding, classifying and grouping existing components into a family matrix and deriving out of this matrix a set of standard plans that can be used and modified later to become process plans for new components.

(*b*) The production stage of a process planning system involves coding and classifying new components so the family that most closely matches them can be found. The standard plan for the family is retrieved and modified to produce the plan for the new component see figure.

II. Group technology

The purpose of group technology is to organize the vast amount of manufactured components which construct a product. Like in biology, where millions of living organisms are classified into genus and species. The method whereby manufactured components are classified into part families. This method has the advantage of providing a tractable database where information about a part is easily managed, retrieved and implemented in computer algorithms.

III. Codium and classification

Coding and grouping components is done with the help of a coding system. Coding systems, which are the subject of group technology, involve the application of a matrix, where a coding system of four digits is presented. The first digit corresponds to primary shape, the second digit corresponds to secondary shape, the third to the auxiliary shape, and the fourth to the initial form of the raw material. The values for these four digits depend upon the particular geometric features of the component, and are systematically presented in the matrix shown in table.

Table 2.3: Coding system

	Rational	Primary shape	Steps with round cross sections Secondary shape	Holes Auxiliary shape	Initial form
0		$\frac{L}{D} \leq 0.05$	No, shape element	No shape element	Round bar
1		$0.05 < \frac{L}{D} < 3$	No shape element	No shape element	Hexagonal bar
2		$\frac{L}{D} \geq 3$	With screw thread	With screw thread	Square bar
3		$\frac{L}{D} \leq 2$ with deviation	With functional groove	With functional groove	Sheet
4		$\frac{L}{D} \geq 2$ with deviation	Rotational cross section	Drill with pattern	Plate and slab
5		Flat	Rectangular cross section	Two or more from 2-4	Cast or Forged

The coding system in variant process planning is the first step in establishing a family formation procedure which allows the classification of existing parts and their process plans into families to be used for creating standard process plans. Generally speaking, the family formation procedure follows some similarity rules. If these rules are strict, they will lead to the formation of a large number of relatively small families, while if they are loose, a small number of large families will be formed. For every component an operation plan is established which entails a number of operation codes.

An operation code is usually an alphanumeric expressions describing the operations that take place in one set-up on the machine for one part. An ordered set of operation codes provides the operation plan. Thus, one step in the family formation procedure into establish an operation plan for every component that is to be placed with the group I.

Current trends toward wide product variety and smaller lot sizes driving a move to cell-type shop organization (to minimize routing paths), which is essentially based on group technology. Some advantages of group technology are:

Group technology facilitates the storage and retrieval of existing designs, minimizing duplication of effort. It also promotes standardization of design feature (example: chamfers, corner radii), leading to standardization of production tools and holding fixtures.

- More efficient material handling through cell organization.
- Decreased WIP and lead times due to reduction in setup and material handling.

***Table 2.4:** Preparation plans and operation code*

Operation code	*Operation plan*
01. SAW 01	Cut to size
02. LATHE 02	Face end
	Centre drill
	Drill
	Ream
	Bore
	Turn straight
	Turn groove
	Chamfer
	Cut off
	Face
	Chamfer
03. GRIND 05	Grind
04. INSP 06	Inspect
	Dimensions
	Inspect finish

(*a*) Operation plan code (OP code) and operation plan

01. SAW 01

02. LATHE 02

03. GRIND 05

04. INSP 06

(*b*) OP Code Sequence

2.6.2.2 Generative Approach

Generative process planning synthesizes manufacturing information, particularly regarding the capabilities of different manufacturing process, and creates process plans for new components. An ideal generative process planning system receives information about the design of the part and generates the process plan, including processes to be used and their sequences, without human intervention. Unlike the variant approach, which uses standardized process-grouped family plans, the generative approach is based on defining the process planning logic using methods like.

2.6.2.2.1 Process planning logic

- Decision trees.
- Decision tables.
- Artificial intelligence based approach.
- Axiomatic approach.

Generative process planning systems are to be rapid and consistent in generating process plans. They should create process plans for entirely new components, unlike variant systems, which always need a standard plan for entirely new components, unlike variant systems, which always need a standard plan of previously existing components; and they must allow the integration. Of these activities with the design of a part (upstream) and the creation of tapes for numerically controlled machines, etc. (downstream).

- Generative process planning attempts to imitate the process planners thinking by applying the planners decision-making logic. These are three areas of concern in a generative process planning system.
- Component decision or the representation of the design in a precise manner so it can be "understood" by the system.
- Identification, capture, and representation of the knowledge of the process planner and the reasoning behind the different decisions made about process selection, process selection, process sequence, etc.
- Component definition and planners logic should be compatible within the system.

Most of the generative process planning system use "built-in" decision logic which checks condition requirements of the component. Some systems have "canned" process, plan fragments which correspond to particular geometric features, which are combined in a final process plan.

In general, generative process planning can be executed either in a forward fashion, where planning starts from the initial raw material and proceeds by building up the component using relevant processes or backwards, where planning starts from the final component and proceeds to the raw material shape.

One approach to define components is to use group technology concepts, as discussed in the section on variant process planning systems. Another approach is to describe the component using descriptive language. This approach is more general and allows a variety of components to be described. General language can describe a large number of components, however, more effort is required to describe a particular component. Less general language may be adequate for only a set of components but they are easier to apply.

I. Process planning logic

Process planning logic determines what processes will be used for the different geometric features of the component by matching process capabilities with design specifications.

(a) Decision trees

A decision tree is comprised of a root and a set of branches originating from the root. In this way paths between alternate courses of action are established. Branches are connected to each other by nodes, which contain a logic operation such as an "and" or "or" statement. When a branch is true, travelling along the branch is allowed until the next node is reached, where another operation is assigned, or an action is executed. A decision tree figure can be used as a base for developing a flow chart see figure and eventually the code to be used in a generative process plan.

(b) Decision tables

Decision tables organize conditions, actions and decision rules in tabular form. Conditions and actions are placed in rows while decision rules are identified in columns. The upper part of the table includes the conditions that must be met in order for the actions (represented in the lower part of the table) to be taken. When all conditions in a decision table are met, a decision is taken. The information content of both approaches is the same, although decision tables have a modular structure which allows them to be easily modified and written in array format.

(c) Artificial intelligence (AI) Expert systems

Artificial intelligence techniques like formal logic, for describing components and expert systems, for codifying human processing knowledge, are also applicable to process planning problems. An expert system can be defined as a tool which has the capability to understand problem specific knowledge and use the domain knowledge intelligently to suggest alternatively paths of action. Component definition can be done with methods used for declarative knowledge, or more specifically First Order Predicate Calculus (FOPC). Process selection knowledge is procedural knowledge, and as such, production systems which consists of production rules in the form of "if-then" are usually applied. Declarative knowledge using first order predicate calculus is represented by a Well-Formed Formula (WFF), which is an atomic formula including a predicate symbol, a function symbol, and a constant which can be true or false. To represent, for example a hole, as one can write "Depth hole (X) 2.5" where the depth is the predicate symbol, hole is the function symbol, and the constant is 2.5. With procedural knowledge, rules can be structured to relate processes to certain geometric or other features of the component, and with an adequate inference engine a set of processes and their sequences can be defined for a given component.

(d) Axiomatic approach

Axiomatic design was developed at MIT at the laboratory of Manufacturing and Productivity. Its intention is to provide a logical framework for designing products and processes. A set of desired characteristics of the design, known as functional requirements (FRs), must be defined to establish a design range.

Raining	T	F	F
Hot		T	F
Go to arcade	X		
Go to beach		X	
Go to picnic			X

(a) Decision table

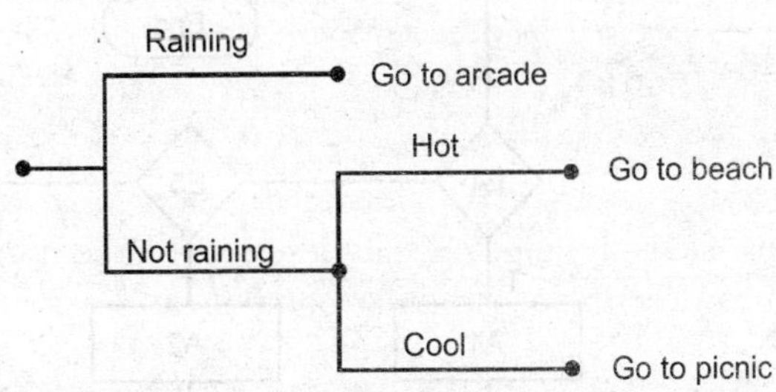

(b) Decision tree

Fig. 2.3: Decision tree and decision table

Information content for each FR has been found, the surfaces needed to be machined by one machine are grouped into surface groups. The information content for each surface group is then calculated. For example, suppose that a particular part has two types of surfaces which require two operations, one on a lathe and one on a cylindrical grinder. The information content discussed above is calculated for each machine and is listed in ascending order, starting from the left-most column see table. Each column represents a possible path of action, the best being the one which best satisfies the axioms.

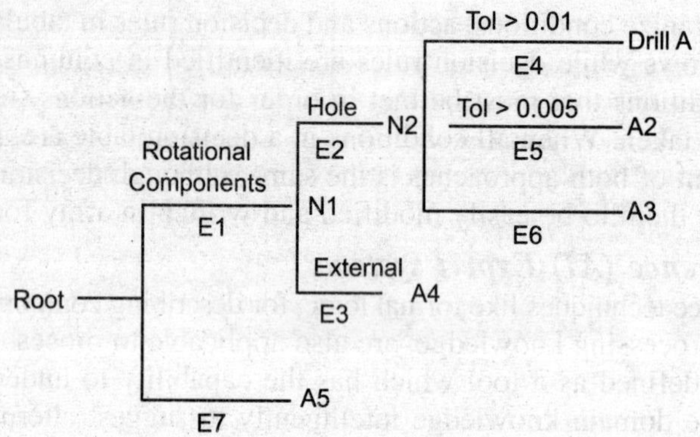

Fig. 2.4: Decision tree for hole drilling

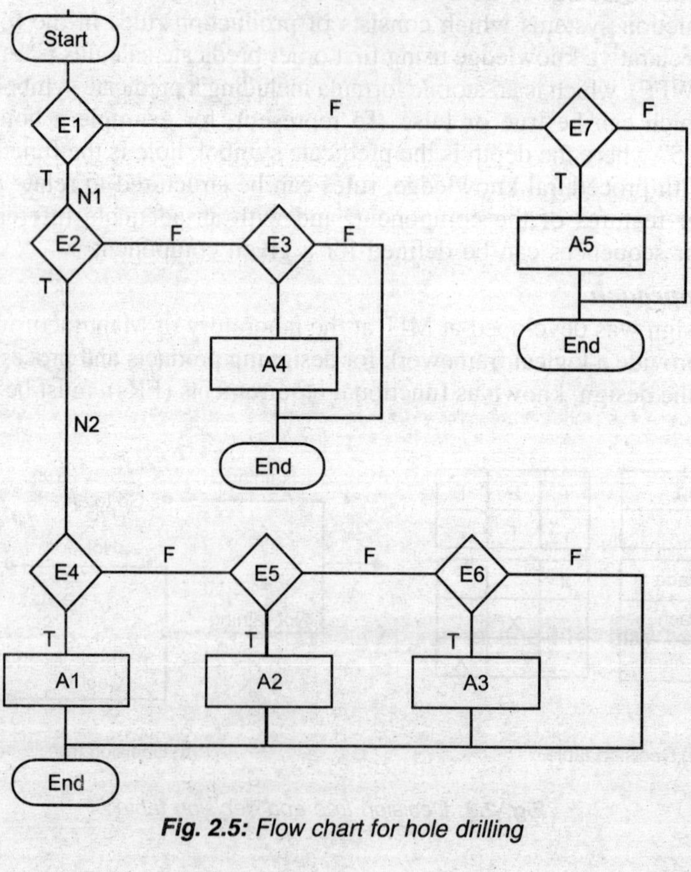

Fig. 2.5: Flow chart for hole drilling

Table 2.5: *Information required to generate the surface groups by various machines*

	Combination			
	1	2	3	4
Surface group 1	L1	1.2	1.3	1.4
Lathe order	1	2	5	24
Information	1.36	1.39	1.94	4.27
Surface group 2	G1	G2	G3	G3
Cylindrical grinder	1	2	3	3
Order information	0.58	2.19	3.73	3.73
Total order	1	21	49	72
Information	1.94	3.58	5.67	8.00

Axiom 1. The independence axiom
Maintain the independence of functional requirements.

Axiom 2. The information axiom
Minimize the information content.

To implement axiomatic design in process planning, the following steps are applied:

1. List all the design (or production) parameters to be evaluated.
2. Divide the surfaces to be produced into surface groups, each of which is to be machined by a single machine.
3. List candidate machines for each surface group.
4. Evaluate all alternatives for the production and machine parameters.
5. Obtain the total information content and select the best machine combination based on the information content.

Table 2.6: *Measured total machine time in seconds*

	Combination			
	1	2	3	4
Surface group I	L1	L2	L3	L4
Lathe	1,453	1.405	1.605	2,487
Measured time				
Surface group II	G1	G2	G3	G3
Cylindrical grinder Measured timex	1,158	G2	1,433	1,481
Total time	2,661	2,6103	098	3,948

In machining operation, the FRs may be surface roughness, dimensional accuracy and cost. The first task is to determine whether these FRs satisfy the first axiom, they can be assumed to be probabilistically independent. Next, the second axiom must be satisfied. The information content of surface roughness can be experimentally determined by measuring the surface roughness given by each machine. In this manner, a lower and upper bound on surface roughness for the system range is defined. The information content associated with dimensional accuracy can be determined in a similar manner so that the system's dimensional accuracy range is bounded. The upper and lower bounds for the system range for cost are determined for each machine by multiplying the maximum and minimum times taken for manufacture by the cost per unit time. Once column in the table has the lowest total information content and should be chosen as the best course of action. To verify this method, an experiment was set up to simulate the analytical problem. The experimental results are tabulated in table 2.6.

2.6.2.3 Semi Generative Approach

Generative forms of process planning in the true sense of the definition do not exist in our estimation. However, a number of "semi generative" exists which combine the decision logic of generative systems with the modification operations of variant systems. The semi-generative approach can be characterized as an advanced application of variant technology employing generative-type features. Hybrid systems can combine variant and generative features in the following ways:

- Within a given product mix, process plans for some products can be produced using generative methods while process plans for the remaining products can be produced using variant planning.
- The variant approach can be used to develop the general process plan, then the generative approach can be used to modify the standard plan.
- The generative plan can be used to create as much of the process plan as possible, then the variant approach can be used to fill in the details.
- The user can select either generative or variant modes for planning a part in order to accommodate fast process plan generation or complicated design features.

2.7 SELECTION PROCESSES

Process selection determines how the product (or service) will be produced. It determines the most economical method of performing an activity. It involves

1. Technological choice.
   (a) Major technological choice.
   (b) Minor technological choice.
2. Specific component choice.
3. Process flow choice.

1. Technological choice

(a) Major technological choice

While considering major technological choice, the following questions should be analysed:

- Does technology exist to make the product?
- Are there competing technologies among which we should choose?
- Should innovations be licensed from foreign countries?

(b) Minor technological choice

Once the major technological choice is made, there may be a number of minor technological process alternatives available. The operations manager should be involved in evaluating alternatives for costs and for consistency with the desired product and capacity plans.

Should the process be continuous, which is carried out for 24 hours a day in order to avoid expensive start ups and shut downs as used by steel and chemical industries.

An assembly line process on the other hand, follows the same series of steps as mass production but need not run for 24 hours a day example: automobile and readymade garment industries.

Job shop processes produce items in small lots, perhaps custom – made for a given customer/ market.

Suppose, we make a job shop choice, the alternatives do not end here. For example, in a factory, the fabrication, joining together and finishing of two pieces of metal may represent only a minuscule part of creating a finished product. There may be numerous ways of casting and molding, several ways of cutting, forming, assembly and finishing.

Deciding on the best combination of processes in terms of costs and the total operations process can be difficult.

2. Specific component choice

While considering the specific component choice, the following questions should be analysed.

- What type of equipment (and degree of automation) should be used?
- Should the equipment be specific purpose or general purpose?
- To what degree should machines be used to replace human labour in performing and automatically controlling the work?

Computer Aided Manufacturing (CAM) and industrial robots are being used increasingly in many manufacturing systems.

3. Process flow choice

- How should the product flow through the operations system?
- The final process selection step determines how materials and products will move through the system.
- Assembly drawings, assembly charts, route sheets and flow process charts are used to analyse process flow.
- Analysis may lead to resequencing, combining or eliminating operations in order to reduce materials handling and storage costs.

The three phases of process selection as discussed above are closely interrelated. In each phase choices should be made to minimize the process operations costs.

2.7.1 Factors Affecting Selection Process

A process is necessary in order to shape, form, condition and join materials and components with the help of machines and labour in order to convert raw material into a finished product.

Break even analysis should be used to find the cheaper process. The relation also depends on the following factors:

1. Availability of machine

If enough work has already been allocated to more efficient equipments, the current work may have to be passed on to less efficient machines to complete the same in time.

2. Delivery date

An early delivery date may

(*a*) Force the use of less efficient machines and,

(*b*) Rule out the use of special tools and jigs as they will take time for design and fabrication.

When the delivery has to be made quickly. Costlier process may have to be selected.

3. Quantity to be produced

Small quantity will not probably justify the high cost of preparation and efficient set-ups. Thus, quite possible they may have to be made on less efficient machines and vice-versa.

4. Quality standards

Quality standards may limit the choice of making the product on a particular machine, etc.

2.7.2 Machine Capacity

1. Capacity

Capacity is a rate of output, a quantity of output in a given time, and it is the highest quantity of output that is possible during that time. Yet, capacity is at the same time a dynamic concept which is subject to being changed and managed. To some extent, it can be adjusted to meet fluctuating sales levels.

2. Machine capacity—definition

Machine capacity may be defined as the time available for work at a machine expressed in machine hours (minutes etc.) For example, a machine may have a maximum capacity of 168 machine hours per week (7 days of 24 hours each). It is also termed as normal machine capacity.

3. Planned machine capacity

If overtime is worked, these extra-hours per week should be added to the normal machine capacity to find the planned machine capacity.

4. Machine down time

It is now necessary to subtract time for maintenance (machine down time), finding the time preferably by reference to the maintenance plan and to a statistical record of past machine break downs.

5. Idle machine time and machine ancillary time

Time must be allowed for idle machine time (waiting for work, no operator etc.) and for machine ancillary time (setting up, cleaning etc.).

6. Machine running time

To find the time actually available for useful work, the machine running time must be corrected up or down, if the average performance in the factory is more or less than the standard performance used in fixing the standard times for work operations.

7. Standard machine running time

The final capacity achieved after making all these corrections is known as the Standard Machine running time and is generally very much less than the maximum 168 hours per week.

Figure 2.6 illustrates these various levels of machine capacity. It will be realized that it would be possible to check load against capacity at a number of these levels, by making the adjustment to correct for lost time, to either the load or the capacity.

<table>
<tr><td colspan="4">Maximum machine capacity = 168 hours/week</td></tr>
<tr><td>Normal machine capacity</td><td colspan="2">Planned overtime</td><td>Not worked</td></tr>
<tr><td colspan="4">Planned machine capacity</td></tr>
<tr><td>Machine running time (planned)</td><td>Idle machine time (forecast)</td><td>Machine ancillary time (forecast)</td><td>Machine down time (forecast)</td></tr>
<tr><td colspan="4">Machine available time (planned)</td></tr>
<tr><td colspan="4">Machine running time (Planned)</td></tr>
<tr><td>Standard machine running time</td><td colspan="3">Low performance (forecast)</td></tr>
</table>

Fig. 2.6: Types of capacity

2.7.3 Analysis of Machine Capacity

The process of obtaining accurate information regarding the capacity of the available machines to produce the desired output is known as machine analysis.

An objective of machine analysis is to obtain the answers to certain definite questions in regard to the use of manufacturing machines.

1. How long will a certain machine take to perform its operation on a unit quantity of material?
2. How many units of material can be processed on this machine per day, week or month?
3. What is the maximum plant capacity per day for each process on each material?

The first of these three questions can be answered either

(a) From standard data,
(b) By actual experiment and trial or,
(c) By reference to records of past performance.

The second question can be answered when the machining time and set-up time are known and when an adequate allowance has been made for the inevitable idle time.

The third question is answered by aggregating the number of units which can be processed by similar machines to give the total plant capacity in units of product.

From this information it is possible to determine the maximum capacity of each process and the plant as a whole. Machine load charts, showing the work ahead of each machine, can also be prepared.

Certain ratios related to this topic are:

(i) Machine availability $= \dfrac{\text{Machine available time}}{\text{Total machine time}} \times 100$

(ii) Machine utilization $= \dfrac{\text{Actual running time}}{\text{Machine available time}} \times 100$

(iii) Machine efficiency $= \dfrac{\text{Standard running time}}{\text{Actual running time}} \times 100$

(iv) Machine effective utilization $= \dfrac{\text{Standard running time}}{\text{Machine available time}} \times 100$

2.7.4 Process and Equipment Selection Procedure

The formal steps of the process and equipment selection procedure are:

1. Developing a general statement of the manufacturing operations to be performed.
2. Establishing a provisional process to provide each individual feature identified by the product designer several additional inputs are necessary before beginning the selection of the provisional process. They are:
   - *(a)* Establish targets for facility and piece costs.
   - *(b)* Specify raw material.
   - *(c)* Determine hourly production volume preparatory for establishing machine capacity.
   - *(d)* Establish timing.
   - *(e)* Select the provisional process.

As part of the selection of the provisional process, the manufacturing engineer will estimate the number of steps and consequent stations necessary to provide all the design features identified on the blueprint. This will require visualization of each individual sequence, an estimate of manpower required and a rough approximation of the necessary layout provisions to accommodate each step of the process.

No process should be selected with a confidence level below that acceptable to the particular management (0.92 is a suggested minimum).

   - *(f)* Based on the provisional process, the manufacturing engineer will develop judgemental costs of facilities and materials and with the assistance of the industrial engineering function, will develop the preliminary piece cost of the components for the final assemblies.

3. Upon completing the provisional processing steps, the manufacturing engineer should develop a list of process alternatives, particularly for those areas where detailed analysis of the preliminary processing has shown high cost, questionable performance, or places where the confidence level of achieving the requirements of the individual operator is judged to be marginal of assistance in developing these opportunities are the historical data relative to similar operations.
4. A careful step-by-step comparison between each phase of the provisional process with each phase of the alternative process will allow the manufacturing engineer to select the compromised position, which optimizes all the elements of cost, quality, flexibility and inherent risk.

All the engineering management and manufacturing considerations being equal, production processes will be chosen on the basis of the most favourable return on investment or other financial criteria.

5. Upon completion of process selection it is communicated to the product engineering, industrial engineering, plant and maintenance engineering, industrial relations and financial departments.

This will provide co-ordination and communication among all concerned which is essential for the successful adaptation of new technology to existing plant and staff.

6. Performing detailed processing.

When the process has been selected and communicated to all affected departments, the final detailed processing upon which all actions depend is initiated.

As the detailed processing proceeds, the manufacturing engineer will make extensive use of the body of engineering knowledge that resides with the machine and equipment suppliers.

As in the establishment of the provisional process, the starting point in establishing the detailed processing is to assemble the latest information relative to product design, production rate, facility cost and part cost targets.

Detailed processing follows the same format as did the provisional processing, except that each element of the process will be completely identified and documented through the use of process estimate sheets.

Information is included on the source of the material for each process from rough stock to finished piece. The subsequent operation should be identified on each process sheet so that there can be an orderly part flow through each of the manufacturing operations.

2.7.5 Process Sheet Description

To examine the required amount of processing documentation, a particular example a machining operation will be used.

- The basic principle involved is that the instructions detailed in the manufacturing engineering document, that is the process sheet, be sufficiently explicit that operational personnel can perform every function necessary to produce the finished component and that operations can establish staffing and piece cost from which to judge operation efficiency during and after physically launching the operation.
- The process sheet contains columns for recording the operation number, a description of operation, numbers and types of machines required, effective operational rates, labour distribution, and minute costs; provision is also made for recording facility and tool costs.
- The process engineer will fill out those portions of the process sheet that relate to establishing the process and selecting the machinery; the plant engineer will enter data relating to the installation cost of the machinery; and the industrial engineer will approximately as certain and register the direct labour minutes of each operation, and so on.
- The sample entry on the process sheet shows the manner in which the manufacturing engineer describes each step in manufacturing process. The engineer numbers and names the operation, namely drill. He indicates the features, namely, the holes, and establishes, their limit, that is their size and depth.

With this information, it is possible to identify the machine(s) required to carry out this specific step. In the example, the machine can be a single-spindle or multi-spindle and can be part of additional automation that is transfer line or a dial machine. All of this information is included on the process sheet.

Number of machines required to meet the production volume and the space required to complete the description of this individual process sheet. If fixtures or tools are required, they should be individually listed and costed as durable tools or special tools in the space provided. Each subsequent operation is identified in the exact detail until the part 18 finished.

2.7.6 Determination of Man, Machine and Material Requirements

2.7.6.1 Manpower Requirement

If a worker works for one hour, it is known as one man hour. Thus in a shift, the worker works for 8 hours giving 8 man hours.

Plant ..... Department ......

Program No.	Party Name.					Issue	Part No.	Sheet of
For models	Material				WT/kg. RGH FIN	dates	Release	
Operation No.	**Operation description**	**Tool-M/c equipment description**	**M/cs reqd. capacity**	**Net hrly**	**Est. minutes**	**Facility and durable tool cost TBF1**	**Special tool cost + TD**	**Expense cost BLIT**
10.	Drill (3) locator holes 10 ϕ 30 deep	Single spindle Drill press locating fixture reqd.	1	16	3.75			

Total

Remarks

Process Engr.	PLT layout	Design	Material Engr.	Daily service	Reqd. per vehicle	Next Assy.	
Ind. Engr.	Qc. contr.	Plant Engr.	Prodn.	Daily PLT planning volume	Requirements Pc/hr	Supersedes	Order
*T-Total	F-Frieght	*T-Total	BL-Build				
B-Basic	I-Installation	D-Design	IT-Inst. Tryout.				

Fig. 2.7: *Typical process sheet*

The manpower needed is calculated as follows:

1. Number of man hours required for the load on hand for the year = H_1 hrs.
2. Number of man hours required due to new load for the year (from the process sheet) = H_2 hrs.
3. Allowance for absentism, leave etc. = H_3 hrs.
4. Total man hours requirement for the year = $H_1 + H_2 + H_3$ hrs.
5. Available man hours = H_4 hrs.
6. Additional man hours required = $H_1 + H_2 + H_3 - H_4$ (Assume 2000 man hours per man per year)
7. Number of additional men required = $\dfrac{H_1 + H_2 + H_3 - H_4}{2000}$

In addition to this the number of helpers, supervisors etc. are also calculated.

2.7.6.2 Machine and Equipment Requirement

The requirement of machine and equipment is calculated as follows

Let,

1. The load on machines for the year due to the work on hand $= H_1$ hrs.
2. The new load on machines for the year based on the process sheet $= H_2$ hrs.
3. Therefore total load on machines for the year $= (H_1 + H_2)$hrs.
4. Time required for maintenance and machine setting (20% of total load) $= H_3$ hrs.
5. Number of machine hours per year for one machine $= h$ hrs.
6. Therefore No. of machines required $= \dfrac{H_1 + H_2 + H_3}{h} = N_1$
7. Available machines $= N_2$
8. Additional machines required $= N_1 - N_2$

In calculating the available machine-hour per machine for the year, the following factors are considered:

(*a*) Number of shifts per day.

(*b*) Giving allowance for rest break and other delays. Assume only 40 machine-hour per week per single shift (instead of 48 hours).

(*c*) Similarly, giving allowance for different holidays, we assume only 50 working weeks per years. Hence, total working hour per machine for single shift is $50 \times 40 = 2000$ hrs. per year.

2.8 MATERIAL REQUIREMENT

It has become a subject requiring study, because selection of material has become complicated by the great increase not only in the kinds of materials but also in the various forms in which any one material may be available.

Material should be of right quality and chemical composition as per the product specifications. Shape and size of material should restrict the scrap (i.e., material removed for getting the product shape).

2.8.1 Bill of Material

The most common method of analyzing a product into component parts is through the use of bills of material or specification sheets. Bill of material is a means of determining, purchasing and production order requirements. It should indicate if the part is to be manufactured or purchased.

The production control department uses the bill of material to determine manufacturing and scheduling dates. Process engineering uses it as a checklist to complete their work. Methods engineering uses it in the preparation of time allowances for assembling operations.

Accumulations are made by the stores department according to the bill of material. They in turn set up the shortage lists for use by expediters of the production-control department.

Releases by assembly units are made by the finished stores department in accordance with the bills of material.

The design of the bill of material varies slightly in minor details, depending upon the various uses made of it by individual companies. The information usually required on the bill of material form includes

1. The product name.
2. Product code identification.
3. Sheet number.
4. Use.
5. Date of preparation.
6. Name/initials of preparer.
7. Name/initials of checker.
8. Item numbers.
9. Make/purchase designations.
10. Subassembly part numbers and names.
11. Quantity requirements, and
12. Material used in each part.

Note: Bill of material is also known as part list.

Item switch, Y 30 — Sheet No.1 of 2,

Drawing = 5 — Assembly 5 HP motor

Date :

Part No.	*Part*	*No/item*	*Material*	*Quantity per item*	*Cost per item*	*Remarks*
SJ-64	Drive spring	2	Sprg steel	-	Rs.5/-	Purchase
Made by...................					Checked by................	

Fig. 2.8: Bill of materials

The requirement of material is calculated as follows:

1. Material required for work already on hand = Q_1
2. Material required for the new work as per the bill of material (including wastage) = Q_2
3. Total material requirement = $Q_1 + Q_2$
4. Material available in stores = Q_3
5. Additional material to be purchased = $(Q_1 + Q_2) - Q_3$.

Selection of jigs, fixtures and other special attachments

These supporting devices are necessary:

- To give higher production rate.
- To reduce cost of production per piece.

Selection of cutting tools and inspection gauges:

They, respectively, are necessary to

- Reduce production time.
- Inspect accurately and at a faster rate.

Tools, jigs and fixture requirements

The tools requirements is worked out considering the following:

1. Number of tools already available.
2. Number of new tools required.
3. Time required for designing the new tools.
4. Taking (make or buy) decision for new tools.
5. Finding out when the new tools will be ready for use.

2.8.2 Machine Tool Replacement

Whether the existing machines and tools should be replaced with new and more modern equipment is a problem frequently faced by the management of a company. The wearing out of the equipment as well as its being made obsolete by new developments and improved devices makes this an every present problem. Some major reasons for machine replacement or purchase of new machine tool are

1. To increase productivity i.e., 'the production of an ever increasing amount of parts per unit of time, per unit of floor space, per unit of material, light, heat and power'.
2. To improve product quality.
3. To accommodate changes in product size.
4. To increase flexibility of use of machine tools by addition of new features.
5. To extend the range of use of new product kind or style.
6. To eliminate safety hazards.
7. To reduce an indirect cost associated with the machine or the product it produces.
8. To obtain maximum rate of return.

2.8.3 Factors Influencing Choice of Machinery

Choice of machines for production of a product depends on the following factors:

1. Accuracy

The machine should be capable of giving the accuracy required. Accuracy is the key factor for the product sales. High accuracy machines produces high quality products whereas low accuracy machines leads to low quality products.

The accuracy of the machine is selected depending upon the required product. If the product to be produced is very important in the system or functional part of the system, high quality is required, example, pressure relief valve in the steam boiler, piston's used in automobile engines etc.

In this case high accuracy machines should be selected.

If the product to be produced by the machine is not so important or not a functional part of the system, low quality is enough and low quality machines should be selected.

Example 2.1

Base of the machines such as lathe bed, universal drilling machine bed etc.

2. Rate of output

The machine should be capable of giving the required rate of output.

The machine to be selected is depending upon the rate of output required. If the output required is less we have to select conventional machines such as lathe, drilling machine, shaper, planner etc. If the output required is more, the automatic machines such as capstan and turret lathes, NC machines, CNC machines etc. to be selected.

3. Cost

The machine producing the given quantity of product at the least cost should be selected.

2.8.4 Selection of Machinery

While selecting the machine for a particular product (or) process, the following methods are used:

1. Selection among the two suitable machines.
2. Break-even point analysis.
3. Production cost comparison.
4. Process-cost comparison.

2.8.4.1 Selection among Suitable Machines

If for a job, the choice lies between two suitable machines, then the machine with the lower cost per unit of production will be selected. For this, the unit cost for each machine is calculated in the following manner:

Let,

C = First cost of first machine (installed).
c = First cost of second machine (installed).
N = Annual production of first machine.
n = Annual production of second machine.
L = Annual labour cost on first machine.
l = Annual labour cost on second machine.
B = Annual labour burden on first machine, %
b = Annual labour burden on second machine, %
I = Rate of interest, %
T = Rate of taxes and insurance, %
D = Annual allowance for depreciation on first machine %
d = Annual allowance for depreciation on second machine, %

M = Annual allowance for maintenance on first machine, %
m = Annual allowance for maintenance on second machine, %
P = Annual cost of power for first machine.
p = Annual cost of power for second machine.
X = Unit production cost on first machine.
x = Unit production cost on second machine.
F = Saving in floor space per year, of first over second machine.

Annual cost of a machine is given as,

Total cost = Fixed cost + Variable cost.

For the first machine,

Fixed cost = C(I+T+D+M)

Variable cost = L+BL+P

$$\therefore \quad X = \frac{L + BL + P + C(I + T + D + M) - F}{N}$$

$$\text{Similarly,} \quad x = \frac{l + bl + p + c(I + T + d + m)}{n}$$

If the use of first machine results in a loss rather than a saving in floor space, the sign of F must be changed to plus in equation 2.1.

Example 2.2

The annual requirement of an article (about 4000 pieces) can be met by one semi-automatic turret lathe or by two engine lathes. The cost of turret lathe is Rs.80,000(installed) and that of the engine lathe is Rs.32,000. The useful life of each type of machine is 10 years. The turret lathe takes up the same floor space as one engine, lathe, saving Rs.480 per year in floor space. The turret lathe can produce 4000 parts in 2256 hours including set up time. Its operator receives Rs.4 per hours. One operator is required on each engine lathe, the wage rate being Rs.5 per hour.

Both engine lathes are operated for 2300 hours and produce a total of 3800 pieces. I = 6%, T = 4%, D = d = 10%, M = m = 6%, B = b = 55%. A 4-hp motor is used on turret lathe and a 2 ½ hp motor on each of the engine lathe. The power rate is Rs.0.35 per kwh. Which type of machine should be selected for the job?

Given data:

C = Rs. 80,000
c = 32000×2 = Rs. 64000
N = 4000
n = 3800
L = 2256×4 = Rs. 9024
l = $2300 \times 2 \times 5$ = Rs. 23000
I = 6%
T = 4%
D = d = 10%; Turret lathe motor power = 4 hp.
M = m = 6%; Engine lathe motor power = 2 ½ hp.
B = b = 55%; Power rate = Rs.0.35 per kWh.

To find

Type of machine should be selected for the job.

Solution

$$\text{Annual cost of power} = \frac{\text{Motor power} \times 746 \times \text{Total machine hours} \times \text{Power rate (kWh)}}{1000}$$

$$P = \frac{4 \times 746 \times 2256 \times 0.35}{1000}$$

$$= \text{Rs. } 2356$$

$$p = \frac{2 \times 2.5 \times 746 \times 2300 \times 0.35}{1000}$$

$$= \text{Rs. } 3002$$

$$F = \text{Rs. } 480$$

$$\therefore \quad X = \frac{L + BL + P + c\left(I + T + D + M\right) - F}{N}$$

$$= \frac{9024 + 0.55 \times 9024 + 2356 + 80000 \left(0.6 + 0.04 + 0.10 + 0.06 - 480\right)}{4000}$$

$$= \text{Rs. } 9.16 \text{ per piece}$$

$$x = \frac{l + bl + p + c\left(I + T + d + m\right)}{n}$$

$$= \frac{23000 + 0.55 \times 2300 + 3002 + 64000 \left(0.06 + 0.04 + 0.10 + 0.06\right)}{3800}$$

$$= \text{Rs. } 14.55 \text{ per piece.}$$

Result

One turret lathe will be more economical than two-engine lathe. [$\because$ x < X].

2.8.4.2 Break Even Point Analysis

(a) Break even point analysis is also used to make a choice between two machines tools to produce a given component.

To determine which of the two machines is most economical, the total cost of the two machines (fixed cost + variable cost) is plotted against the number of units. The point at which the two lines representing the total costs of the two machines meet each other, is termed as break even point.

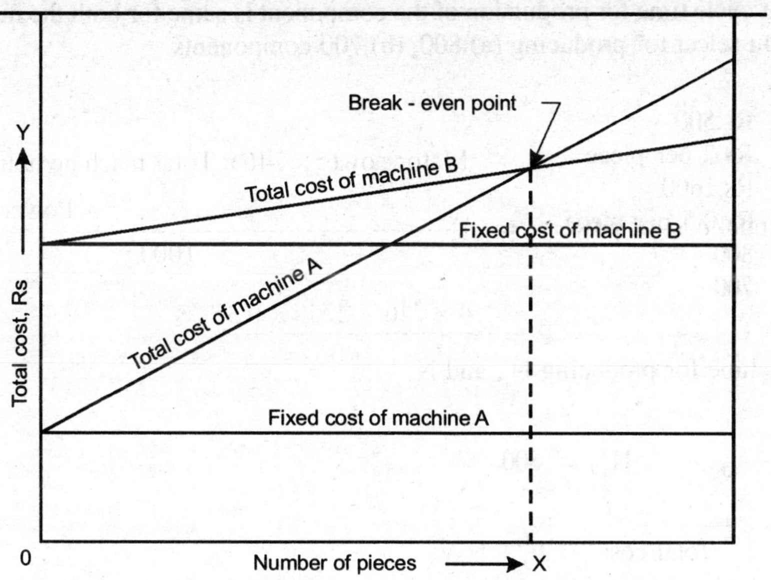

Fig. 2.9: Break even point

Towards the left of break even point figure 2.9, machine. A is economical than machine B and if the quantity of production is more than that corresponding to break even point, machine B becomes economical than machine A.

Mathematically, the above discussion can be written as,

$$F_A + Q \times V_a = F_B + Q \times V_B,$$

$$\therefore \quad Q = \frac{F_B - F_A}{V_A - V_B}$$

where,
F_A = Fixed cost of machine A, Rs.
F_B = Fixed cost of machine B, Rs.
V_A = Variable cost of machine A, Rs.
V_B = Variable cost of machine B, Rs.
Q = Required Quantity.

This would give a positive value when fixed cost of a process is greater and variable cost less than those of the other process. If both fixed cost and variable cost are lower than the other process, then the latter process is always uneconomical whatever may be the production quantity.

This can also be done by graphical method.

Example 2.3

A component can be produced on either a capstan lathe or an automatic lathe. The different cost factors for the two machines are given below.

Machine I

Fixed cost = Rs.500
Variable cost = Rs.3 per piece

Machine II

Fixed cost = Rs.1500
Variable cost = Rs.1 per piece

Assume that cycle time for production of the component is same for both the machines. Which machine will you select for producing (a) 800, (b) 700 components.

Given data:

F_A = Rs.500
V_A = Rs.2 per piece
F_B = Rs.1600
V_B = Rs.0.5 per piece
N_1 = 800
N_2 = 700

To find

Type of machine for producing N_1, and N_2

Solution

(a) Let $N_1 = 800$

Machine I

Total cost $= F_A + N_1 V_A$
$= (500 + 800 \times 2)$
$=$ Rs.2100

Machine II

Total cost $= F_B + N_1 V_B$
$= (1600 + 800 \times 0.5)$
$=$ Rs.2000

We select machine II as the total cost is less.

(b) Let $N_1 = 700$

Machine I

Total cost $= F_A + N_2 V_A$
$= 500 + (700 \times 2)$
$=$ Rs.1900

Machine II

Total cost $= F_B + N_2 V_B$
$= (1600 + 700 \times 0.5)$
$=$ Rs.1950

We select machine I as the total cost is less.

Result

N_1 = 800 = machine II, and
N_2 = 700 = machine I.

Example 2.4

The initial cost for machine A is Rs.12000 and the unit production cost of the machine is Rs.6.00 each. For the other machine B, the initial cost is Rs. 48000 and the unit production cost is Rs.1.20 each. Do the break even analysis.

iven data

$$\text{Fixed cost of A, } F_a = \text{Rs. } 1200$$

$$\text{Variable cost of A, } V_A = \text{Rs. } 6.00$$

$$\text{Fixed cost of B, } F_B = \text{Rs. } 48000$$

$$\text{Variable cost of B, } V_B = \text{Rs. } 1.20$$

o find

Break even analysis.

olution

At the break even point,

Total cost of machine A = Total cost of machine B

Total cost = Fixed cost + variable cost

Variable cost = Unit production cost × number of pieces

∴ If 'Q' is the quantity of production at break-even point, then,

$$F_A + Q \times V_A = F_B + Q \times V_B$$

$$Q = \frac{F_B - F_A}{V_A - V_B}$$

$$= \frac{48000 - 12000}{6 - 1.2}$$

$$= 7500 \text{ pieces}$$

esult

If production does not exceed 7500 pieces, it is more economical to purchase machine A. For igher quantity production, the economy lies with machine B.

xample 2.5

he following information is available for two machines:

	Item	*Capstan Lathe*	*Automatic (Single spindle)*
(i)	Tooling cost	Rs. 300	Rs. 300
(ii)	Cost of cams	–	Rs. 1500
(iii)	Material cost per piece	Rs.2.50	Rs.2.50
(iv)	Operation labour cost	Rs. 5 per hour	Rs. 2 per hour
(v)	Cycle time per piece	5 min.	1 min.
(vi)	Setting up labour cost	Rs. 20 per hr.	Rs. 20 per hr.
(vii)	Setting up time	1 hr.	8 hr.
(viii)	Machine over heads (setting and operation)	300% of (iv)	1000% of (iv)

Find the break-even quantity for a component which can be produced on either the capstan athe or the single spindle automatic.

Solution

1. Capstan Lathe

$$\text{Overheads} = \frac{300}{100} \times 5 = \text{Rs.15 per hr}$$

$$\begin{aligned}
\text{Fixed cost} &= \text{Tooling cost + Setting up labour cost + Setting up overhead} \\
&= 300 + 20 \times 1 + 15 \times 1 \\
&= \text{Rs. } 335 \\
\text{Variable cost per piece} &= \text{Material cost + Labour cost + Operation overheads} \\
&= 2.50 + 5 \times 5/60 + 15 \times 5/60 \\
&= \text{Rs. } 4.16
\end{aligned}$$

2. Automatic

$$\begin{aligned}
\text{Overheads} &= \frac{1000}{100} \times 2 \\
&= \text{Rs. 20 per hr.} \\
\text{Fixed cost} &= (300 + 1500) + (20 \times 8) + (20 \times 8) \\
&= \text{Rs. } 2120 \\
\text{Variable cost per piece} &= 2.50 + (2 \times 1/60) + 20 \times 1/60 \\
&= \text{Rs.}2.863
\end{aligned}$$

∴ If 'Q' is the break even quantity, then,

$$\begin{aligned}
F_A + QV_A &= F_B + QV_B \\
335 + Q \times 4.16 &= 2120 + Q \times 2.863 \\
Q &= 1373 \text{ pieces}
\end{aligned}$$

Result

(a) Its production does not exceed 1373 pieces, it is more economical to produce the component on capstan lathe. For higher quantity production, the component is to be produced on automatic lathe.

(b) Some companies use a formula to calculate the break even point between two machines. The formula is based on known or estimated elements that make up the production costs. The formula is given as

$$Q = \frac{pP(SL + SD - sl - sd)}{P(ltd) - p(L + D)}$$

where,
Q = Quantity of pieces at break even point.
P = Number of pieces produced per hour by the first machine.
p = Number of pieces produced per hour by the second machine.
S = Set up time required on the first machine, hrs.

l = Labour rate for the first machine, Rs.

L = Labour rate for the second machine, Rs.

d = Hourly depreciation rate for first machine (based on machine hours)

D = Hourly depreciation rate for second machine (based on machine hours).

Example 2.6

The following data is given for turret lathe and automatic lathe.

Turret lathe	*Automatic lathe*
p = 10 pieces per hour	P = 30 pieces per hour
s = 2 hour	S = 4 hours
l = Rs.4 per hour	L = Rs. 4 per hour
d = Rs.1.50 per machine hour	D = Rs.4.50 per machine hour

Find the break even quantity which can be produced on either the turret lathe or the automatic lathe.

Solution

Putting the values in equation.

$$Q = \frac{pP\left(SL + SD - sl - sd\right)}{P(ltd) - p(L + D)}$$

$$= \frac{10 \times 30\left(4 \times 4 + 4 \times 4.50 - 2 \times 4 - 2 \times 1.50\right)}{30\left(4 + 1.50\right) - 10\left(4 + 4.50\right)}$$

$= 86$ pieces.

2.8.4.3 Production Cost Comparison

Another simple approach to do break even point analysis is to compare the cost of production by the two machines, by considering the following items of cost.

(a) Time to produce a part.
(b) Set up.
(c) Direct labour cost.
(d) The overheads.

Let For,

1st machine	*2nd machine*
t = Time/piece, min.	T = Time/piece, min.
o = Overhead cost/hr.	O = Overhead cost/hr.
s = Set up time, hr.	S = Set up time, hr.
sr = Set up rate/hr.	Sr = Set up rate/hr.

For first machine

Fixed cost = Set up cost = ssr

Variable cost = Direct labour cost + Overhead cost

$$= \frac{t}{60}(1 - o) \text{per piece}$$

$$\therefore \quad \text{Total cost} = ssr + \frac{t}{60}(1+o).Q$$

Similarly for second machine,

$$\text{Total cost} = SSr + \frac{T}{60}(L+o).Q$$

$\therefore$ For break even point,

$$SSr + \frac{t}{60}(1+o).Q = SSr + \frac{T}{60}(L+o).Q$$

$$\therefore \quad Q = \frac{60\,(SSr - SSr)}{t\,(1+o) - T\,(L-o)}$$

Example 2.7

Do the break even analysis for engine lathe and turret lathe, from the following data.

Engine lathe	***Turret lathe***
t = 12 min.	T = 5 min.
l = Rs. 7 per hr.	L = Rs. 5 per hr.
o = Rs. 4 per hr.	O = Rs. 8 per hr.
s = 2 hrs.	S = 8 hrs.
sr = Rs. 8 per hr.	Sr = Rs. 8 per hr.

Solution

From equation.

$$Q = \frac{60\,(SSr - ssr)}{t\,(1+o) - T\,(L+O)}$$

$$= \frac{60\,(8 \times 8 - 2 \times 8)}{12\,(7+4) - 5\,(5+8)}$$

$$Q = 43 \text{ pieces}$$

Result

Thus a job of 43 or more pieces should be done on turret lathe.

Example 2.8

A semi automatic turret lathe costs. Rs. 80000 and it produces 16 pieces per hour and its operator receives Rs. 2 per hour. An engine lathe which costs Rs. 32000 produces to pieces per hour and its operator receives Rs. 2.50 per hour. Calculate the minimum number of pieces which makes turret lathe more economical.

Given data:

Semi automatic turret lathe

$$\text{Fixed cost, } F_A = \text{Rs. } 80000$$

$$\text{Variable cost, } V_A = \text{Rs. 2 per hour.}$$

No. of pieces produced per hour = 16

Engine lathe

$$\text{Fixed cost, } F_B = \text{Rs. } 32000$$

$$\text{Variable cost, } V_B = \text{Rs. } 2.50 \text{ per hour.}$$

No. of pieces produced per hour = 10

To find

Minimum no. of pieces which makes turret

Solution

Lathe more economical, Q

Total cost of turret lathe = Total cost of engine lathe

(Fixed cost + Variable cost) of turret lathe

= (Fixed cost + Variable cost) of engine lathe

∴ If Q is the minimum number of pieces, then

$$F_A + Q \times V_A = F_B + Q \times V_B$$

$$V_A = \text{Rs. } 2 \text{ per hour}$$

$$V_A = 2/16 \text{ per piece}$$

Similarly,

$$V_B = 2.5/10 \text{ per piece}$$

$$\therefore \quad Q = \frac{F_A - F_B}{V_B - V_A} = \frac{80000 - 32000}{\frac{2.5}{10} - \frac{2}{16}}$$

$$Q = 384000 \text{ pieces}$$

Result

The minimum no. of pieces which makes turret lathe more economical, Q is 384000 pieces.

2.8.4.4 Process Cost Comparison

For a given job, more than one manufacturing process may be used. The most economical process is that which gives the lowest total cost per part.

Let,

Nf = Total number of parts to be produced in a single run.

Q = Number of parts for which the unit cost will be equal for each of the two compared methods A and B break even point (figure 2.10).

Ta = Total tool cost for methods 'A'

Tb = Total tool cost for methods 'B'

Pa = Units tool process cost for method 'A'

Pb = Unit tool process cost for method 'B'

Ca = Tool unit cost for method 'A'

Cb = Tool unit cost for method 'B'

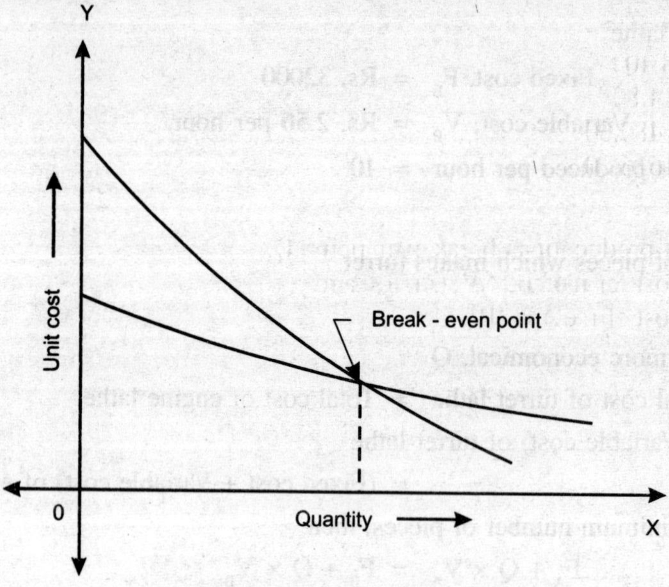

Fig. 2.10: Break even point

Equating the total cost of the two methods

$$Ta + Q \cdot Pa = tb + Q \cdot Pb$$

$$\therefore \quad Q = \frac{Ta - Tb}{Pb - Pa}$$

Now, total unit cost = Fixed cost + Variable cost

$\therefore$ For method 'A',

$$Ca \times Nt = Ta + Pa \times Nt$$

$$\therefore \quad Ca = \frac{Ta + Pa \times Nt}{Nt}$$

Similarly

$$Cb = \frac{Tb + Pb + Nt}{Nt}$$

Example 2.9

The aircraft flap nose rib can be produced either by hydropress or by steel draw die. The following data is available for Nt = 500.

Pa	=	Rs. 8.40	Pb	=	Rs. 14.80
Ta	=	Rs. 6480.00	Tb	=	Rs. 1616.00

Determine the quantity of production at 'break even point' and tool unit cost for method 'A' and method 'B'.

Given data:

Nt = 500
Pa = Rs. 8.40
Pb = Rs. 14.80
Ta = Rs. 6480.00
Tb = Rs. 1616.00

To find

(*a*) Quantity of production at break even point, Q.
(*b*) Tool unit cost for method 'A', Ca, Rs, and
(*c*) Tool unit cost of method 'B', Cb, Rs.

Solution

(*a*)
$$Q = \frac{Ta - Tb}{Pb - Pa}$$
$$= \frac{6480 - 1616}{14.80 - 8.40}$$
$$Q = 760 \text{ pieces}$$

(*b*)
$$Ca = \frac{Ta + Pa \times Nt}{Nt}$$
$$= \frac{6480 + 8.40 \times 500}{500}$$

(*c*)
$$Cb = \frac{Tb + Pb + Nt}{Nt}$$
$$= \frac{1616 + 14.80 \times 500}{500}$$

Result

(*a*) Q = 760 pieces.
(*b*) Ca = Rs. 21.36
(*c*) Cb = Rs. 18.032

2.9 SET OF DOCUMENTS FOR PROCESS PLANNING

(Already discussed in 2.5.2).

2.10 DEVELOPING MANUFACTURING LOGIC AND KNOWLEDGE

(Already discussed in 2.6.2.2.1).

2.11 PROCESS TIME CALCULATION

Machining time in time during when the work pieces or job is being changed to the desired size, shape or form on the machine tool. Machining time can be computed after determining the revolutions per minute feed of tool number of cuts etc.

2.12 SELECTION OF COST OPTIMAL PROCESS

In some cases, a number of alternative processes may be available and a process planner has t choose a particular manufacturing process. For instance, the turning operation on a part of componen may be performed on an automatic lathe, an engine lathe or turret lathe. Process research ma have to be carried out to select the best process. Decisions regarding select of manufacturin process depend upon both economic and non-economic considerations. The incremental cost c each alternative and the volume of manufacture are important economic considerations.

Non-economic considerations may differ from situation to situation. For example, machin availability may be an important consideration in the intermittent production of custom built part Similarly, in case of very difficult job, a machine that holds closer tolerance may be a better choice

In addition to the selection of manufacturing process, the process planner, is expected to specif the machines to be used, the type of tools required, the speed under which process should be carrie out.

REVIEW QUESTIONS

1. Define process planning.
2. What is the purpose of process planning?
3. Explain the concept of process planning with sketch.
4. What are the objectives of process planning?
5. List the informations required to do process planning.
6. Explain the activities involved in process planning.
7. Explain the process sheet and its necessity.
8. What are the various approaches of process planning?
9. Explain variant approach of process planning.
10. Explain generative approach of process planning.
11. What do you mean by artificial intelligence?
12. What is axiomatice approach?
13. Explain the selection process.
14. What are the factors affecting selection process?
15. Explain the steps involved in process and equipment selection procedure.
16. Explain break even analysis with a sketch.
17. What is break even analysis?
18. What are the reasons for machine tool replacement?
19. What are the factors influencing choice of machinery?
20. Explain the methods used for selection of machinery.

Unit–3

INTRODUCTION TO COST ESTIMATION

3.0 INTRODUCTION

Cost estimation may be defined as the process of forecasting the expenses that must be incurred to manufacture a product. These expenses take into consideration all expenditures involved in design and manufacturing with all the related service facilities such as pattern making, tool making as well as portion of the general administrative and selling costs. Cost estimates are the joint product of the engineer and the cost accountant.

Estimating is the calculation of the costs which are expected to be incurred in manufacturing a component in advance before the component is actually manufactured.

Costing may be defined as a system of accounts which systematically and accurately records every expenditure in order to determine the cost of a product after knowing the different expenses incurred in various department.

3.1 REASONS FOR DOING ESTIMATES

Cost estimates are developed for a variety of different reasons. The most important reasons are shown below.

Should the product be produced? When a company designs a new product, a detailed estimate of cost is developed to assist management in making an intelligent decision about producing the product. This detailed estimate of cost includes an estimate of material cost, labour cost, purchased components and assembly cost.

In addition to product cost, many other elements must be estimated. These include all tooling costs. A cost estimate must be developed for jigs, fixtures, tools, dies and gauges. Also, the cost of any capital equipment must be entered into the estimate. These figures are usually supplied through quotation by vendors. An estimate of this nature will include a vast amount of details, because if management approves the project, the estimate now becomes the budget.

Estimates as temporary work standards. Many companies that produce product in high volume, such as automotive companies, will use estimates on the shop floor as temporary work standards. Temporary work standards are replaced with time studied work standards as rapidly as possible.

Cost control

A job shop (contract shop) will use a cost estimate for cost control purposes because lot of sizes are small and job shops seldom estimate work standards for what they produce. This use of an estimate for this purpose is different from temporary standards in that it uses the "meet or beat" philosophy.

Make-or-buy decision

When a company sets out to produce a new product, many components in the bill of materials are subject to a make-or-buy decision. A cost estimate is developed for comparison purposes. There are usually considerations aside from piece part cost. These may include tooling cost, vendor quality, and vendor delivery.

Determine selling price

An estimate is used to determine selling price. The estimate is always a reflection of actual cost. In most organizations the marketing department has the responsibility of establishing a selling price, which can be substantially different from the cost estimate. There are many reasons for this. For example, a contract shop might be willing to sell the first order at something less than the estimate to develop a new customer.

Check vendor quotes (purchase analysis)

An estimating function is often established for the sole purpose of checking vendor quotations on outsourced work. One automobile company has an entire department of cost estimators devoted to this task.

3.2 DEFINITION

Cost estimating may be defined as the process of forecasting the expenses that must be incurred to manufacture a product. These expenses take into consideration all expenditures involved in design and manufacturing with all the related service facilities such as pattern making tool making, as well as a portion of the general administrative and selling costs.

Cost estimating also includes predetermination of the quantity and quality of material, labour required etc. Estimating requires highly technical knowledge about manufacturing methods and operation times etc.

Cost estimates are the joint product of the engineer and the cost accountant, and involves two factors.

1. Physical data.
2. Costing data.

1. Physical data

The engineer as part of his job of planning and manufacturing determines the physical data.

2. Costing data

The cost accountant compiles and applies the costing data.

3.2.1 Importance of Estimating

Estimating is of great importance to a concern because it enables the factory owner to decide about the manufacturing and selling policies. It is obvious that too high estimates will not get jobs to the firm by quoting higher rates according to over estimate whereas under estimating will put the owner to a loss and will lead the concern to utter failure. So, estimation should be carried out accurately. The persons preparing estimates should be highly qualified and experienced. They should be chosen from shops or should be first trained in all the shop methods and their estimates preparation.

3.3 OBJECTIVES OR PURPOSE OF ESTIMATING

The main purpose or objective of estimating are

(i) To establish the selling price of a product.

(ii) To ascertain whether a proposed product can be manufactured and marketed profitably.

(iii) To determine how much must be invested in equipment.

(iv) To find whether parts or assemblies can be more cheaply fabricated or purchased from outside (make or buy decision).

(v) To determine the most economical process, tooling or material for making a product.

(vi) To establish a standard of performance at the start of project.

(vii) For feasibility studies on possible new products.

(viii) To assist in long term financial planning.

(ix) To prepare production budget.

(x) To help in responding to tender enquiries.

(xi) To evaluate alternate designs of a product.

(xii) To set a standard estimate of costs.

(xiii) To initiate programs of cost reduction that result in economics due to the use of new materials, which produce lower scrap losses and which create savings due to revisions in methods of tooling and processing, and

(xiv) To control actual operating costs by incorporating these estimates into the general plan of cost accounting.

3.4 FUNCTIONS OF ESTIMATING

(i) To calculate the cost of new material needed to manufacture a product.

(ii) To find the cost of parts to be purchased from outside vendors.

(iii) To find the cost of equipment, machinery, tools, jigs and fixtures etc. required to be purchased to make the product.

(iv) To calculate the direct and indirect labour cost associated with the manufacture of the product, based upon work study.

(v) To calculate various overhead charges associated with the product.

(vi) To decide about the profit to be charged, taking into consideration other manufacturers of same product in the market.

(vii) To calculate the selling price of the product.

(viii) To maintain records of previous estimating activities of the company for future references.

(ix) To decide the most economical method of making the product.

(x) To submit cost estimates with the competent authority for further action.

3.5 COST ACCOUNTING OF COSTING

It is the determination of an actual cost of a component after adding different expenses incurred in various departments or it may be defined as a system which systematically records all the expenditures to determine the cost of manufactured products. The work of cost accountings begins with the pre-planning stage of the product. It ends only after the whole lot of the product has been fully manufactured. Costing progresses with the progress of the product through the plant.

3.6 IMPORTANCE OF COSTING

Costing is an essential work for the efficient management of any enterprise and gives most useful information for the preparation of financial accounts. It enables a business not only to find out what various jobs or processes have costed but also what they should have costed. It indicates where losses are wastage are occurring before the work is finished, so that immediate action may be taken to avoid such loss or waste. Also all expenditure are localized and thereby controlled in the light of information provided by the cost records.

Costing shows which type of output will yield a profit and which type does not. Thus, it makes up the deficiency. A planned system of cost accounting will point out the weak spots and thus enable the administration to have a clear picture and show up immediately the essential facts in such a way that the responsible persons can put forth their efforts to bring improvements and reduce costs.

Costing has proved so beneficial that nowadays almost every concern has adopted the cost accounting system.

3.7 AIMS OF COST ACCOUNTING

The purpose of costing are:

1. To compare the actual cost with the estimated cost to know whether the estimate had been realistic or not.
2. Wastages and undesirable expenses are pointed out requiring corrective measures.
3. The costing data helps in changing the selling price because of change in material cost of labour cost etc.
4. It helps to locate the reasons for the increase or decrease of loss of profits of a company.
5. It helps in determining the discount on catalogue or market price of the product.
6. The actual cost helps the company to decide whether to continue with the manufacture of a product or to buy it from outside.
7. It helps the enterprise to prepare its budget.
8. The costing data helps to formulate policies and plans for the pricing of a new job.
9. It helps in regulating from time to time the production of a job so that it may be profitable to the company.

3.8 DIFFERENCE BETWEEN COST ESTIMATING AND COST ACCOUNTING

Point of comparison	*Cost estimating*	*Cost accounting*
1. Type of cost	It gives an expected cost of the product based on the calculations by means of standard formulae or certain established rules.	It gives actual cost of the product based on the data collected from the different expenditures actually done for a product.

Contd...

2. Duration of process	It is generally carried out before actual production of a product. Due to certain unforeseen or unexpected expenses coming to light at a later stage, estimate may be modified or revised.	It usually starts with the issue of order for production of a product and ends after the product is dispatched for sale. For sale commitments like free repair or replacement, the process continues upto the expiry period of guarantee or warranty because the overhead expenses incurred in the above case will be included in the production cost.
3. Nature of quality	A qualified technical person or engineer having a thorough knowledge of the drawings and manufacturing process is required. Thus, it is a technical work, instead of a clerical one.	It can be done by a person qualified for accounts instead of a technical person. The cost accountant develops his knowledge of technical person. The cost accountant develops his knowledge of technical terms and process while working. Thus, this work instead of being of technical nature is more of a clerical nature.
4. Main objectives	*(i)* To set standard for, with actual cost.	*(i)* To help in comparison of cost with estimates to know if they are over, under realistic as well as to know where the actual costs involve unnecessary wastage of men, materials, machines and money.
	(ii) To help in setting up market price for a proposed product to be manufactured.	*(ii)* To facilitate the budget preparation as well as to provide cost data for future estimates of new products of their pricing plans.
	(iii) To decide whether it is economical to buy or manufacture a product under prevailing market conditions.	*(iii)* To facilitate in deciding output targets time to time.
	(iv) To facilitate in filling up of tenders or quotation of products for supply. After receipt of supply order from the buyers the production will be started.	*(iv)* To facilitate in meeting certain legal obligations or regulations.

3.9 DIFFERENCE BETWEEN FINANCIAL ACCOUNTING AND COST ACCOUNTING

- Accounting information is vital for showing the indebtedness of a business accounting uses words and figures to communicate the transactions which have been entered into.
- Both financial accounting and cost accounting are concerned with the recording of transactions so as to enable to calculate profit (or loss) for one or more transactions and to show the assets and liabilities owned or incurred by the business.

- Financial accounting is concerned with the external transactions and, therefore, record all dealings with the outside world. Any purchase or sale of goods and services and fixed assets, whether for cash or on credit are covered.
- Cost accounting, on the other hand, deals with the internal affairs of a business. It attempts to show the results of the operations carried out and emphasizes throughout the measurement and achievement of efficiency.
- Fixed assets, workers and materials are brought together with the object of transforming the resources employed and thereby obtaining a saleable product or service.
- Generally special attention is paid to the control aspect of the quantities and prices of the resources necessary for the transformation.

3.10 METHODS OF COSTING

(*a*) Process costing.
(*b*) Job costing.
(*c*) Batch costing.
(*d*) Hybrid costing systems.

(a) Process costing

Process cost sheet						
Accounting Period..................						
Date Ref. Mat. Labour Over/head Cost-Center-I				***Cost Center-2***		
(OH)	***Mat.***	***Labour***	***O.H.***	***Mat.***	***Labour***	***O.H.***

Summary:

Center-1	Rs.	Rs.	Production
Materials	XXX		No.of Units
Labour	XXX	———	Cost per unit. Rs.
Overhead	XXX	XXX	
Center-2			
Materials	XXX		
Labour	XXX		
Overhead	XXX	XXX	
	Rs.	XXX	

- This method is employed when a standard product is being made which involves a number of distinct processes performed in a definite sequence.

- In oil refining, chemical manufacture, paper making, flour milling, and cement manufacturing etc., this method is used.
- The object i.e., record and trace cots for each distinct stage.
- While costing, the by-products of each process should be considered.
- This method indicates the cost of a product at different stages as it passes through various processes.
- The total time spent and materials used on each process, as well as services such as power, light and heating are all charged. For this purpose cost sheet may be employed.

The process cost sheet is a summary of all operations for the month. The current operating charges are entered on the sheet showing

1. The transfer cost from the previous operation.
2. The costs incurred by each operation showing materials, labour and overhead in separate columns.

This separation of transfer cost and conversion cost is extremely important for the charges incurred by a department are its measures of efficiency.

The sheet can be used as a basis for:

1. Closing entries at the end of each month.
2. Operating statements, without need to lookup the ledger accounts.

Within the cost ledger an account is kept for each process. The direct material, direct labour and factory overhead costs are transferred from the process cost sheet. There are debited to the process account, and then any completed units are credited to cover the transfer to the next process. The balance on the account represents the work-in-progress at the end of the period, which, of course, becomes the opening balance for the next period.

(b) Job costing or order costing

- Job costing is concerned with finding the cost of each individual job or contract. Examples are to be found in general (job order) engineering industries, ship building, building contracts, etc.
- The main features of the system is that each job has to be planned and costed separately.
- Overhead costs may be absorbed on jobs on the basis of actual costs incurred or on predetermined costs.
- The process of determining in advance what a job or order will cost is known as estimating. It involves consideration of the following factors for each job/order:
  1. Materials requirements and prices to arrive at the direct material cost.
  2. Labour hours and rates to determine labour costs.
  3. Overhead costs.
  4. Percentage added to total cost to cover profit.

A record of above costs per unit time is kept in separate cost sheets.

(c) Batch costing

- Batch costing is a form of job costing. Instead of costing each component separately, each batch of components are taken together and treated as a job. Thus, for example, if 100 units of a component, say a reflector are to be manufactured, then the costing would be as far a single job. The unit price would be ascertained by dividing the cost by 100.

- Besides maintaining job cost sheets it may also be necessary to keep summary sheets on which the cost of each component can be transferred and the cost of the finished product can be calculated. This applies in general engineering where many hundreds of components may go towards making the finished machine or other product.

(d) Hybrid costing systems

- Many costing systems do not fall nearly into the category of either job costing or process costing. Often systems use some features of both main costing systems.
- Many engineering companies use batch costing, which treats each batch of components as a job and then finds the average cost of a single unit.
- Another variation is multiple costing, used when many different finished products are made. Many components are made which are subsequently assembled into the completed article, which may be bicycles, cars, etc. Costs have to be ascertained for operations, processes, units and jobs, building together until the total cost is found.
- Different names may be used to describe either process costing or job costing. Thus, for example, unit costing is the name given to one system where there is a natural unit, such as sack of flour, a barrel of beer etc.
- In unit costing method, the expenses on various items are charged per unit quantity or production.
- Operation costing is a variation of unit costing, and is used when production is carried out on a large scale, popularly known as mass production.
- Operation costing is the term applied to describe the system used to find the cost of performing a utility service such as transport, gas, water or electricity.
- In this method, the cost per unit is found on the basis of operating expenses incurred on various items of expenditure.
- Unit costing, operation costing and operating costing are variations of process costing.
- Contract or terminal costing is the name given to job costing employed by builders and constructional engineers.
- All these methods ascertain the actual cost.

Departmental costing method

In big industries like steel industry or automobile industry each department is producing independently one or more components. Departmental costing method is used in such industries and the actual expenditure of each department on various products is entered on the separate cost sheet and the costing for each department is separately undertaken.

3.11 ELEMENTS OF COST INTRODUCTION

For the successful functioning of an industrial enterprise, one of the most important consideration is to reduce the cost of manufacture of the product or article, as much as possible without affecting the quality. This will help in earning higher profits. To achieve the idea of reducing cost one must be familiar with elements which make up the total cost of a product. The total cost is made up of three main elements (figure 3.1).

1. Material.
2. Labour.
3. Expenses.
4. Overhead.

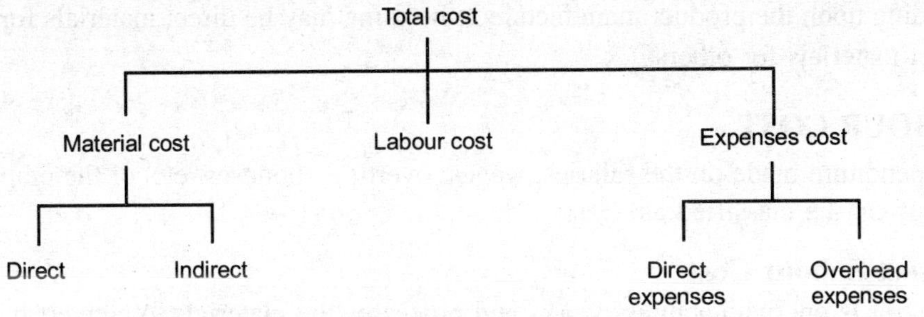

Fig. 3.1

3.12 MATERIAL COST

Material cost consists of the cost of materials which are used in the manufacture of product. It is divided into the following:

3.12.1 Direct Material Cost

It is the cost of those materials which are directly used for the manufacture of the product and become a part of the finished product. This expenditure can be directly allocated and charged to the manufacture of a specific product or job and includes the scrap and waste that has been cut away from original bar or casting.

The procedure for calculating the direct material cost is as follows:

(i) From the product drawing, make a list of all the components required to make the final product.

(ii) Calculate the volume of each component from the drawing dimensions after adding machining allowances, wherever necessary.

(iii) The volume of component multiplied by the density of material used gives the weight of the material per component.

(iv) Add process rejection and other allowances like cutting allowance to get the gross weight per component.

(v) Multiply the gross weight by the rate of material per unit weight to get the cost of raw material per component.

(vi) The cost of raw material for all the components is, similarly, calculated and added up which gives the cost of direct material for the product.

3.12.2 Indirect Material Cost

In addition to direct materials a number of other materials are necessary to help in the conversion of direct materials into final shape. Though these materials are consumed in the production, they don't become part of the finished product and their cost cannot be directly booked to the manufacture of a specific product. Such materials are called indirect materials. The indirect materials include oils, general tools, greases, sand papers, coolants, cotton waste etc. The cost associated with indirect materials is called indirect material cost.

In some cases certain direct materials like nails, screws, glue, putty etc. are used in such small quantity that it is not considered worthwhile to identify and charge them as direct materials. In such cases these materials are also charged as indirect materials.

Depending upon the product manufactured, the same may be direct materials for one concern and indirect materials for others.

3.13 LABOUR COST

It is the expenditure made on the salaries, wages, overtime, bonuses, etc. of the employees of the enterprise. It can be classified as

3.13.1 Direct Labour Cost

Direct labourer is one who actually works and processes the materials to convert it into the final shape. The cost associated with direct labour is called direct labour cost. The direct labour cost can be identified and allocated to the manufacture of a specific product. Examples of the direct labour are the workers operating lathes, milling machines or welders, or assemblers in assembly shop. The direct labour cost may be allocated to a product or job on the basis of time spent by a worker on a job.

3.13.2 Determination of Direct Labour Cost

Determination of labour is much more complicated problem than calculating material cost. To find the labour cost one must have the knowledge of all the operations which are carried out for production of the product, tools and machines to be used and the departments in which the product is to be manufactured.

For calculation purposes, the operation time and rate per hour of different operation must be known. For calculating time required for a particular job following considerations should be taken into account:

(a) Setup time.
(b) Operation time.
  (i) Handling time.
  (ii) Machining time.
(c) Tear down time
(d) Down (or) lost time.
(e) Miscellaneous allowances:
  (i) Personal allowance.
  (ii) Fatigue allowance.
  (iii) Tool sharpening and changing allowance.
  (iv) Checking allowance.
  (v) Other oiling and cleaning.
  (vi) Filling coolant reservoirs.
  (vii) Disposing of scraps and surplus stocks.

Setup time

Before starting any operation, first we have to set the job, tools and other auxiliary equipment. So, set up time is the time required for setting and fixing the jobs and tools on the machine. Time to study the drawings, blueprints, time to make adjustment for getting the required size are all included in set up time. This time is also known as setting time.

Man (or) handling time

This is the time the operator spends loading and unloading the work, manipulating the tools and the machine and making measurements during each cycle of operation.

Machinery time

This is the time during each cycle of operation that the machine is working or the tools are cutting.

Example

Let us take the example of a drill press operation which has the following sequence of elements of handling and machining

Pick up part	
Place the jig	
Fit in the jig	Handling time
Position under drill	
Advance drill to work	
Drill hole through part	Machining time
Clear the drill from the work	
Move jig into clear position	
Release part from jig	Handling time
Remove part from jig	

Tear down time

Tear down time is the time required to remove the tools from the machine and to clean the tools and the machine after the last component of the batch has been machined. This time is usually small. It will seldom run over 10 minutes on the average machine in the shop. It may require only a few minutes to tear down a set up on a drilling press and 10 to 15 minutes on the turret lathe. In exceptional case, it may go up to as high as 30 minutes on very large boring mills and large milling machines.

Down (or) lost time

This is the unavoidable time lost by the operator due to breakdowns, waiting for the tools and materials etc.

Miscellaneous allowances (allowances in estimation)

A worker cannot work for 8 hours continuously without rest. Also efficiency decreases as the time passes due to fatigue etc. He also requires for tool sharpening, checking measurements and personal calls. All these allowances come under this category. These allowances generally consumes 15 to 20% of total time.

(a) Personnal allowances

This is the time allowed for a worker for his personal needs like going to rest rooms, smoking, having a cup of tea, going to Lavatories to take water for personal cleanliness etc. This is generally about 5% of the total working time.

(b) Fatigue

The efficiency of the worker decreases due to fatigue (or) working at a stretch and also due to working conditions such as poor lighting, heating (or) ventilation. The efficiency is also affected by the psychology of the worker. It may be due to domestic worries, job securities etc.

For normal work, the allowance for fatigue is about 5% of the total time. This allowance can be increased depending upon the type and nature of work and working conditions.

(c) Total sharpening and changing allowance

It is the time required to remove the tool and its holder, to walk up to the grinder to grind the tools, to come back to the machine and then to fix the tool again in the machine.

(d) Checking allowance

It is the time taken for checking the dimensions. Rough dimensions take less while accurate dimensions require more time. This allowance should be considered only when the operator is doing checking only and no work on the machine. If the checking is done during machining time it should not be considered. The checking times for the various instruments are given below to check one dimension.

With rule	0.10	minute
Vernier caliper	0.50	minute
Inside caliper	0.10	minute
Outside caliper	0.05	minute
Inside micrometer	0.30	minute
Outer micrometer	0.15	minute
Depth micrometer	0.20	minute
Dial micrometer	0.30	minute
Thread micrometer	0.25	minute
Plug gauge	0.20	minute
Snap gauge	0.10	minute

(e) Oiling and cleaning

It is the time required for cleaning the machine and to lubricate its various parts for smooth functioning of the machine.

(f) Filling coolant reservoirs

It is the time required for filling the reservoirs of the coolant which are used for cooling the jobs and tools.

(g) Disposing off scraps and surplus stocks

It is the time consumed for disposing off the scraps and other surplus stocks.

The miscellaneous allowances should be added to the set up, the operation and tear down times to complete the element.

3.13.3 Indirect Labour Cost

Indirect labourer is one who is not directly employed in the manufacturing of the product but his services are used in some indirect manner. The indirect labour includes supervisors, foreman, storekeeper, gatekeeper, maintenance, staff, crane driver etc. The cost associated with indirect labour is called indirect labour cost. The indirect labour costs cannot be identified with a particular job or product but are charged on the total number of products made during a particular period in a plant.

To make the concept of direct and indirect labour cost clear, consider an operator working on drilling machine. The operator in this case is direct labour whereas the man supervising the job, inspector and store man supplying the material are indirect labour.

3.14 EXPENSES

Apart from material and labour cost in each factory there are several other expenditures such as cost of special layouts, designs, etc. hire of special tools and equipments; depreciation charges of plants and factory building; building rent; cost of transportation, salaries and commissions to salesman etc. All these expenditures are known as overheads or expenses. So, from above it is clear that except for direct material and direct labour cost, all other expenditures are known as expenses. The expenses include indirect material cost and indirect cost and such other expenses.

3.14.1 Direct Expenses

Direct expenses also known as chargeable expenses include any expenditure other than direct material or direct labour incurred on a specific cost unit. These are the expenses which can be charged directly to a particular job and are done for that specific job only. For example, hire of special tools and equipment, cost of special jigs and fixtures or some special patterns and its maintenance cost, costs of layouts, designs and drawings or experimental work on a particular job etc.

3.14.2 Indirect Expenses (Overheads)

These are known as overhead charges, burden or on cost. All the expenses over and above prime cost are indirect expenses. Overhead is the sum of indirect labour cost, indirect material cost and other expenses including service which cannot be conveniently charged to specific cost unit. These can be further classified as

1. Production expenses/Factory expenses.
2. Administrative expenses.
3. Selling expenses.
4. Distribution expenses.

(i) Production expenses

These expenses cover all indirect expenditures incurred by the undertaking from the receipt of the order until its completion ready for dispatch. Production expenses are also known as factory on cost, production overhead, factory overhead, work on cost, works overhead etc. Some examples of factory expenses or production expenses are:

(i) Rent, rates and insurance chargeable against the works.
(ii) Indirect labour example: supervision such as salaries of foreman, supervisors, factory manager etc.
(iii) Consumable stores and all forms of indirect material such as cotton waste, grease, oil etc.
(iv) Depreciation, maintenance and repair of buildings, plant, machine tools etc.,
(v) Power such as steam, gas, electricity, hydraulic or compressed air, internal transport etc.

(ii) Administrative expenses

These expenses include all the expenses on managerial or administerial staff for the planning and policy making work. Some examples of administrative expenses are:

(i) Salaries of directors and managing directors.
(ii) Salaries of cost, finance and secretary office staff including clerks and peons.
(iii) Expenses of direct amenities like telephone, coolers and other modern equipments.
(iv) Travelling expenses for attending meetings etc.

(v) Charges for electric consumption for light, heating and cooling.
(vi) Stationary, auditing expenses.
(vii) Insurance of building and employees, repairs, maintenance and depreciation of building and furniture.

(iii) Selling expenses

These consist of the expenditures spent towards securing orders, and finding or retaining markets for the products manufactured. Following is the list of selling expenses:

(i) Advertising and publicity expenses.
(ii) Salaries of the sales department staff including sales manager, salesman etc.
(iii) Travelling expenses of sales engineers.
(iv) Cost of preparing tenders and estimates.
(v) Expenses of making blocks and posters.
(vi) Sales stock storage charges.

(iv) Distribution expenses

These are the expenses which are paid for the distribution of the product. It includes the expenditure made on holding finished stock, packing cost and dispatching them to the customer. This type of expenses include

(i) Finished stock storages.
(ii) Lost of packing.
(iii) Loading, unloading charges, freight and warfare.
(iv) Expenses of transportation and vehicles.
(v) Salaries of dispatch clerks and labourers.

3.15 COST OF PRODUCT (LADDER OF COST)

The elements of cost can be combined to give following types of cost:

1. Prime cost: It consists of direct material cost, direct labour cost and direct expenses.
   Prime cost = Direct material cost + Direct labour cost + Direct expenses.
   Prime cost is also called as direct cost.
2. Factory cost: It consists of prime cost and factory expenses.
   Factory cost = prime cost + factory expenses.
   Factory cost is also named as works cost.
3. Office cost: It consists of factory cost and administrative expenses.
   Office cost = Factory cost + Administrative expenses
   It is also named as manufacturing cost (or) cost of production.
4. Total cost: It includes manufacturing cost and selling and distribution expenses.
   Total cost = Manufacturing cost + selling and distribution expenses.

Selling price

If the profit is added in the total cost of the product, it is called selling price. The customers get the articles by paying the price which is named as selling price.

Selling price = Total cost + Profit
= Total cost – Loss

Making price (or) catalogue price: Some percentage of discount allowed to the distributors of product is added into the selling price. The result obtained is called the market price (or) catalogue price (figure 3.2).

				Profit (or) Loss	
			Selling + Distribution expenses		
		Administrative expenses	Office cost (or) production	Total (or) selling cost	Selling price (or) Market price
	Factory expenses	Factory cost (or)	(or) Manufacturing cost	(or)	Catalogue price
Direct material	Prime cost (or)	Works cost	(or)		
Direct labour	Direct cost				
Direct expense					

Fig. 3.2: Ladder of cost

REVIEW QUESTIONS

1. List some of the reasons for doing estimates.
2. Define cost estimating.
3. Explain the importance of estimating.
4. What is the objective of estimating?
5. Explain the function of estimating.
6. What is costing?
7. Explain briefly the importance of costing.
8. What are the aims of cost accounting?
9. What is the difference between cost estimating and cost accounting?
10. Explain the difference between financial accounting and cost accounting.
11. Explain "Methods of costing".
12. What are the elements of cost?
13. Explain in detail about the elements of cost and its types.
14. What is expenses?
15. What are the types of expenses?
16. What is meant by ladder of cost with a neat sketch?

Unit–4

COST ESTIMATION

4.0 INTRODUCTION

In this rapid developing and competitive age, it is necessary for a factory that the advance information about the cost of a job or a manufacturing order to be put through should be available before taking up the actual production. Estimating which is predetermination of cost is mainly concerned with the factory owner. It helps him to decide about the manufacturing, and selling prices.

4.1 TYPES OF ESTIMATE

Estimates can be developed in a variety of different ways depending upon the use of the estimates and the amount of detail provided to the estimator.

Importance of understanding estimating methods. Every estimator should understand every estimating method and when to apply each, because no one estimating method will solve all estimating problems.

4.1.1 Guesstimates

Guesstimates is a slang term used to describe as estimate than lacks detail. This type of estimate relies on the estimators experience and judgment. There are many reasons why some estimates are developed using his method. One example can be found in the tool and die industry. Usually, the tool and die estimator is estimating tool cost without any tool or die drawings. The estimator typically works from a piece part drawing and must visualize what the tool or die looks like. Some estimators develop some level of detail in their estimate. Material cost, for example, is usually priced out in some detail, and this brings greater accuracy to the estimator by reducing error. If the material part of the estimate has an estimating error of plus or minus 5 per cent and the reminder of the estimate has an estimating error of plus or minus 10 per cent, the overall error is reduced.

4.1.2 Budgetary

The budgetary estimate can also be a guesstimate but is used for a different purpose. The budgetary estimate is used for planning the cost of a piece part, assembly, or project. This type of estimate is typically on the high side because the estimator understands that a low estimate could create real problems.

4.1.3 Using Past History

Using past history is a very popular way of developing estimates for new work. Some companies go to great lengths to ensure that estimates are developed in the same way actual cost is conducted. This provides a way past history in developing new estimates. New advancements in group technology now provide a way for the microcomputer to assist in this effort.

4.1.4 Estimating in Some Detail

Some estimators vary the amount of detail in an estimate depending on the risk and dollar amount of the estimate. This is true in most contract shops. This level of detail might be at the operation level where operation 10 might be a turning operation and the estimator would estimate the setup time at 0.5 hours and the run time at 5.00 minutes. The material part of the estimate is usually calculated out in detail to reduce estimating error.

4.1.5 Estimating in Complete Detail

When the risk of being wrong is high or the dollar amount of the estimate is high, the estimator will develop the estimate in as much detail as possible. Detailed estimates for machinery operations, for example, would include calculations for speeds, feeds, cutting times, load and unload times and even machine manipulations factors. These time values are calculated as standard time and adjusted with an efficiency factor to predict actual performance.

4.1.6 Parametric Estimating

Parametric estimating is an estimating method developed and used by trade associations. New housing constructions can be estimated on the basis of cost per square. There would be different figures for wood construction as compared with brick and for single strong construction as compared with multilevel construction.

Some heat-beating companies price work on a cost per pound basis and have different cost curves for different heat-treating methods.

4.1.7 Project Estimating

Project estimating is by far the most complex of all estimating tasks. This is especially true if the project is a lengthy one. A good example of project estimating is the time and cost of developing a new missile. The project might take 5 years and cost millions of dollars. The actual manufacturing cost of the missile might be a fraction of the total cost. Major projects of this nature will have a PERT network to keep track of the many complexities of the project. A team of people with a project leader is usually required to develop a project estimate.

4.2 HOW ESTIMATES ARE DEVELOPED?

Estimates are developed in a variety of ways depending on a number of different factors. These factors include the purpose of the estimate, how the company is organized, the amount of lead time to prepare the estimate, and the complexity of what is being estimated.

Estimating accuracy and consistency

Another very important factor in how estimates are developed is the need to control accuracy and consistency of the estimate one person making an estimate will be for more consistent than an entire department participating in the estimate's development.

4.2.1 Single Person

In many companies, especially smaller ones, one person develops a cost estimate. This person usually has been in the business for several years and has had experience in both manufacturing whatever is being estimated as well as estimating experience; a single person estimate tends to be more consistent than a group estimate, if estimates are consistent.

4.2.2 Committee Estimating

They can be made accurate by application of maths formulas such as leaving curves. Committee estimating is used especially when there is a lack of detail about the product being estimated. In developing a budgetary estimate for a helicopter transmission, for example, there are no detailed part drawings at this stage of the helicopter's development. Assembly sketches are provided to illustrate the transmission size and weight. The collective judgment of the committee will provide a better estimate than the judgement of the individual. Also, parametric estimating is frequency used in this situation. The cost of spiral bevel gears can be estimated very accurately based on weight and number teeth.

4.2.3 Department to Department

Some companies develop estimates by moving the estimating paperwork through each department that can contribute to the estimate. Purchasing provides material cost, manufacturing engineering provides the process, industrial engineering provides the time values, and production control provides the machine loading. There are advantages and disadvantages to this procedure in developing an estimate. The chief advantage is that each person contributing information to the estimate is an expert in his or her field. The chief disadvantage is the amount of turnaround time to develop the estimate. Each person who makes a contribution to the estimate has other duties, and estimating new work usually is not a high priority.

4.2.4 Reporting Relationships

Reporting relationships are very important, especially in manufacturing firms. The estimating function usually reports to the person in charge of manufacturing, typically the manufacturing manager. The theory behind this is that if people who rep out to the CEO of the manufacturing contribute information to the estimate, they must live with it if the project is booked. Another reason for their reporting relationship is that marketing is usually given some authority over price but not over cost. Conventional organization wisdom will rarely permit marketing to govern estimating.

4.3 STANDARD DATA

Standard data are defined as standard time values for all the manual work in an estimate standard data provide the opportunity for the estimator to be consistent in developing an estimate.

4.3.1 How Standard Data are Developed?

Standard data are developed in a variety of ways depending on the industry that uses them. Experience shows that it is easier to develop standard data for machinery operation as compared with fabrication operation. This is because machinery operations can be calculated by using speeds, feeds and lengths of cut to determine time values. Most of the work content of a fabrication operation is manual effort rather than machine time, and for this reason reliable standard data for the fabrication industry are difficult to find. Listed below are the basic methods used to develop standard data.

4.3.2 Past History

Many companies use past history or actual performance on joules produced to develop standard data. Developing standard data this way rarely considers the best method of organizing work. This method is popular in smaller companies that do not have industrial engineers or time study engineers.

4.3.3 Time Study

Larger, well-organised companies will develop standard data from stop-watch time studies. Time studies are used to establish rates of production. However, when time studies are also used to establish standard data, care must be taken in defining element content so work content can be isolated. Time study engineers must be taught how to establish the element content of their studies in a way that will permit the development of standard data.

4.3.4 Predetermined Time Standards

Another approach in the development of standard data is to use one of the many predetermined time standard systems like MTM or MOST. This method has its advantages and disadvantages. The chiefly advantage is consistency of data, and the chief disadvantage is the amount of time necessary to develop the data. Some predetermined time standard systems are now computerized, which shortens the development time.

4.3.5 Standard Data Specific to a Shop and Lot Size

It should be pointed out that "all standard data are specific to a given shop and lot size."

Standard data developed in a high-production shop under ideal methods are of little value to a job shop that runs lot, sizes of 10 parts each. The reverse is also true. The use of efficiency factors or off standard factors can assist in using the same data for both conditions, but this is less than ideal. The reverse use of learning curves, that is, backing up the curve, is a better method of repricing work for small lot sizes using this method, the same standard data can be used for high and low production.

4.4 MATERIALS AVAILABLE TO DEVELOP AN ESTIMATE

Materials available for developing an estimate vary widely depending on what is being estimated. In most cases the quality of the estimate will depend on the amount of materials to makc the estimate.

Estimating materials shown below is a listing of the materials available for making an estimate.

No drawings

In many cases there are no drawings of what is being estimated. One clear example of this is tool estimating. The estimator will develop an estimate for a progressive die, for example, by reviewing the price part drawing. Some die estimators will develop a strip layout for the part and then estimate the die cost station by station.

Sketches

Sometimes sketches of the parts represent the only information available. This is typically true for a budgetary estimate.

Line drawings

Loftings or line drawings are used for estimating in some industries. The pleasure boat industry represents an example. A full-scale lofting of a deck and hull is used to estimate both the material and labour for a new fiber glass boat.

Complete drawings

Complete drawings and specifications are available for estimating some work. The aircraft industry is one good example. Many times the estimator will spend more time reading the specifications than developing the estimate. This is necessary because the specifications will often determine the part process.

4.5 METHODS OF ESTIMATES

4.5.1 Computer Estimating

Computer estimating has become very popular in recent years primarily because of the advent of the micro computer. Early efforts of computer estimating date back to the early 1970s but were cumbersome to use because they were on a mainframe and were card-driven. No less than 15 U.S. companies now offer estimating software for a microcomputer. Because the computer estimating industry is new, there are no real standards for estimating programs. Some programs are nothing more than a way to organize the calculations of an estimate, while others calculate all the details of the estimate.

Advantages and disadvantages

Shown below are some of the major advantages of computer cost estimating.

Accuracy versus consistency

Computer estimates are very consistent, provided they calculate the detail of an estimate. Because these estimates are consistent, they can be made to be accurate. Through the use of consistent efficiency factors or leaving curves, estimates can be adjusted up or down. This is one of the chief advantages of computer cost estimating.

Levels of details

Some computer estimating systems provide different levels of estimating cost. The level of detail selected by the user depends on the dollar risk. Many estimators produce an estimate in more detail because the computer can calculate speeds and feeds, for example, much faster than an estimator can a hand-held calculators.

Refinements

Some computer estimating systems provide many refinements that would be impossible for the estimator to do in any timely manner. One example is to adjust speeds and feeds for material hardness. Typically, the harder the material the more slowly a part will be turned or bored. Another refinement is the ability to calculate a feed state and adjust it based on the width of a form tool.

Source code

Some companies offer the source code uncompiled to their users. This is important because it affords the user the opportunity to customize the software. In addition, many companies have written their own software to do something that is not available on the market. If the source code is not compiled, the users can build upon a computer estimating system.

Disadvantages

The chief disadvantage of computer estimating is that no one estimating system can suit everyone's need. This is especially true if the source code is compiled and not customizable.

Another problem with computer estimating is that the estimator will, in all probability, have to change some estimating methods. Computer software for estimating cost is seldom written around one method of estimating.

4.5.2 Group Technology

Group technology is not new. It was invented by a Russian engineer over 30 years ago. Unfortunately the subject is not taught in many of our colleges and universities. Group technology (GT) is a coding system to describe something.

Several proprietary systems are on the market. One such system, the MICAPP system, uses four code lengths, a 10-,15-,20-,25- digit code. The code length selected is based on the complexity of the piece part or tool being described.

Use for group technology

Shown below are several uses for group technology along with several examples of use both internally and externally.

Cost estimating

GT can be used very efficiently in estimating cost. Assume a company manufactures shaft-type parts. Also arsum there is a computer data base named SHAFT that contains 10-digit code followed by a part number, that is, code part number, and so on. When an estimator must estimate the cost of a new shaft, the process starts by developing a code that describes the characteristics of the part. The first digit in the code might be assigned the part length, while the second digit is assigned the largest diameter and so on. Next, the code is keyed in and the computer finds all the parts that meet the numeric descriptions and points out the part numbers. The best fit is selected to be modified into a new part. All the details of each description are retrieved. These include diameter, length of cut, number of surfaces, and the like. The estimator can alter these features and make the old part into a new one.

Actual performance

As the part is being produced, thc cstimatcd information is updated with actual performance and refined. This gives the estimator the ability to improve estimating accuracy, because the next time, the computer finds that part as one to be modified into a new one, the estimator is working with actual performance.

Other use for GT

There are many other uses for group technology one that is similar to estimating is variant process planning, in which a standard process plan is on file for each operation and can be modified into a new plan.

One carbide tool manufacturer produced a line of carbide drills and reamers and in their series 10 line and they had 758 different designs. After a matrix to describe these tools was developed, a code for each tool was developed and the database was established. The company conducted a redundancy search and found that 9% of the existing designs were either look-alikes or very similar. Now the company conducts a database search first when confronted with a new design.

4.5.3 Parametric Estimating

Parametric estimating is the act of estimating cost or time by the application of mathematical formulas. These formulas can be as simple as multiplices or as complex as regression models. Parametric estimating, sometimes refused as statistical modeling, was first documented by the Rard Corporation in the early 1950's in an attempt to predict military hardware cost.

Use of parametric estimating

Many companies use some form of parametric estimating to develop sales forecasting. The four examples cited below will give the reader a good feel of how parametric estimating is used in a variety of different industries.

Construction industry

In developing a cost estimate for residential buildings, some cost estimators use a dollar value per square foot. The estimator constitutes curves based on different construction such as wood on brick buildings and single or multi-storey dwellings. These numbers can then be multiplied by the number of square feet in the building. Some construction companies have refined this process to provide additional detail carpeting, for example, could have a separate multiplier.

Heat treating

Most commercial heat-treating companies price their work based on a cost per pound and heat-treating method. Heat-treating costs are very difficult to define because many times more than one type of part is in the heat-treating furnace at the same time. It is difficult to think of a more effective way to estimate cost for this type of industry.

Tool and die industry

As pointed out earlier, estimating cost for a progressive die can be very difficult because the estimator seldom has a die drawing to work from some tool and die shops have developed parametric estimating methods that take out some of the guestimating. This method is known as the "unit value" method over a period of time, the estimator collects actual time values about dies being produced. Once the estimator is satisfied that the data are correct, they are over aged into usable hours. As an example, this might include 4 hours for every inch of forming or 3 hours for every hole under 2 inches in diameter. The unit value can stand for several meanings. For flowing it is a number of inches being formed. For holes under 2 inches, in diameter, it represents the number of holes.

The estimator might establish a factor of 40 hours for a degree of difficulty. If the scrap cutter is 'Standard" the unit value is 1. If the scrap cutter is more difficult, the unit value might have a value of 1.5 where the hours allotted would be 60.

Helicopter transmission

A helicopter transmission is a large complicated assembly comprised of a planetary gear system, bevel gears, shafting, and housings. Budgetary estimates for a transmission are usually developed using a variety of parametric methods. The housing costs are based on weight. The bevel gear cost is based on number of teeth, and the planetary gear cost is based on gear face width and number of teeth:

If methods like these were not employed, it would take hundred man-hour to produce an estimate.

Collecting and testing data

The single most important activity in parametric estimating is data collection and testing. Once the estimator develops the estimating methods, enough sample data should be collected for a natural bell curve. Statistical testing of the curve is also very important. Once the parametric data are used for estimating it is important to continually test them against actual performance and refine them as necessary.

(a) Other factors that affect cost estimating

There are other factors that affect the accuracy of a cost estimate. Several of these are cited below.

Project estimating

Inflation analysis and risk analysis come into play in project estimating. A multi-year estimate, such as many government contracts, is especially sensitive to both these factors.

Inflation

When the estimate is being developed for future time periods, inflation rates are very important considerations. The three most popular measurements of inflation are the wholesale price index, the implicit price index, and the consumer index, the last being the most quoted.

Because inflation rates are difficult to estimate accurately most multi-year contracts have some provisions reopeners to renegotiate. An after-tax evaluation of a multi-year project provides a more accurate assessment because it take into consideration costs that are not sensitive to inflation. These costs might be loans repayment, leases, and depreciation costs.

Risk analysis

Risk analysis is a series of methods used to quantify uncertainty. Most of these methods are math models. Three broad classifications of risk associated with a project are cost, schedule, and performance. Some of the most popular methods of risk analysis are:

1. Program Evaluation and Review Technique (PERT).
2. Probabilistic Analysis of Network (PAN).
3. Risk Information System and Network Evaluation Technique (RISNET).

4.5.4 Statistical Estimating

The analysis of data through the use of statistical methods has been used for centuries. These data can be cost versus other information that leads to cost development. The practitioner must have a well-founded background in the use and application of statistical methods because an endless array of methods is available, several of which are described below.

Parametric estimating

Statistical estimating is another form of parametric estimating. The parametric methods made industry oriented whereas the methods discussed below are universal.

Regression analysis

They form most popular of regression analysis are simple regression, multiple regression, log-linear regression and curvilinear regression. Each math model is different and is designed for a specific use.

Information can be regressed along a straight line or along a curve. Statistical estimating methods are very useful in parametric estimating. To use any of these methods also requires the user to have a sound knowledge of "goodness of data fit". Math models are available to determine how well data fit a straight line, curve or log-linear relationship.

Computers

Because of the complex nature of statistical estimating, the use of a computer is required. Fortunately, many good commercial programs, many of which are not expensive, are available on the market.

4.6 IMPORTANCE OF REALISTIC ESTIMATES

If the estimated cost of a product proves later on, to be almost same as the actual cost of that product, it is a realistic estimate.

The cost estimate may prove to be

(i) A realistic estimate,
(ii) An over-estimate, or
(iii) An under-estimate.

- An over-estimate, later on, proves to be much more than the actual cost of that product.
- An under-estimate, later on, proves to be much lower than the actual cost of that product.
- Both over-estimate and under-estimate may prove to be dangerous and harmful for a concern. Assume that on the basis of an estimate, the concern has to fill up a tender enquiry. The over estimate means the concern will quote a higher rate and thus will not get the job or contract. In case of an under-estimate, the concern will get the contract but it will not be able to complete the work within that small quoted amount and hence will suffer heavy losses.

This emphasizes the importance of making realistic estimates. Realistic estimates are very essential for the survival and growth of a concern.

4.7 ESTIMATING PROCEDURE

The estimating department is generally attached with the planning department and is controlled by production manager. The total procedure is considered to have three stages.

(i) Fixing of design, accuracy and finish.
(ii) Proper working of estimating department.
(iii) Obtaining a delivery promise from the progress department in view of existing load on the shop.

The planning department sets down the requirements and specifications, type and quantities of materials, make out the drawing, lays down the methods and sequence of operations, machines to be used, allowed times and rates of labour etc. Main items to be estimated in order of sequence are as follows:

1. *Price list:* To prepare the list of all the components of the product.
2. *Buy or Manufacture:* To decide which components should be made in the factory itself and which component should be procured from the market.
3. *Weight of material:* Determination of the weight of the materials with various allowances.
4. *Material cost:* Determination of the material cost either at market price or at a forecast price.

5. *Outside purchases:* Determination of prices of outside purchases.
6. *Machinery or processing data:* Determination of cutting speeds and feeds for the materials selected and machining times for all operations.
7. *Labour cost:* Determination of labour cost of each operation from performance times and wage rates, including manufacturing and assembly and testing.
8. *Cost of tools and equipment:* Determination of cost of necessary special tools or equipment etc.
9. *Prime cost:* Determination of prime cost by adding labour cost into material cost.
10. *Factory overheads:* Determination of factory on cost and general overhead charges.
11. *Package and delivery charges:* Determination of package and delivery charges and also insurance charges if necessary.
12. *Total cost:* To calculate the total cost.
13. Standard profit and sales price: To decide standard profit and adding this into total cost so as to fix the sale price.
14. *Discount to be allowed:* To decide discount allowed to the distributors and adding this into sale price to get market price or catalogue price.
15. *Time of delivery:* Determination of time of delivery in collaboration with the progress department.
16. *Approval of management:* When the estimate is complete, it is entered into the 'Estimate form' and submitted to the directors and sales department for dispatch of the quotation or tender.

Estimate Form

Description.................... Date..........................

Quantity........................ Enquiry No..................

Drawing No.................... Customer.....................

	Item			*Total Cost*	*Cost of Item*
1.	Material (............)	No. of Components Batch No............			
2.	Operation *(a)* *(b)* *(c)* *(d)* Total: (Factory cost)	Labour	Overhead		
3.	Office and Administrative Expenses. Total: (Induction cost)				
4.	Selling Expenses *(a)* Packing and Carriage *(b)* Advertisement and Publicity *(c)* Other Allied Expenses Total: (Ultimate cost)				
5.	Profit Total: (Selling price)				

4.8 DIVISION OF ESTIMATING PROCEDURE

The above said procedure for simplicity can be divided into following major groups:

1. Material Cost.
2. Direc Labour Cost.
3. Direct Expenses.
4. Various Overhead Expenses.

1. Material cost

This estimation is most important in cost estimation. In calculating material cost both direct and indirect materials should be taken into account. The estimation of materials for this job or product includes the calculation of quantities to be provided including allowances for scrap and wastage in cutting, punching, turning etc. and for spoilage in processing. After calculating weights or volumes of materials required, the cost of materials is estimated from rate of material. The estimator should have full information about the availability of the material.

2. Labour cost

Next stage is the estimation of labour cost. For this purpose the estimator must have the knowledge of the operations which will be performed, tools to be used, machine that will be employed and the department in which the product is to work for different operations. The labour cost is calculated by multiplying hourly rate of the worker by total time spent in processing a job. The total time spent includes the set up time, tear down time, operation time and other miscellaneous allowances such as personal, fatigue, tool sharpening and charging, checking etc.

3. Direct expenses

It includes any expenditure other than direct material and direct labour incurred on a specific cost unit such as

(*i*) Hire charges of special tools or equipments for a particular production order or product.
(*ii*) Cost of special layout, design or drawing.
(*iii*) Cost of jigs and fixtures/pattern specially meant for the particular job only.

4. Various overhead expenses

All expenses other than direct material, direct labour and other direct expenses are called overhead expenses. These include the expenses such as

(*i*) Indirect material cost: These expenses include the cost of oil greases, coolants, cotton waste, etc.
(*ii*) Industrial labour cost: These expenses include the salaries of supervisors, foreman, draftsman, designers, chowkidars, storekeepers, etc.

4.9 CONSTITUENTS OF A JOB ESTIMATE

The various constituents of estimating the cost of a product may be sub-divided as under:

(*a*) Design time.
(*b*) Drafting time.
(*c*) Method studies, time studies, planning and production time.
(*d*) Design, procurement and manufacture of special patterns, cores, core boxes, flasks, tools, dies, jigs and fixtures etc.
(*e*) Experimental work.

(f) Materials.
(g) Labour.
(h) Overheads.

Design time

The time required for designing a product is estimated either on the basis of similar product previously manufactured or on the judgement of the designer. This time is generally considerable in quantity. It should be taken as the important.

(i) Repairs and maintenances expenses of machines and tools.
(ii) Insurance premium on building and plants.
(iii) Expenses of power such as steam, gas, electricity, etc.
(iv) Depreciation on building, furniture and equipment.
(v) Administrative overhead or expenses: These expenses include the salaries of high officials, persons working in general office, telephone telegraph, stationary etc.
(vi) Selling expenses: These expenses include the salaries of salesman, commission to salesman, advertising, publicity expenditure.
(vii) Light and power expenses.
(viii) Packing expenses.
(ix) Supervisory staff expenses.

Planned as regard the various processes and time to be taken by each. In case of routine or repetitive jobs, the planning would be available in the records. This may be checked up and the necessary modifications required may be made. In case of new jobs its method studies and time studies must be carried out. The jobs should be broken down into its elements. For each part, sub-assembly and complete assembly, the type and sequence of operation should be studied and planned. Times for various operation and the schedules for doing the work should be seen. This time setting effect both the delivery date as well as the cost. In case of a special order requiring considerable time, a special calculation should be made by making some allowance factor in estimating the cost of the product. The standard man hour rate should be used for calculating the cost of the designing time.

Drafting time

The next step after the design of the component is the preparation of its drawing to be used by the worker during production. An experienced draughtsman is required to prepare them. He also estimates the time and cost of drafting a new product. The probable time for drafting and the cost of drafting are estimated on the basis of drawing of similar previous components, and the standard man hour rate.

Method studies, time studies, planning and production time

Before the product is actually put into production, the material situation and purchase requisition are investigated for different materials required for the product. Now, the job must be produced.

The main points to be considered for this purpose are cost of the equipment, labour, material, depreciation, overheads, repair and maintenance, special buildings if required, supervision and the time required to conduct the experimental work.

Materials

It is the most important factor in cost estimation of any component. While computing the cost of material both the direct and indirect material should be taken into account. For this purpose the calculations of the quantities of raw materials allowances for scrap, spoilage and wastage during cutting, punching, turning etc. should be made. Now the cost of the material is estimated from the rate of the material design, procurement and manufacture of special patterns, core boxes etc.

The cost of special patterns, core boxes, tools, jigs, fixtures, gauges, consumable cutting fads etc. required for manufacturing a product should be considered for estimation. This cost should be added to the estimated cost. This cost is generally estimated in close coordination with Tool Department.

Experimental work

Certain types of experimental work has to be carried out in case of new type of products or inventions. The main purpose of experimental work is to find the quickest, easiest, and cheapest way of manufacture product. When estimating the cost of the new or undeveloped type of products the estimator should be very careful to make proper allowances to the experimental work.

Labour

For estimating the labour cost, the estimator is to go into greater details. He must be in knowledge of the various operations to be performed, tool to be used, machines employed and the departments in which the product is to be manufactured. He must also be conversant with the wage rate for different operations. For time calculations we must consider. "The set up time; the operation time including the handling and machine time; the tear down time and various allowances like personal fatigue, tool sharpening or changing, checking etc.

4.10 COLLECTION OF COST

The various components of cost of any product manufacturing in any production concern are

1. Prime cost = Direct material cost + Direct labour cost + Direct expenses (if any)
2. Factory cost = Prime cost + Factory overheads
3. Cost of production = Factory cost + Administrative overheads + Miscellaneous overheads (if any)
4. Total cost = Cost of production + Selling and distribution overheads

The selling price of any product manufactured can be arrived at by adding a certain percentage of profit to total cost.

The given stepped diagram explains the step-by-step procedure of arriving at selling price of any product manufactured.

4.11 ALLOWANCES IN ESTIMATION

A worker cannot work continuously without rest. His efficiency decreases as time passes due to fatigue etc. He also requires time for tool sharpening checking measurements and for personal calls. All these allowance are called miscellaneous allowances. The allowances amount to 15% of total time.

Miscellaneous allowances are classified as personal fatigue, tool changing of grinding, checking, oiling and cleaning allowances, filling coolant reservoir and disposing off scraps and surplus, stock, etc.

REVIEW QUESTIONS

1. What are the types of estimate?
2. What is meant by Guesstimates?
3. Explain how estimates are developed with its types?
4. What is standard data?
5. How standard data are developed?
6. What is time study?
7. Explain the materials available to develop an estimate.
8. What is predetermined time standards?
9. Explain the methods of estimates in detail.
10. What is group technology?
11. What is cost estimating?
12. What is parametric estimating?
13. What are the factors that affect cost estimating?
14. What is statistical estimating?
15. Explain the importance of realistic estimates.
16. What is the procedure for estimating?
17. Explain division of estimating procedure.
18. What are the costituents of a job estimate?
19. What is design time?

Unit–5

PRODUCTION COST ESTIMATION

5.0 INTRODUCTION—PRODUCTION COST ESTIMATION

In this rapid developing and competitive age it is necessary for a factory that the advance information about the cost of a job or a manufacturing order to be put through should be available before taking up actual production. Estimating which is predetermination of cost is mainly concerted with factory owner. It helps him to decide about the manufacturing the selling prices.

Estimation is calculation of cost when are expected to be incurred in manufacturing a component in advance before the component is actually manufactured.

5.1 ESTIMATION OF MATERIAL COST

5.1.1 Determination of Material Cost

To calculate the material cost of the product the first step is to study drawing of the product and split it into simple standard geometrical shapes and to find the volume of the material in the product and then to find the weight. The volume is multiplied by density of the metal used in the product. The exact procedure to find the material cost is like this:

1. Study the drawing carefully and break up the component into simple geometrical shapes. (Cubes, prisms, cylinders, etc.)
2. Add the necessary machining allowances on all sides which are to be machined.
3. Determine the volume of each part by applying the formulae of mensuration.
4. Add the volumes of all the simple components to get total volume of the product.
5. Multiply the total volume of the product by the density of the material to get the weight of the material.
6. Find out the cost of the material by multiplying the cost per unit weight to the total weight of the material.

5.1.2 Mensuration in Estimating

Introduction

Mensuration is the science which deals with the calculation of length of lines, areas of surfaces and volumes of solids by means of mathematical rules and formulae. An estimator is often required to calculate the length, area of volume of a job he is going to perform. Hence, he must be thoroughly acquainted with the rules and formulae of mensuration.

The general formulae for calculating the volume of a simple solid having a uniform cross-sectional area throughout in the direction normal to the section considered, is to find the product of the cross-sectional area and the length of the solid in the direction normal to the section considered.

To calculate the volume of a complex solid, it should be divided into a number of sample geometric solids. The volume of all these parts are calculated separately and then added together to get the total volume.

The volume of a solid of revolution, as generated by the rotation of a plane area about a given axis in its plane, is equal to the product of the area of the revolving section and the length of the path covered by its centroid in describing a circle about the axis. This theorem was given by Guldinus. Volume of a circular ring, a half-round rib surrounding the boss of a fly wheel, and V-groove of a V-belt pulley may be calculated by Guildinus theorem.

Centroids and area of plane figures

Name	*Figure*	*Centroid*	*Surface area*
Triangle	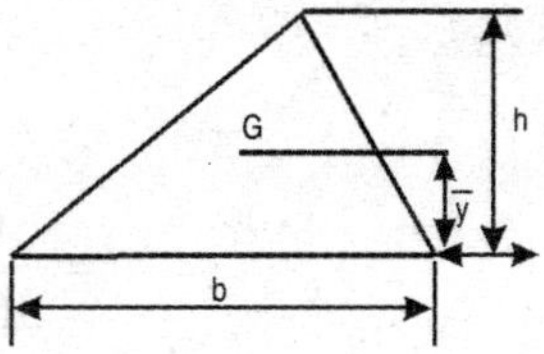	$\bar{y} = \frac{h}{3}$	$A = \frac{1}{2}bh$
Trapezium	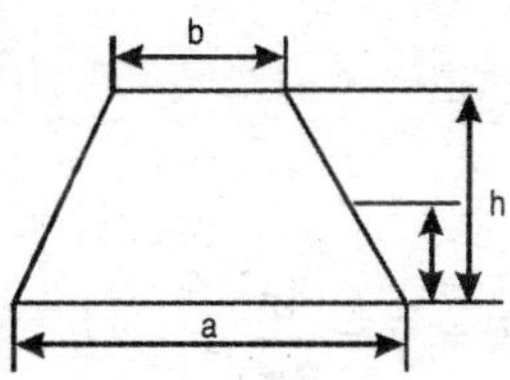	$\bar{y} = \frac{h\ 2a + b}{3\ a + b}$	$A = \frac{1}{2}(a+b)h$
Semi circle	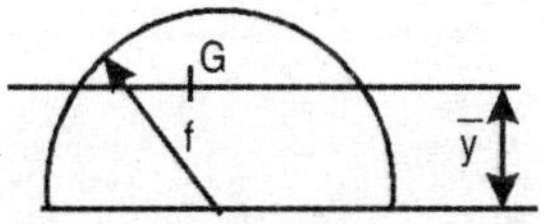	$\bar{y} = \frac{4r}{3\pi}$	$A = \frac{\pi r^2}{4}$
Ellipse	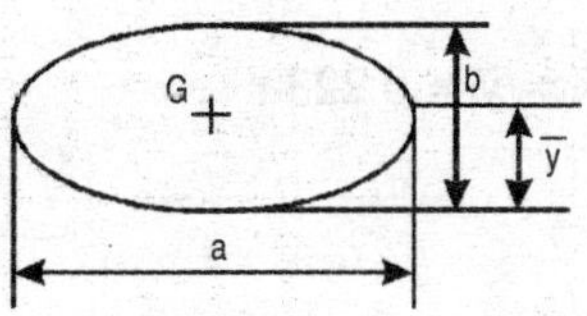	$\bar{y} = \frac{b}{2}$	$A = \frac{\pi ab}{4}$
Regular hexagon	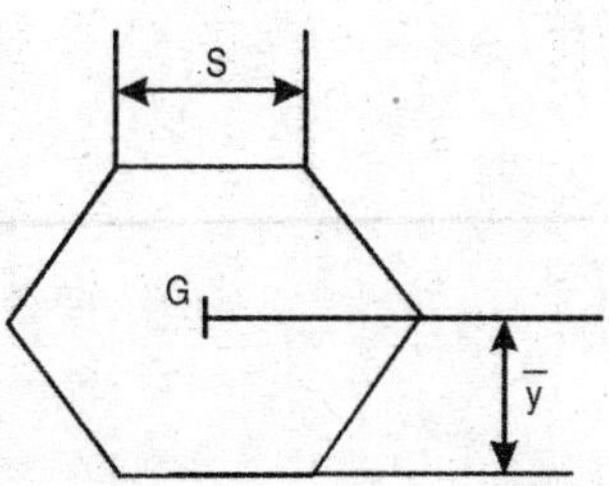	$\bar{y} = \frac{\sqrt{3}}{2}S$	$A = \frac{3\sqrt{3}}{2}S^2$

Any regular polygon	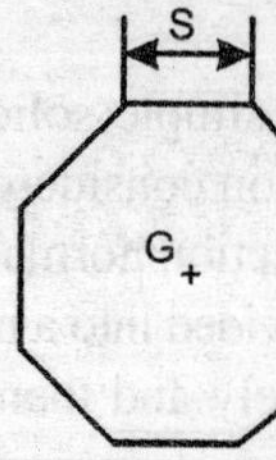	-	$A = S^2 \frac{n}{4} \cot \frac{180^\circ}{n}$

Sector and segment of a circle

Name	*Figure*	*Centroid*	*Surface area (A)*
Segment of a circle	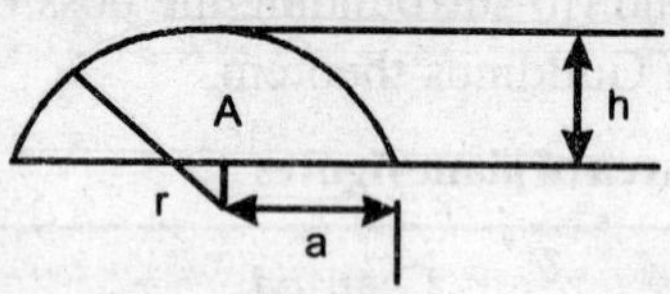	-	$A = \frac{4}{3} h \sqrt{a^2 + \frac{2}{5} h^2}$
Sector of a circle	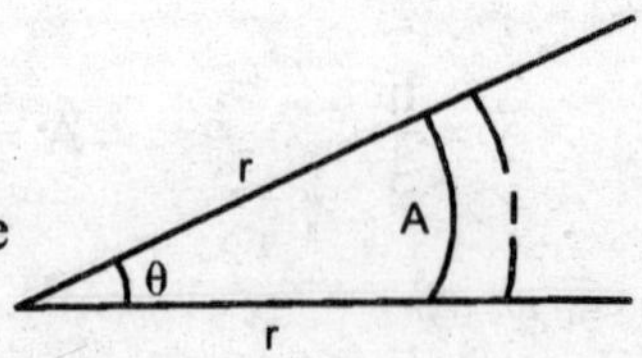	-	$A = \frac{1}{2} lt$ $= \frac{\theta}{360^\circ} \pi r (\theta \text{ in degree})$
Quadrant of a circle	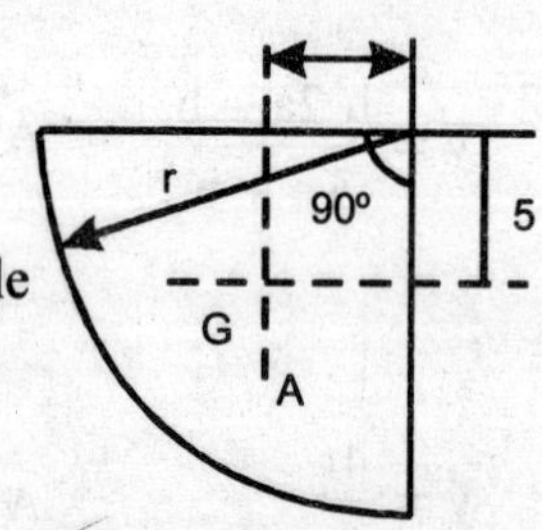	$\bar{x} = \bar{y} = \frac{4r}{3\pi}$	$A = \frac{\pi r^2}{4}$
Circular fillet	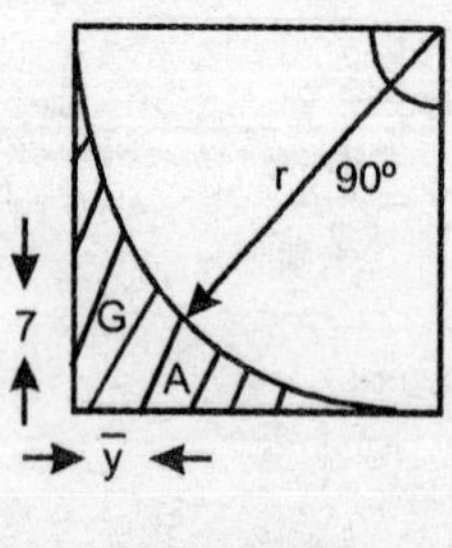	$\bar{x} = \bar{y} = 0.223\ r$	$A = r^2 - \frac{\pi r^2}{4}$ $= \frac{1}{5} r^2$

Volumes and surface areas of solids

Name	*Figure*	*Surface area (A)*	*Volume (V)*
Hollow cylinder	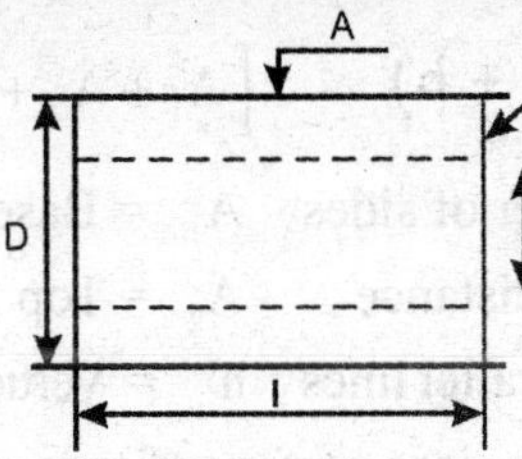	Outer curved surface area $A = \pi Dt$ Flat surface area on each end $A^1 = \frac{\pi}{4}\left(D^2 - d^2\right)$	$V = \frac{\pi}{4}\left(D^2 - d^2\right)t$
Right sphere	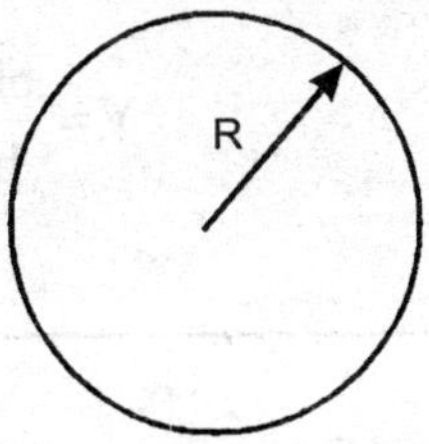	$A = 4\pi R^2$	$V = \frac{\pi}{3}\pi R^3$
Right circular cone	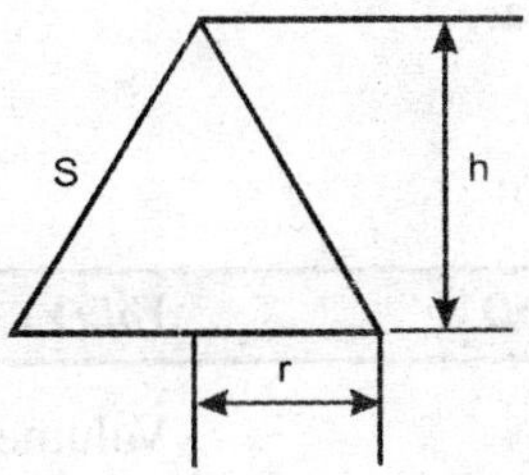	Curve surface area $A = \pi rS$ $= \pi r\sqrt{r^2 + h^2}$ $\left[S = \sqrt{r^2 + h^2}\right]$	$V = \frac{1}{3}\pi r^2 h$
Segment of a sphere	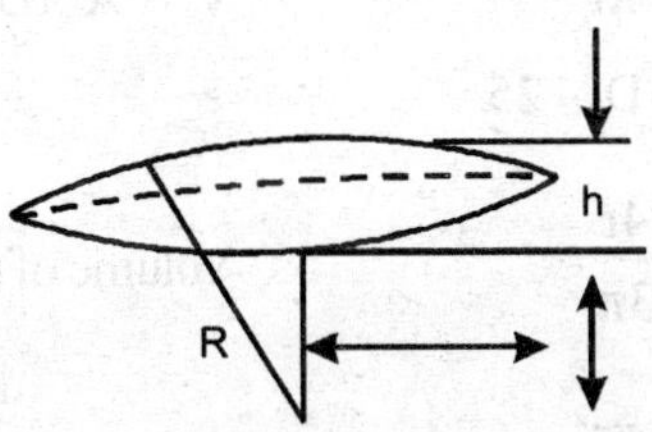	Curved surface area $A = 2\pi Rh$	$V = \frac{\pi h}{6}\left[3r^2 + h^2\right]$ $= \frac{\pi h^2}{3}\left[3R - h\right]$
Right truncated cone	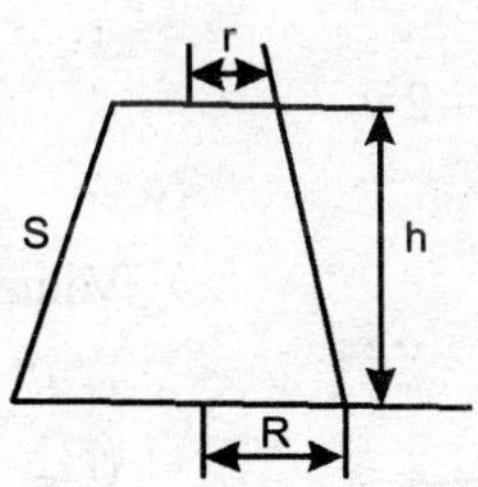	Curved surface $A = \pi (R + r)3$ [When S = Slant height] $= \sqrt{\left\{l(R-r)^2 + h^2\right\}}$	$V = \frac{\pi h}{3}$ $\left[R^2 + r^2 + Rr\right]$

Regular truncated pyramid	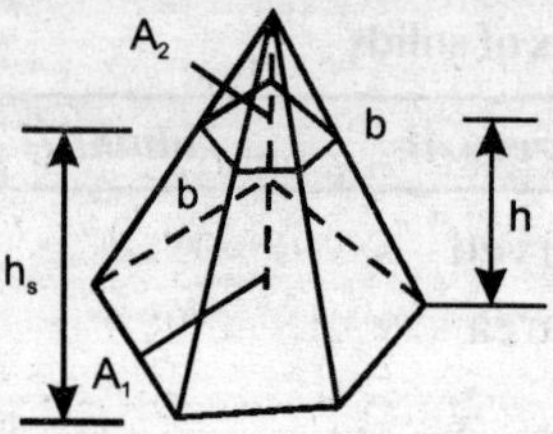	Slant surface area $A = \frac{nhs}{2}(a + b)$ n = Number of sides h_s = Perp. distance between parallel lines ab along the slant surface of truncated pyramid.	$V = \frac{h}{3}\left[A_1 + A_2 + \sqrt{A_1 A_2}\right]$ A_1 = Base area A_2 = Top flat area h = Vertical height
Wedge	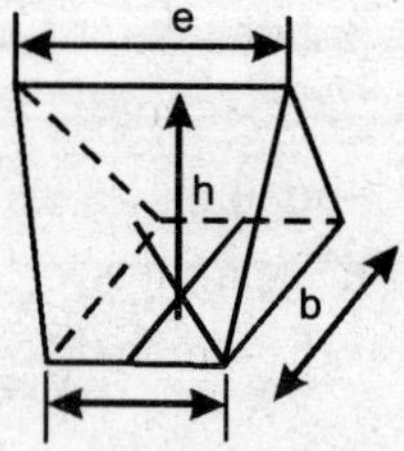		$V = \frac{bh}{b}(2l + e)$

Volumes of revolution (Guldinus theorem)

$\bar{y}$ = Position of C.G. (G): A = Gross-sectional area:

D_G = Diameter of path of C.G.:

V = Cross-sectional area × Length of path of C.G:

Name	***Figure***	***J, A and D_G***	***Vol (V)***
Circular ring		$\bar{y} = r$ $A = \pi r^2$ $D_G = D - 25$	Volume of the ring $V = A\,\pi D_G$
Half round groove	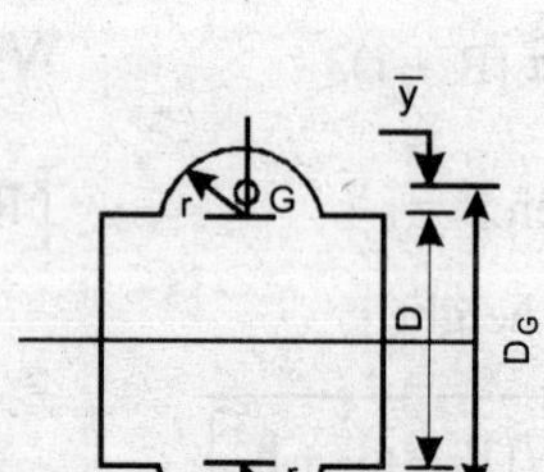	$\bar{y} = \frac{4r}{3\pi}$ $A = \frac{\pi r^2}{2}$ $D_G = D - 2\bar{y}$	Volume of the groove $V = A\pi\, D_G$
Half round rib	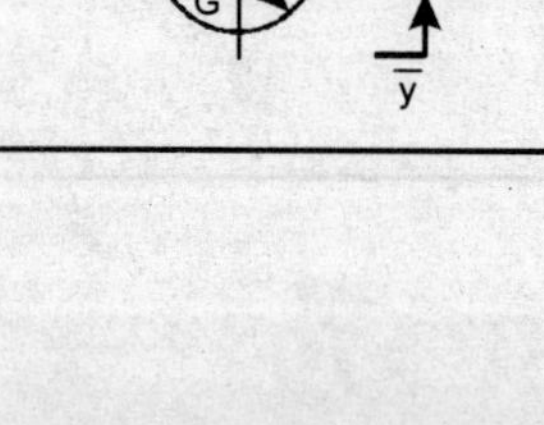	$\bar{y} = \frac{4r}{3\pi}$ $A = \frac{\pi r^2}{2}$ $D_2 = D + 2\bar{y}$	Volume of rib $V = A\pi D_G$

r groove

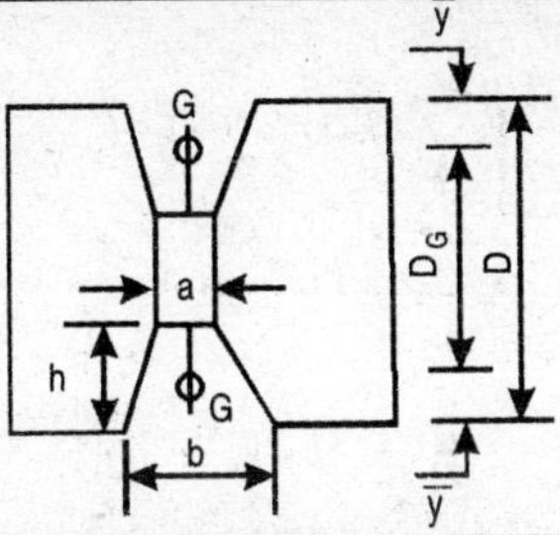

$$\bar{y} = \frac{h}{3} \times \frac{2a+b}{a+b}$$

$$A = \frac{a+b}{2} \times h$$

$$D_G = D - 2\bar{y}$$

Volume of V-groove

$$V = A\pi\, D_G$$

5.1.3 Solved Problems in Material Cost

Example 5.1

The wedge shown in the figure 5.1 below is to be made of 38.1 mm diameter stock by forging. Calculate the length of the bar if the volume remains unchanged.

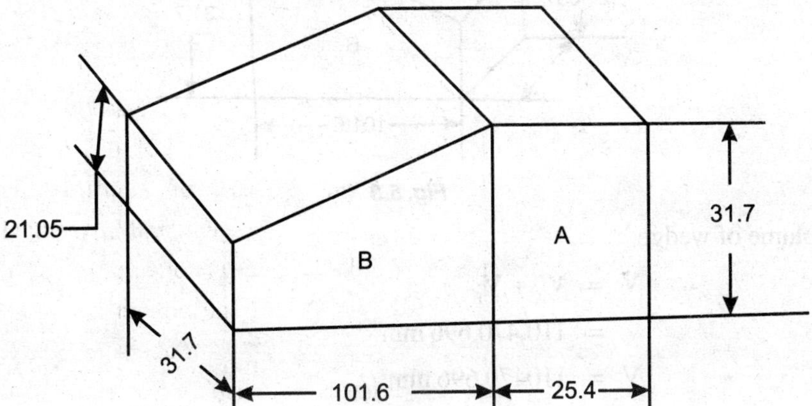

Fig. 5.1

Solution

Divide the wedge into components A, B. Consider component A. It is a simple RECTANGLE.

Hence, Surface area $A_A = l \times b$

and Volume $V = l \times b \times h = A \times h$

Now, $V_A = l \times b \times h = A \times h$

$= 31.7 \times 25.4 \times 31.7$

$V_A = 25{,}524.206 \text{ mm}^3$

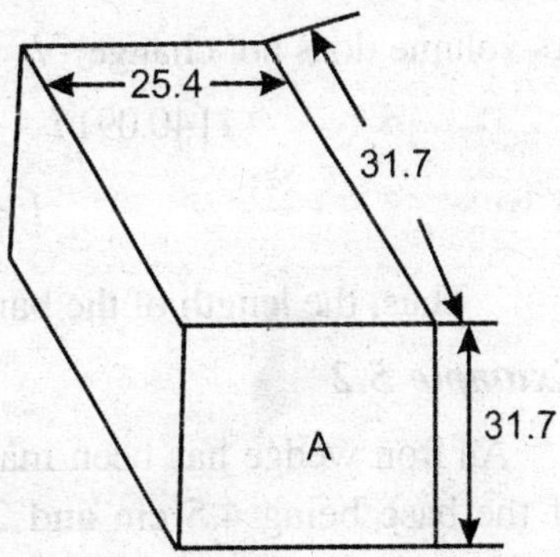

Fig. 5.2

Consider component B

Surface area $A_B = \frac{1}{2}(a + b)\,h$

Here $a = 21.05$

$$b = 31.7$$

$$h = 101.6$$

Hence, $A_B = 2679.7$

Volume. $V_B = A_B \times \text{Thickness}$

Volume of part B, $V_B = 2679.7 \times 31.7$

$$= 84,946.49$$

$$V_B = 84,946.49 \text{ mm}^3$$

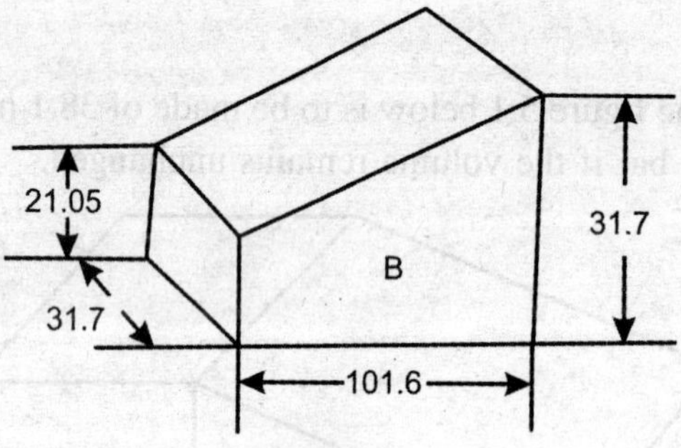

Fig. 5.3

Total volume of wedge

$$V = V_A + V_B$$

$$= 110,470.696 \text{ mm}^3$$

$$V = 110470.696 \text{ mm}^3$$

Now, volume of the cylindrical bar stock (from which the wedge is to be forged) is given as

$$V_1 = \frac{\pi}{4} d^2 l \qquad d = \text{Dia of stock}$$

$$= \frac{\pi}{4} (38.1)^2 l \qquad l = \text{Length of stock}$$

$$V_1 = 1140.091 l$$

As volume does not change $V_1 = V$

$$1140.091 l = 114070.696$$

$$l = 96.89 \simeq 96.9 \cong 97 \text{ mm}$$

Thus, the length of the bar stock is 97 mm or 9.7 cms.

Example 5.2

An iron wedge has been made by forging a 3 cm diameter bar stock. The length and breadth of the base being 4.5 cm and 2.5 cm. Length 4 cm and height 12 cm. If the density remains unchanged after forging. What length of bar is required to make the wedge?

All diamensions are in cms.

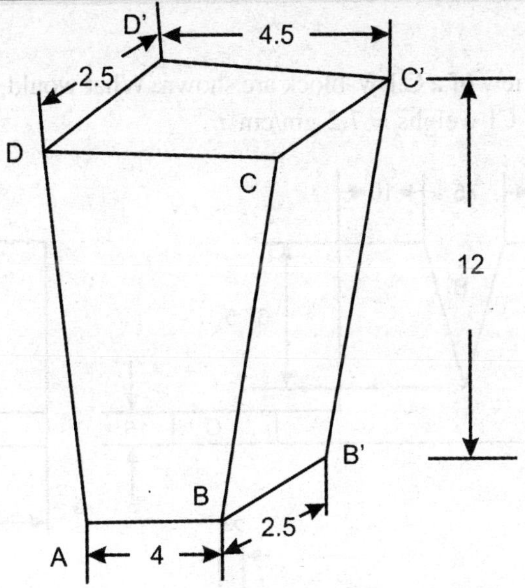

Fig. 5.4

Solution

The wedge represents a solid, vertical TRAPEZIUM.

We know, Surface area; $A = \frac{1}{2}(a+b)\,h$

Volume $V = `A \times t$

Here $a = 4$

$b = 4.5$

$h = 12$

$t = 2.5$

$\therefore$ Volume, $V = \frac{1}{2}(4+4.5) \times 12 \times 2.5$

$= 127.5 \text{ cm}^3 = 127.5 \text{ cu.cm}$

Hence, volume of the wedge is 127.5 cm^3.

Now, the volume of the cylindrical bar stock (from which the wedge is forged) is

$$V_1 = \frac{\pi}{4} d^2\, l$$

Now, as density remains unchanged in forging (given, volume also remains unchanged)

Hence, $V = V_1$

Hence, $127.5 \text{ cm}^3 = \frac{\pi}{4}(3)^2\, l \text{ cm}^3$

$l = 18.037 \text{ cm} = 180.3 \text{ mm}$

The length of the cylindrical bar stock is 180.3 mm.

Example 5.3

Three orthographic view of a C.I. V-block are shown. What would be the weight of the material required for the block if CI weighs = 7.2 gm/cm³?

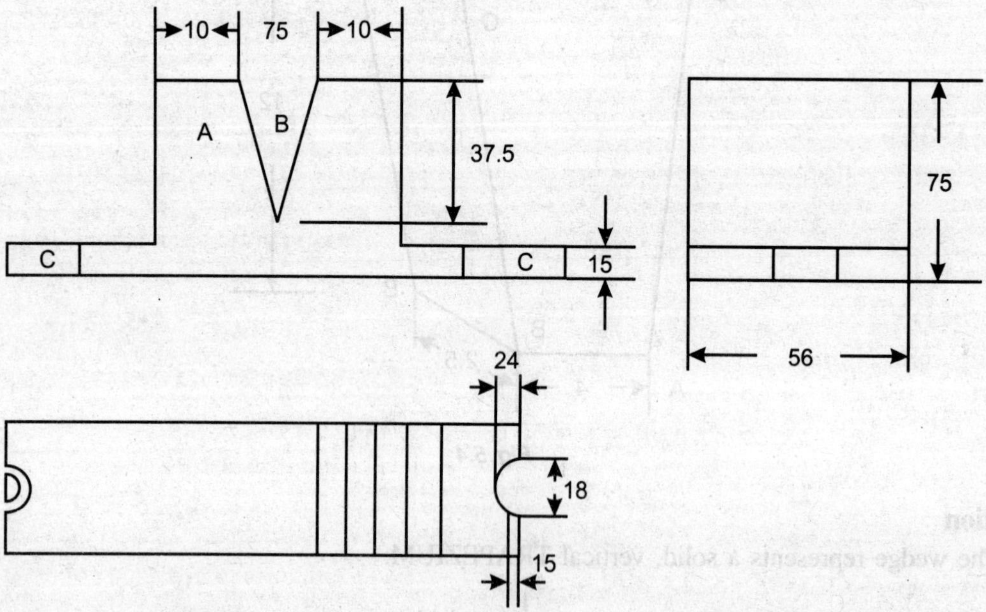

Fig. 5.5

Solution

The total volume of the V-block is calculated as follows,

$$V = V_A + V_C - V_B - V_D$$

Volume of the section A, $V_A = l \times g \times h = 95 \times 56 \times 75$

$$V_A = 3{,}99{,}000 \text{ mm}^3$$

Volume of the section B $V_B = \frac{1}{2}(l \times b \times h) = (75 \times 37.5 \times 56) \times \frac{1}{2}$

$$V_B = 78{,}750 \text{ mm}^3$$

Volume of section C $V_C = 2\,(l \times b \times h) = 2\,(38 \times 15 \times 56) = 63{,}840 \text{ mm}^3$

Volume of section D $V_D = 2\left[(bh) + \frac{1}{2}\left(\frac{\pi}{4} d^2\, l\right)\right]$

$$= 2\left[(15 \times 18 \times 15) + \frac{1}{2}\left(\frac{\pi}{4} 18^2 \times 15\right)\right]$$

$$= 11917.035 \text{ mm}^3$$

Hence, total volume $V = V_A + V_C - V_B - V_D$

$$= 372{,}171.43 \text{ mm}^3$$

Weight of the block $= 372171.43 \text{ mm}^3 \times 7.2$

$$= 2679.6 \text{ gm} = 2.67 \text{ kg}$$

The weight of the block is 2.67 kgs.

Example 5.4

The following product is manufactured by forging process from a block of cast iron. Find the weight of the material required for the block if cast iron weighs 7 gms/cm^3.

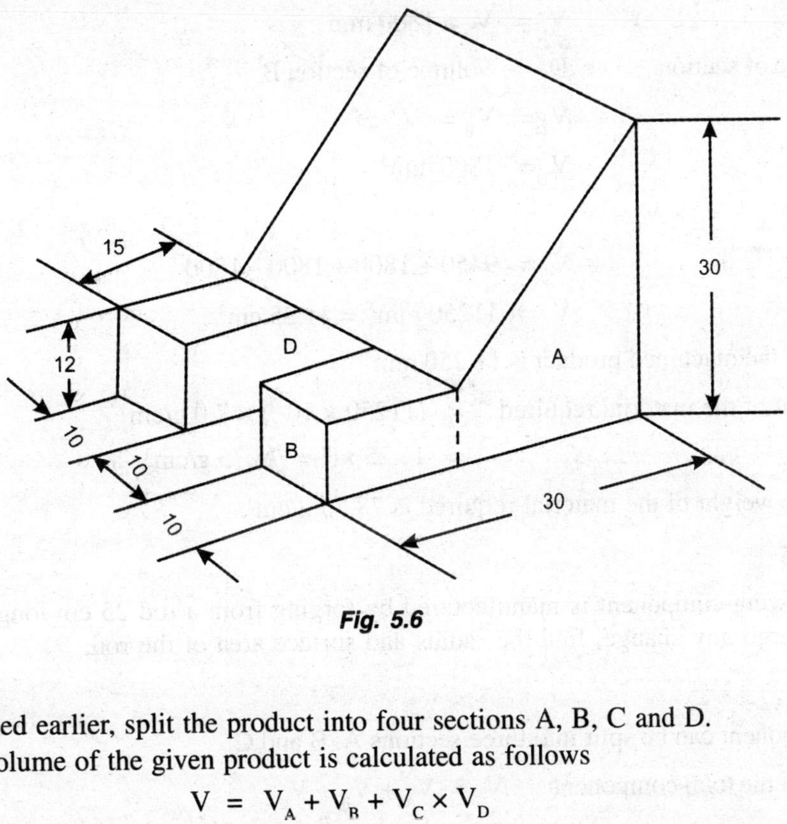

Fig. 5.6

Solution

As performed earlier, split the product into four sections A, B, C and D.
The total volume of the given product is calculated as follows

$$V = V_A + V_B + V_C \times V_D$$

Volume of section A is $V_A = \frac{1}{2}(a + b)\, h \times t$

Here
$$a = 12 \text{ mm}$$
$$b = 30 \text{ mm}$$
$$h = 15 \text{ mm}$$
$$t = 30 \text{ mm}$$

$$V_A = \frac{1}{2}(12 + 30) \times 15 \times 30$$

$$V_A = 9450 \text{ mm}^3$$

Volume of section B, $V_B = l \times b \times h$

Here $l = 15$ mm

$b = 10$ mm

$h = 12$ mm

$V_B = 15 \times 10 \times 12 = 1800 \text{ mm}^3$

$V_B = 1800 \text{ mm}^3$

Volume of section C = Volume of section B

$\therefore$ $V_C = V_B = 1800 \text{ mm}^3$

Volume of section D = Volume of section B

$V_D = V_B = V_C$

$V_D = 1800 \text{ mm}^3$

Now $V_A + V_B \times V_C - V_D = V$

$V = 9450 + 1800 + 1800 - 1800$

$V = 11250 \text{ mm}^3 = 11.25 \text{ cm}^3$

Volume of the machined product is 11,250 mm³

The weight of the material required $= (11250 \times 10^{-3}) \times 7.0 \text{ g/cm}^3$

$= 11.25 \times 7 = 78.75 \text{ g/cm}^3$

Hence, the weight of the material required is 78.75 g/cm³.

Example 5.5

The following component is manufactured by forging from a rod 25 cm long. If the volume does not undergo any change, find the radius and surface area of the rod.

Solution

The component can be split into three sections A, B and C.

Volume of the total component $V = V_A + V_B + V_C$

Consider section A,

Volume, $V_A = \frac{1}{2}(a + h) \times h \times t$

$a = 15$ mm

$b = 30$ mm

$h = 15$ mm

$t = 15$ mm

$V_A = \frac{1}{2}(15 + 30) \times 15 \times 15$

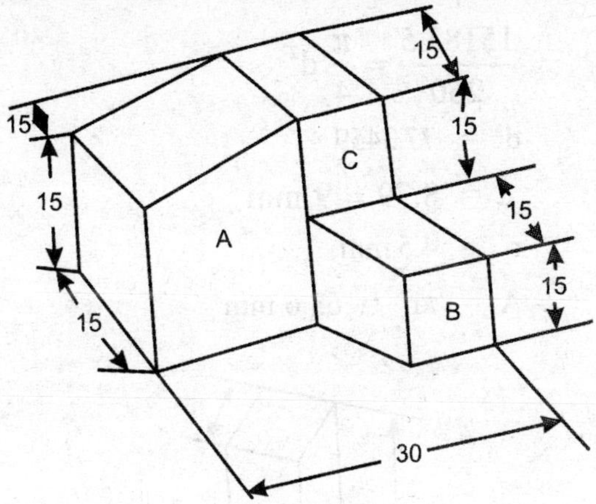

Fig. 5.7

$$V_A = 5062.5 \text{ mm}^3$$

Consider section B $\quad V_B = l \times b \times h$

$$= 15 \times 15 \times 15 \ (l = b = h = 15)$$

$$= 3375 \text{ mm}^3$$

$$N_B = 3375 \text{ mm}^3$$

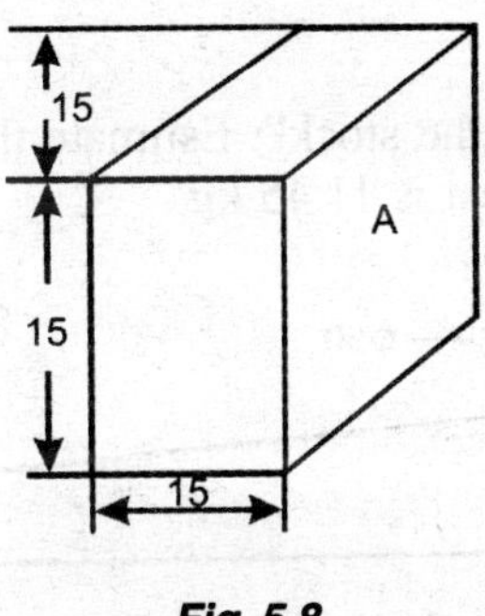

Fig. 5.8

Consider section C $\quad V_C = l \times b \times h$

$$= 30 \times 15 \times 15 = 6750$$

$$V_C = 6750 \text{ mm}^3$$

Total volume

$$V = V_A + V_B + V_C = 15187.5$$

$$V = 15187.5 \text{ mm}^3$$

Fig. 5.9

Now total volume = Volume of bar stock

$$\Rightarrow \quad 15187.5 = \frac{\pi}{4} d^2 \, l$$

$$\frac{15187.5}{250} = \frac{\pi}{4} d^2$$

$$d^2 = 77.3459$$

$$d = 8.79 \simeq 9 \text{ mm}$$

$$r = 4.5 \text{ mm}$$

$$\therefore \quad A = \pi r^2 = 63.6 \text{ mm}^2$$

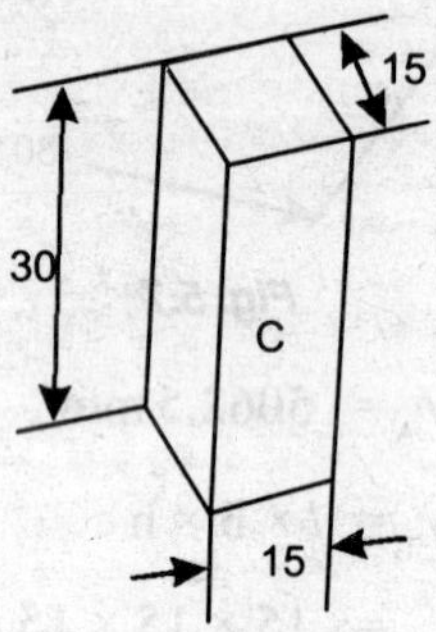

Fig. 5.10

Hence, radius of bar stock is 4.5 mm and the surface area is 63.6 mm².

Example 5.6

The following figure shows a "lathe stock". Estimate the weight and cost of material if C.I. weighs 7.787 gm/cm³ and material cost is 11.45 kg.

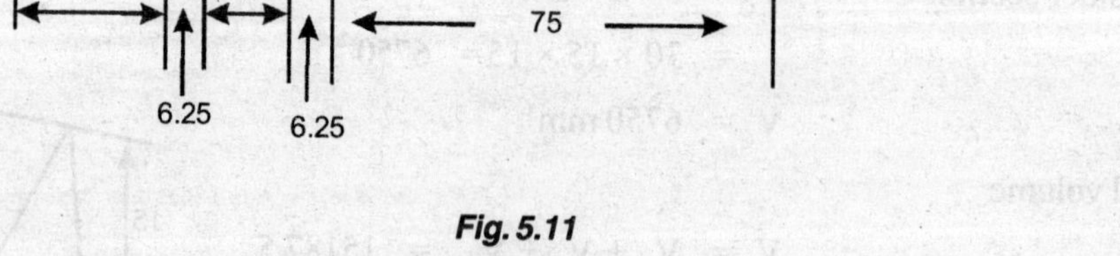

Fig. 5.11

Solution

The dimensional figure is divided into five sections A, B, C, D and E.

Section A is a FRUSTUM of A cone.

Now, Volume of frustum of cone $\quad V_A = \left[(a_1 + a_2) + \sqrt{a_1 a_2}\right]\frac{h}{3}$

Here $a_1 = \frac{\pi}{4}(d_1^2)$ $h = 75$ mm

$d_1 = 31.25$ mm

$$a_1 = \frac{\pi}{4}(31.25)^2$$

$$a_2 = \frac{\pi}{4}(50)^2$$

$$V_A = \left(\frac{\pi}{4}(31.25^2) + \frac{\pi}{4}(50^2)\right) + \left(\frac{75}{3}\sqrt{a_1 a_2}\right)$$

$$= 33410.10 \text{ mm}^3 = 33.410 \text{ cm}^3$$

Section B

Volume of section B, $V_B = \frac{\pi}{4} d^2 l = \frac{\pi}{4}(50)(6.25)$

$$= 12271.84 \text{ mm}^3$$

$$V_B = 12.271 \text{ cm}^3$$

Section C

Volume of section C, $V_C = \frac{\pi}{4} d^2 l$

$$= \frac{\pi}{4}(37.5)^2 \times 25 = 27611.65 \text{ mm}^3$$

$$V_C = 27.611 \text{ cm}^3$$

Section D

Volume of section D, V_D = Volume of B

$$V_D = V_B = 12.276 \text{ cm}^3$$

Section E

Section E is a cone with base 50 mm. We have to determine the slant height 'l' of the cone.

We know that, $\tan\theta = \frac{\text{Half base}}{\text{Slant ht.}}$

$$\tan = 60 = \frac{25}{l}$$

$$l = \frac{25}{1/\sqrt{3}}$$

$$l = 25\sqrt{3} \text{ mm}$$

$$V_E = \frac{1}{3} \times \text{Area of base} \times l$$

$$= \frac{1}{3} \times \frac{\pi}{4}(50)^2 \times 25\sqrt{3} = 28.4 \text{ cm}^3$$

Total volume of the lathe centre

$$V = V_A + V_B + V_C + V_d + V_E$$

$$= 113.63 \text{ cm}^3$$

Weight of the material $= \dfrac{113.63 \times 7.787}{1000}$

$$= 0.887 \text{ kg} \approx 0.89 \text{ kg} \approx 890 \text{g}$$

Cost of the material (cm)

$$\text{cm} = \text{Weight of material} \times \text{Bar stock cost}$$

$$= .890 \times 11.45 = \text{Rs. } 10.1905$$

The cost of the material is Rs. 10.1905/kg.

Example 5.7

Estimate the weight of the aluminium shaft. Aluminium weighs 9 gms/cm³. Also evaluate the material cost if 1 kg Aluminium costs Rs. 8 kg.

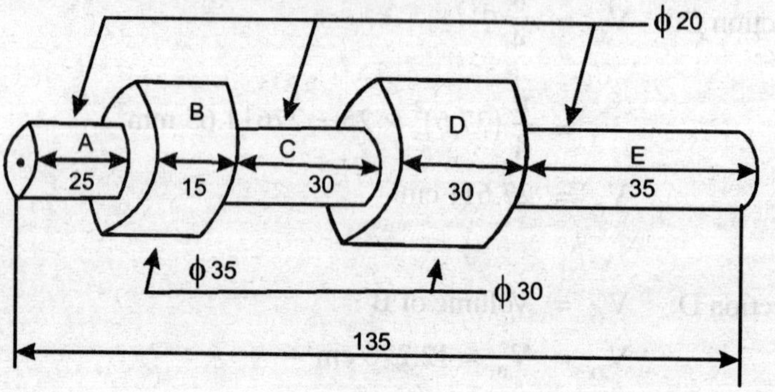

Fig. 5.12

Solution

Let us disintegrate the given shaft into five different sections as shown below consider section A.

$$V_A = \frac{\pi}{4} d^2 \, l = \frac{\pi}{4}(20)^2 \times 25$$

$$V_A = 10{,}000 \times \frac{\pi}{4} = 7853 \text{ mm}^3$$

Volume of section B $\quad V_B = \dfrac{\pi}{4} d^2 \, l$

$$= \frac{\pi}{4}(35)^2 \times 15$$

$$V_B = 14431.69 \text{ mm}^3$$

Volume of section C $V_C = \frac{\pi}{4} d^2 l$

$$= \frac{\pi}{4}(20)^2 \times 30$$

$$V_D = 21205.75 \text{ mm}^3$$

Volume of section E $V_E = \frac{\pi}{4}(20)^2 \times 35$

$$= 10{,}995.57 \text{ mm}^3$$

$$V_E = 10{,}995.57 \text{ mm}^3$$

Total volume of the shaft $V = V_A + V_B + V_C + V_d + V_E$

$$= 63{,}911.776 \text{ mm}^3$$

$$V = 63.911 \text{ cm}^3$$

Weight of the material of the shaft $W = 63.911 \times 9 = 575.205 \text{ g}$

$$= 0.575 \text{ kg}$$

The weight of the material is 0.585 kgs.

Material cost (cm)

$$\text{cm} = 0.575 \times 8 = \text{Rs. } 4.6$$

Hence, the cost of material required to forge a shaft is Rs. 4.6/kg.

Example 5.8

The following figures show brasses for a particular bearing. Determine material cost and weight if brass weighs 8.4 g/cm^3 and 1 kg brass costs Rs. 27.50.

Solution

The brasses diagram is split into individual volumes and the total volume is found as

$$V = \left(2 \times \frac{\pi}{4} \times 120^2 \times 25\right) + \left(2 \times \frac{\pi}{4} \times 90^2 \times 15\right)$$

$$+ \left(\frac{\pi}{4} \times 80^2 \times 60\right) - \left(\frac{\pi}{4} \times 40^2 \times 200\right)$$

$$= (806.60 \text{ mm}^3)$$

$$V = 806.60 \text{ cm}^3$$

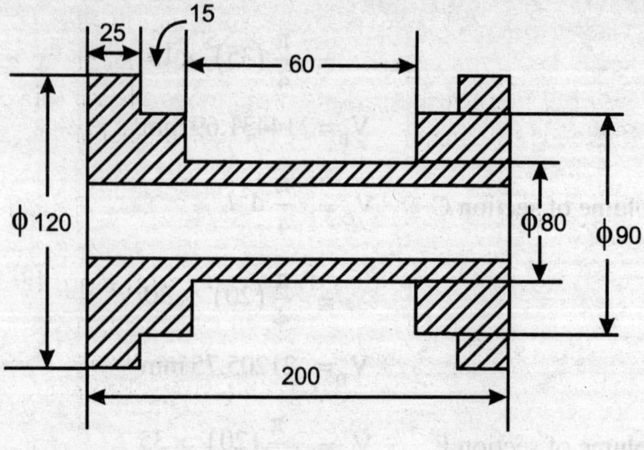

Fig. 5.13

Weight of brass required (W),

$$W = 806.66 \times 8.4 = 6775.4 \text{ g}$$

$$= 6.775 \text{ kg}$$

Thus, 6.775 kgs of brass the required to manufacture the brasses

Cost of required brasses (C)

$$C = 6.775 \times 27.50 = 186.32 \approx 187 \text{ Rs./kg}$$

The cost of the required brasses are Rs. 198.

Example 5.9

Estimate the weight of the forged shaft shown if steel weighs 8.1 gm/cc. (Dimensions are in cm).

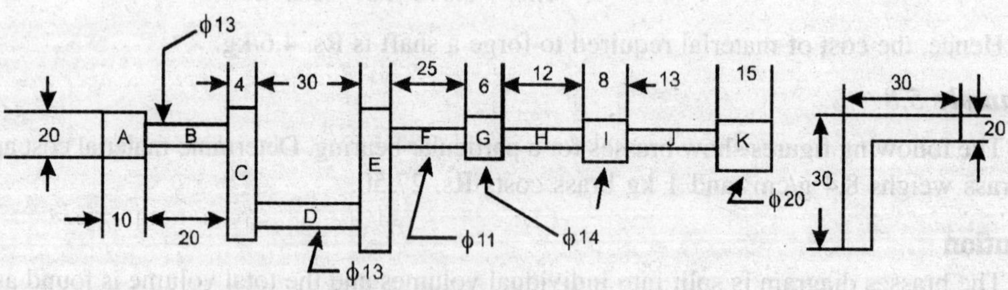

Fig. 5.14

Solution

The shaft is split into 11 sections.

$$\text{Total volume, } V = V_A + V_B + V_C + V_D + V_E + V_F + V_G + V_H + V_I + V_J + V_K$$

$$V_A = \frac{\pi}{4}(20)^2 \times 10 = 3141.59 \text{ cm}^3$$

$$V_B = \frac{\pi}{4}(13)^2 \times 20 = 2654.64 \text{ cm}^3$$

$$V_C = 4 \times 30 \times 20 = 2400 \text{ cm}^3$$

$$V_D = \frac{\pi}{4}(16)^2 \times 30 = 6031.85 \text{ cm}^3$$

$$V_E = V_C = 2400 \text{ cm}^3$$

$$V_F = \frac{\pi}{4}(11)^2 \times 25 = 2375.82 \text{ cm}^3$$

$$V_G = \frac{\pi}{4}(14)^2 \times 6 = 923.62 \text{ cm}^3$$

$$V_H = \frac{\pi}{4}(11)^2 \times 12 = 1140.39 \text{ cm}^3$$

$$V_I = \frac{\pi}{4}(14)^2 \times 8 = 1231.50 \text{ cm}^3$$

$$V_J = \frac{\pi}{4}(11)^2 \times 13 = 1235.43 \text{ cm}^3$$

$$V_K = \frac{\pi}{4}(20)^2 \times 5 \times 15 = 4712.38 \text{ cm}^3$$

$$V = V_A + V_B + V_C + V_D + V_E + V_F + V_G + V_H + V_I + V_J + V_K$$

$$V = 28{,}247 \times 8.1$$

Weight of steel required

$$W = 28{,}247 \times 8.1 = 22{,}8802.9418 \text{ gms}$$

$$W = 228.8 \text{ kg}$$

Hence, 228.8 kg of steel are required to forge a shaft.

Example 5.10

Estimate the weight of steel is gms/cc if about 200g of steel are required to forge a shaft as shown.

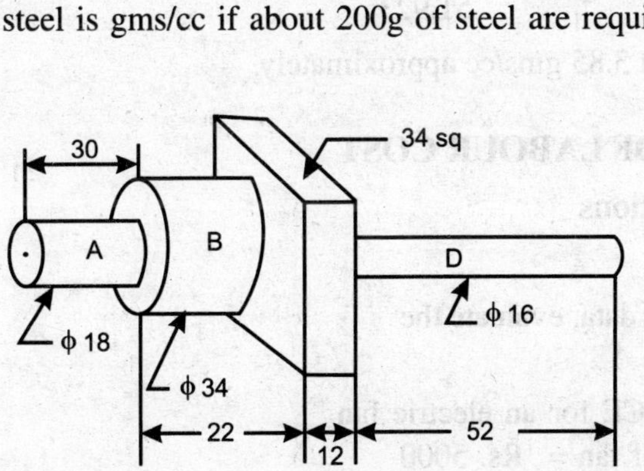

Fig. 5.15

Solution

Divide the shaft into four sections.

Total volume of solid

$$V = V_A + V_B + V_C + V_D$$

$$V_A = \frac{\pi}{4}(18)^2 \times 30 = \frac{\pi}{4} \times 324 \times 40$$

$$= 7634.070 \text{ mm}^3 = 7.63 \text{ cm}^3$$

$$V_A = 7.63 \text{ cm}^3$$

$$V_B = \frac{\pi}{4}(34)^2 \times 22 = 19{,}973.8 \text{ mm}^3$$

$$V_B = 19.973 \text{ cm}^3$$

$$V_C = 34 + 34 + 12 = 13{,}872 \text{ mm}^3$$

$$V_C = 13.87 \text{ cm}^3$$

$$V_D = \frac{\pi}{4}(16)^2 \times 52 = 10{,}455.2 \text{ mm}^3$$

$$V_D = 10.45 \text{ cm}^3$$

Total volume $V = V_A + V_B + V_C + V_D$

$$= 51.923$$

Weight of required steel material is 200 gms

$$W = 200 \text{ kgs} = 200 \text{ gms}$$

Also $W = V + (\text{Weight of steel mg/cc})$

$$\therefore \quad \text{Weight of steel in g/cc} = \frac{200}{51.923} = 3.85 \text{ g/cc}$$

Hence, steel weight 3.85 gms/cc approximately.

5.2 ESTIMATION OF LABOUR COST

Selling price calculations

Example 5.11

From the following data, evaluate the

(i) TOTAL COST

(ii) SELLING PRICE for an electric fan.

- Material cost of fan = Rs. 5000
- (Aluminium blades, steel cage etc.)

- Mfg wages = Rs. 3500
- Factory overheads to the manufacturing wages = 100%
- Non-manufacturing overheads = 15%
- Profit on total cost = 12%

Solution: Data given as

Direct material cost = Rs. 5000

Direct labour cost = Rs. 3500

Factory overheads = 100% of 3500 = Rs. 3500

(FC) Factory Cost = Direct Material Cost + Labour + Overheads cost

= 5000 + 3500 + 3500

(FC) = Rs. 12,000/-

Non-manufacturing overheads = 15% of factory cost

$$= \frac{15}{100} \times 12000$$

Non-manufacturing overheads = Rs. 1800

(i) Total cost determination

Total cost = Factory cost + Non-manufacturing overheads

= 12000 + 1800 = 13800

Total cost = Rs. 13,800/-

Profit on total cost = 12%

= 12% of total cost

= 12% of 13800

$$= \frac{12}{100} \times 13800 = 1656$$

Profit = Rs. 1656/-

(ii) Selling price determination

Selling price = Total cost + Profit

= 13,800 + 1656 = 15,456

Selling price = Rs. 15,456/-

Example 5.12

The direct cost of material per unit of a parker pen is Rs. 10.25. The direct man hours required for 50 units of the product is 225 hours the factory. The factory overheads are calculate on the basis of 100% of direct labour cost. The mean labour overhead wages are estimated as Rs. 5 per hour. The administrative and selling expenses are taken as 150 per cent of factory expenses. A discount of 20% is given for the distribution on the list price. The price of the product is fixed on the basis of 20% marking on the total cost as profit. Fix the list price per unit of the product.

Solution

Total units = 50

Direct material cost = Cost/Unit × Number of units

= 10.25 × 50 = Rs. 512.5/-

Labour wage per hour = Rs. 5/-

Total direct labour cost = Wage/hr × Number of man hours

= 5 × 225 = Rs. 1125/-

∴ Prime cost = Direct material cost + Direct labour cost

= 512.5 + 1125 = Rs. 1637.5/-

Factory overhead = 100% Direct labour cost

$$= \frac{100}{100} \times 900 = \text{Rs. } 900/-$$

Production = Prime cost + Factory overhead

= 1637.5 + 900 = Rs. 2537.5/-

Administrative and selling overhead

= 150% of factory expenses

$$= \frac{150}{100} \times 900 = \text{Rs. } 1350/-$$

Total cost = Production cost + Administrative and selling overhead

= 2537.5 + 1350 = Rs. 3887.5/-

Profit = 20% of the total cost

$$= \frac{20}{100} \times 3887.5 = \text{Rs. } 777.5/-$$

Example 5.13

From the records of an oil mill, the following data are available,

(a) Raw materials

Opening stock	= Rs. 1,40,000
Closing stock	= Rs. 1,00,000
Total purchases during the year	= Rs. 2,00,000

(b) Finished goods

Opening stock	= Rs. 20,000

Closing stock = Rs. 30,000

Sales = Rs. 6,00,000

(*c*) Direct wages = Rs. 1,00,000

(*d*) Factory expenses = Rs. 1,00,000

(*e*) Non-manufacturing expenses = Rs. 85,500

Find out what price should be quoted for a product involving an expenditure of Rs. 35,000 in material and Rs. 45,000 wages. Factory expenses to labour cost is 100%.

Solution

Direct material cost = Opening stock + Total purchases – Closing stock

= 1,40,000 + 2,00,000 – 1,00,000

= Rs. 2,40,000

Direct material cost = Rs. 2,40,000

Direct wages = Rs. 1,00,000

Factory expenses = Rs. 1,00,000

Factory cost = Direct material + Direct labour + Factory overheads

= 2,40,000 + 1,00,000 + 1,00,000

= Rs. 4,40,000/-

Non-manufacturing expenses = Rs. 85,000

Total cost = Factory cost + Non-manufacturing expenses

= 4,40,000 + 85,000

= Rs. 5,25,000/-

Factory expenses of direct labour cost = 100%

$$\text{Non-manufacturing expenses} = \frac{85000}{4,40,000} = 19.31\%$$

Cost of finished goods = Opening stock + cost of goods – Closing stock

= 20,000 + 5,25,000 – 30,000

= 5,15,000

Cost of finished goods = Rs. 5,15,000/-

Total sales = Rs. 6,00,000

Profit = Rs. 6,00,000 – 5,15,000

$$\text{Profit to sales cost} = \frac{85,000}{5,15,000} = 16.5\%$$

The cost of the product to be quoted is listed down as follows:

Direct material cost = Rs. 35,000

Direct labour cost = Rs. 45,000

Factory expenses = 100% of wages

= Rs. 45,000

Factory cost = Direct material cost + Labour cost + Factory expenses

= 35000 + 45000 + 45000 = 1,25,000

Factory cost = Rs. 1,25,000

Administrative and selling expenses = Non-manufacturing expenses

= 19.31% of factory cost

= Rs. 24,137.50

Total cost = 1,25,000 + 24137.50

= Rs. 1,49,137.50

Total cost = Rs. 1,49,137.50

Profit = 16.5% total cost

= Rs. 24,607.68

Profit = Rs. 24,607,68/-

Quotation price = 1,49,137.50 + 24,607.68

= 1,73,745.1875

Quotation price = Rs. 1,73,745.1875/-

Selling price = Total cost + Profit

= 3410 + 682 = Rs. 4092/-

$$\text{Cost per unit} = \frac{4092}{\text{Number of units}} = \frac{4092}{50} = \text{Rs. } 81.84/-$$

List price = Selling price + Discount

= Selling price + 20% list price

Let us assume 'list price' be ('x/-Rs.')

Now,

$$x = 81.84 + \frac{20}{100}x$$

$$x = 81.84 + 0.2x$$

$$0.8x = 81.84$$

$$x = 102.30$$

List price = Rs. 102.30.

Example 5.14

The cost-detail list for the production of a car is given as follows. Evaluate the selling price.

1. Material in hand - Rs. 30,000/-
2. New material purchased - Rs. 1,25,000/-
3. Director, fees - Rs. 1,750/-
4. Advertising - Rs. 6,000/-
5. Depreciation on sales dept. - Rs. 600/-
6. Printing and stationary charges - Rs. 150/-
7. Plant depreciation - Rs. 2,500/-
8. Wages - Rs. 35,000/-
9. Wages of indirect workers - Rs. 5,000/-
10. Factory rent - Rs. 2,500/-
11. Post and phone - Rs. 100/-
12. Water and electricity - Rs. 500/-
13. Office salaries - Rs. 1,000/-
14. Office rent - Rs. 250/-
15. Showroom rent - Rs. 750/-
16. Commission for salesmen - Rs. 1,250/-
17. Sales dept. expenses - Rs. 750/-
18. Material junk (Wasted) - Rs. 25,000/-
19. Variable direct expenses - Rs. 375/-
20. Plant maintenance - Rs. 1,500/-
21. Heating, lighting - Rs. 1,250/-
22. Distribution cost - Rs. 1,000/-
23. Profit - Rs. 5,000/-

Solution

(a) Material cost

Material cost = Material in hand – Material wasted + New material

= 30,000 – 25,000 + 1,25,000

= 1,30,000

Material cost = Rs. 1,30,000/-

(b) Prime cost = Direct material cost + Labour cost + Direct expenses

= 1,30,000 + 35,000 + 375

= Rs. 1,65,375/-

(c) Factory cost = Prime cost + Factory overhead

= 1,65,375 + (Serial Nos. 7 + 9 + 10 + 12 + 20)

= 1,65,375 + 2,500 + 5,000 + 2,500 + 500 + 1,500

= 1,77,375

Factory cost = Rs. 1,77,375/-

(d) Administrative overheads,

They include serial nos. 3, 6, 11, 13, 4, 21

= 1750 + 150 + 100 + 1000 + 250 + 1250

Admin-Overheads = Rs. 4,500/-

(e) Production cost

Production cost = Factory cost + Admin overhead

Production cost = Rs. 1,81,875/-

(f) Selling and Distribution overheads

They include serial nos. 4, 5, 15, 16, 17, 22

= 6000 + 600 + 750 + 1250 + 750 + 1000

= 10,350

Sales and Distributive overheads = Rs. 10,350/-

(g) Total cost

Total cost = Production cost + Sales overhead

Selling price = Rs. 1,92,225

Selling price = Total cost + Profit

= Rs. 1,97,225/-

Example 5.15

A factory produces 1500 electric bulbs per day. The details are given below

(i) Direct material cost = Rs. 1000/-

(ii) Direct labour cost = Rs. 800/-

(iii) Factory overhead = Rs. 900/-

Assume a 40% profit and 40% overhead of sales and evaluate selling price of one bulb.

Solution

Factory cost = Direct material cost + Labour cost + Factory overhead

= 1000 + 800 + 900 = 2700

Factory cost = Rs. 2700/-

Total cost = Factory cost + Selling overhead

= Rs. 2700 + 40% of 2700 = 3780

$$\text{Total cost} = \text{Selling price} - \text{Profit}$$

$$= \text{S.P.} - 40\% \text{ of S.P.}$$

$$\therefore \quad 0.6 \text{ SP} = 3{,}780 \Rightarrow \text{S.P.} = \text{Rs. } 6{,}300$$

$$\therefore \quad \text{S.P. for 1 bulb} = \frac{6{,}300}{1{,}500} = \text{Rs. } 4.20$$

Example 5.16

A cast foundry employs 30 persons. It consumes material worth Rs. 25,000 pays workers at the rate of Rs. 10/hr and incurs a total overhead of Rs. 20,000. In a particular month (25 days), workers had an overtime of 150 hours and were paid twice the normal rate. Find i) Total cost, ii) Man hour rate of overheads. Assume an 8 hrs workshift per day.

Solution

(i) Labour cost

$$\text{Labour cost} = (\text{Number of working hours}) + (\text{Rate of pay})$$

$$= (25 \times 8 \times 30)\ 10 = \text{Rs. } 60{,}000/-$$

(ii) Overtime expenses

$$\text{Overtime expenses} = \text{Rs. } 150 \times \text{Rs. } 20 = \text{Rs. } 3{,}000/-$$

$$\text{Total labour cost} = 60{,}000 + 3{,}000 = \text{Rs. } 63{,}000/-$$

(i) Total cost

$$\text{Total cost} = \text{Labour cost} + \text{Material cost} + \text{Overhead cost}$$

$$= \text{Rs. } 63{,}000 + \text{Rs. } 25{,}000 + 20{,}000 = 1{,}08{,}000/-$$

(iii) Man hour rate of overheads

$$= \frac{\text{Total overheads}}{\text{Number of total man hours put}}$$

$$= \frac{20{,}000}{25 \times 8 \times 30 + 15} = \text{Rs. } 3.25/-$$

Hence, the man hour rate of overheads in Rs. 3.25/-.

Example 5.17

Two moulders can cost 250 gears per day. Each gear weighs 3 kg and the gear material costs Rs.10/kg. If overhead expenses are 150% of direct labour cost and molders are paid at Rs. 70/ day, calculate the cost of producing one gear.

Solution

(a) Total Cost

$$= [\text{Material cost}] + [\text{Labour cost}] + [\text{Overhead}]$$

$$= (250 \times 3 \times 10) + (70) + \left(\frac{150}{100} \times 70\right)$$

$$= \text{Rs. } 7{,}580.50/-$$

$$\text{Cost/Gear} = \frac{7{,}580.50}{250} = 30.322$$

Approximately a gear costs Rs. 30.322/-.

Example 5.18

Estimate the sales price to be quoted for the product from the given data.

Direct material cost per piece = Rs. 14

Direct labour cost per piece = Rs. 18

Factory overhead = 100% of prime cost

General overhead = 25% of factory cost

Profit = 10% of total cost

Solution

Direct material cost = 14

Labour cost = 18

Prime cost = 14 + 18 = Rs. 32/-

Factory overhead = 100% of prime cost = Rs. 32/-

Factory cost = 32 + 32 = Rs. 64/-

General overhead = 25% of factory cost

$$= \frac{25}{100} \times 65 = \text{Rs. } 16/\text{-}$$

Total cost = Rs. 64 + 16 = Rs. 80

Profit = 10% of Rs. 80 = 8

Selling price = 80 + 8 = Rs. 88/-

Example 5.19

Market price of a CNC lathe is Rs. 50,000 and discount is 20% of market price. Here factory cost is 4 times selling cost and 1 : 4 : 2 is ratio of material, labour and overhead charges. Material cost is Rs. 4000. What is profit value?

Solution

Material cost = 4000

From ratio, Labour cost = 16,000/-

Overheat charges = 8000/-

∴ Factory cost = 4000 + 16000 + 8000 = Rs. 28000/-

$$\text{Now selling price} = \frac{1}{4}(28000) = 7000$$

Total cost = 28000 + 7000 = Rs. 35000/-

Selling price = Market rate – Discount

Profit = Selling price – Total cost

= 40000 – 35000 = 5000

∴ Company incurs Rs. 5000/- as profit.

Example 5.20

A factory produces 100 bolts and nuts per hour on a machine. Material cost is Rs. 375, labour Rs. 245 and direct expense is Rs. 80. The factory on cost is 150% and office on cost is 30%. If sales price is Rs. 11.30 find whether company incurs profit or loss.

Solution

$$\text{Material cost} = 375.00$$

$$\text{Labour} = 245.00$$

$$\text{Direct expenses} = 80.00$$

$$\text{Factory expenses} = 150\% \text{ of labour cost}$$

$$= 245 \times 1.5 = \text{Rs. } 367.50$$

$$\text{Factory cost} = 375 + 245 + 80 + 367.5$$

$$= \text{Rs. } 1067.50$$

$$\text{Office on cost} = 30\% \text{ of factory cost}$$

$$= \frac{1067.50 \times 30}{100} = \text{Rs. } 320.25$$

$$\text{Total cost} = 1067.50 + 320.25 = 13.87/-$$

$$\text{Cost per nut} = \frac{1387.75}{100} = 13.87/-$$

$$\text{Sales price} = 11.30$$

Hence, company incurs a loss of Rs. 2.57/-.

5.3 ESTIMATION OF OVERHEAD COST

5.3.1 Introduction

Overhead expenses are those costs which are incurred by the manufacturer but cannot be indentified and charged directly to any order product. Overhead expenses include all expenditure incurred by the manufacturer on the product except the direct material cost, direct labour cost and direct chargeablc expenses.

In most of the manufacturing organisation the overhead expenses are more than the direct labour costs. In some cases it may be 100 per cent of direct labour costs. In some other cases there may range from 200 per cent to 300 per cent of direct labour cost.

(a) Indirect material expenses.
(b) Indirect labour expenses.
(c) Other indirect.

(a) Indirect material expenses

Indirect materials are those materials which are consumed in the operations and processes in the factory but cannot be indentified as a part of a product. The expenditure incurred on such materials, which do not form a part of the final product but are consumed in the process conversion of raw materials into the finished products, are called indirect material expenses. The direct material expenses include the cost of oil, grease, lubricants, coolants, emery papers, cotton waste, etc. The indirect materials are weighed, counter or measured and then issued to the shop against requisition slip. The cost of such materials may then be worked out to assess the total cost of indirect materials used in manufacture and allocated to the product/products.

(b) Indirect labour expenses

Indirect labour is one who is not actually employed in the manufacturing of the product but his services are used in some indirect manner. The indirect labour includes supervisors, inspectors, foremen, store-keeper, gatekeepers, repair and maintenance staff, crane drivers, sweepers, administrative office staff and sales and distribution staff, etc. Salaries and wages paid to indirect labour in the entire year may be calculated from the records and distributed on the product/products.

(c) Other indirect expenses

All other expenses except direct and indirect materials, direct and indirect labour and direct expenses, incurred on a product are called "other indirect expenses". The other indirect expenses include depreciation of plant and machinery, water and electricity charges, rent of factory building, licence fee, insurance premia stationery, legal expenses, audit fee etc. The cost of all the above may be calculated on yearly basis and charged to the product/products.

5.4 ALLOCATION OR DISTRIBUTION OF OVERHEAD

After estimating the total on-cost, next step is the allocation of this on-cost over the production. To run the business in economical way, it is necessary to know, the variation of on-cost with the variation of production. Several methods are available for the allocation of on-cost. The choice of a particular method depends upon the nature of work, type of organisation and types of machine used, etc.

Following are the different methods of on-cost allocation:

1. Percentage on direct material cost.
2. Percentage on direct labour cost.
3. Percentage on prime cost.
4. Manhour method.
5. Machine hour method.
6. Combination of man hour and machine hour method.
7. Unit of production method.
8. Space rate method.

These methods for estimation the overheads are discussed below:

5.4.1 Percentage on Direct Material Cost

This method is based on the theory that the overhead expense is incurred in proportion to the value of the direct materials consumed. This method is simple, but does not allow for the usual situation where in some of the materials is fabricated without the use of much equipment whereas other material in the same plant requires extensive machinery, requiring considerably more labour, power, maintenance and floor space.

However, for the allocation of material expenses such as purchasing, storage and handling, this method is useful. This method is also useful when major part of the cost is of material line foundries and mines.

$$\text{Overhead rate} = \frac{\text{Total overhead expenses}}{\text{Total direct material cost}}$$

Example 5.21

A foundry department of a factory producing water meter body has Rs. 5.0 lacs as total overheads while the material cost was Rs. 25.0 lacs, calculate the percentage on-cost.

Solution

$$\text{Percentage on-cost} = \frac{\text{Total overhead}}{\text{Total direct material cost}}$$

$$= \frac{5}{25} \times 100 = 20\% \text{ of direct material cost.}$$

5.4.2 Percentage on Direct Labour Cost

In this method, allocation of on-cost depends upon the wages paid to the direct labour. This method is very reasonable and simple in calculation. Therefore, this method is very popular. It is the ratio of the total overhead to the direct labour cost for a particular period.

$$\text{Overhead rate} = \frac{\text{Total overhead for a period}}{\text{Total direct labour for that period}}$$

It is also called as labour burden rate. It is the ratio of the annual total overheads to the annual direct labour cost.

$$\text{Overhead cost} = \text{Overhead rate} \times \text{Direct labour cost/unit.}$$

This is very suitable where production is mainly carried out by hand. It may not be an accurate indicator where machines of greatly different capacity and sizes are operated. Also if two products take the same time but labour rate for both is different then this method will give less overhead cost where labour is cheap and high overhead cost where labour is costly. Therefore, this method increases the cost of a component which has already higher labour cost.

Also, in many case it gives very approximate results because sometimes of overhead such as depreciation and taxes have very little relationship to labour costs.

Example 5.22

The factory overheads of a certain concern for the year 1998-1999 were Rs. 10.0 lacs and total direct wages paid to the labour during the above period were Rs. 40 lacs, find out the percentage on-cost by percentage on direct labour cost method.

Solution

$$\text{Percentage on-cost} = \frac{\text{Total overhead}}{\text{Direct labour cost}} \times 100$$

$$= \frac{10}{40} \times 100 = 20\% \text{ of the direct labour cost.}$$

Example 5.23

The following particulars of a factory manufacturing three types of components X, Y and Z. Annual overhead expenses = Rs. 90,000. Direct labour cost for the component X = Rs. 10.000. Direct labour cost for the component Y = Rs. 15,000 and direct labour cost for the component Z = Rs. 20,000. Allocate the overheads to each components.

Solution

$$\text{Total direct labour cost} = \text{Rs. } 10{,}000 + 15{,}000 + 20{,}000$$

$$= \text{Rs. } 45{,}000/-$$

$$\%\ \text{Overhead rate} = \frac{\text{Total overhead}}{\text{Total direct labour cost}} \times 100$$

$$= \frac{90{,}000}{45{,}000} \times 100 = 200\%$$

∴ Allocation of overhead

1. For components $X = \frac{200}{100} \times 1000 = \text{Rs. } 20000$
2. For components $Y = \frac{200}{100} \times 15000 = \text{Rs. } 30000$
3. For components $Z = \frac{200}{100} \times 20000 = \text{Rs. } 40000.$

5.4.3 Percentage on Prime Cost

This is a very simple method. So it has gained popularity. This method is suitable, where labour and material both play equal role. This method will give the same overhead cost for two products with equal prime cost, even though their labour and material costs will be different. This will be useful where only one type of product is being manufactured and when direct labour and direct materials costs are nearly equal.

$$\text{Overhead rate} = \frac{\text{Total overhead over a period}}{\text{Prime cost over a period}} \times 100$$

Then, overhead cost/unit = Overhead rate × Prime cost/unit.

The method of allocation can be best understood by the following example.

Example 5.24

A factory has total overheads of Rs. 7 lacs, while the prime cost is Rs. 14 lacs. Find out the on-cost of the two products by percentage on prime cost method, if first product has Rs. 100 as direct material and Rs. 200 as direct labour cost, while second product has Rs. 150 as direct labour cost and Rs. 150 as direct material cost.

$$\text{Percentage on-cost} = \frac{\text{Total overhead}}{\text{Prime cost}} \times 100$$

$$= \frac{7}{14} \times 100 = 50\% \text{ of prime cost.}$$

1st product Prime cost $= 100 + 200 = \text{Rs. } 300$

$\therefore$ Overheads $= \frac{50}{100} \times 300 = \text{Rs. } 150$

2nd product Prime cost $= 150 + 150 = \text{Rs. } 300$

$\therefore$ Overheads $= \frac{50}{100} \times 300 = \text{Rs. } 150$

From the above example, it has been seen that both the product will be charged equally for overheads, while product first has labour cost as Rs. 200 and product second has labour cost as Rs. 150. Actually material cost has nothing to do with the overheads. Products which require large manufacturing time should have more overheads. This facts has not been considered in this method. Therefore, this method is a faulty one and is only suitable in the following two cases:

(a) Where only one type of product is being manufactured.

(b) Where direct labour and direct material costs are nearly same.

5.4.4 Man-Hour Rate

This method is very similar to the percentage on direct labour cost method. The difference in the two methods is that in which the basis of allocation was the total direct labour cost, whereas in this basis of the total hours spent by the direct labour and not the wages paid to them. This is an important method over the direct labour cost method.

$$\text{Man-hour rate} = \frac{\text{Total overheads}}{\text{Total direct man hour spent}}$$

It will be more clear by the following solved problem.

Example 5.25

A factory produces two components X and Y. Component X requires 20 hours and is manufactured by the workers paid at the rate of Rs. 10 per hour, while component Y also requires 20 hours but the workers producing it are paid at the rate of Rs. 7.5 per hour. Find out the on-cost of each component, if

(i) It is 40% if the direct labour cost, *(ii)* Rs. 2.00 per man-hour.

Solution

Component X

Labour charges $= 20 \times 10 = \text{Rs. } 200$

(i) Overhead @ 40% direct labour cost $= \text{Rs. } 0.4 \times 200$

$= \text{Rs. } 80$

(ii) Overhead @ Rs. 2.00 per man hour = 20×2 = Rs. 40.00

Component Y

Labour charges = 20×7.5 = Rs. 150

(i) Overhead @ 40% of direct labour cost = 0.4×150 = Rs. 60

(ii) Overhead @ Rs. 2.00 per man hour = 2×20 = Rs. 40

It is clear from the above examples that by considering percentages on direct labour cost method, the component X's on-cost is Rs. 80 while component Y's on-cost is Rs. 60. Actually both the components take same time, therefore, overheads should also be equal but this is not the case. Therefore, percentage on direct labour cost method is not very accurate one this gives less on-cost where labour is cheap and gives high on-cost, while labour is costly.

Therefore, this method increases the cost of component, which has already higher labour cost, irrespective of the time needed for the completion of the job.

From the above example, it is clear, that overheads by a man-hour method for both the components are same. Man-hour method has removed the drawbacks of direct labour cost method. Hence, it is comparatively more accurate method of overhead allocation.

5.4.5 Machine-Hour Rate

This method is generally used where work is done mostly by machines and not by hand. The overhead increased in each shop during a particular period are distributed over a group of similar machines. These expenses are then distributed on the basis of total productive machine hours. Machine hour rate is the rate of the total overheads to the total productive machine hour.

$$\text{Machine-hour rate} = \frac{\text{Total overhead}}{\text{Total productive machine hour}}$$

Total overheads in this system are distributed over the group of similar machines in the following ways:

(i) Power consumption is metered separately.
(ii) Depreciation charges are calculated separately.
(iii) Building rents, insurance, taxes, light charges and indirect labour and indirect materials are distributed on the basis of the floor area occupied by the machines.
(iv) The expenditure of wages paid for the ideal period of machines is not considered in these overheads but is seperately charged from the profit and loss accounts. This method will be clear by the following solved problem.

Example 5.26

A factory has 15 lathes of same make and capacity and 5 shapers of same make and capacity. Lathes occupy 30 m^2 area while shapers occupy 15 m^2. During one calender year, factory expenses for this section area are as follows:

(i)	Building rent and depreciation	Rs. 5000
(ii)	Indirect labour and material	Rs. 15000
(iii)	Insurance	Rs. 2000
(iv)	Depreciation charges of lathes	Rs. 5000

(v) Depreciation charges of shapers Rs. 3000

(vi) Power consumption for the lathes Rs. 2000

(vii) Power consumption for the shapers Rs. 1000

Find out the machine hour rate for lathes and shapers work for 25000 hours and 8000 hours respectively.

Solution

(a) Lathe section

Total overheads for the lathe section will be as follows:

(i) Building rent and depreciation (charged on the basis of floor area occupied)

$$= \frac{5000 \times 30}{(30+15)} = \text{Rs. } 3333.33$$

(ii) Indirect labour and material

$$= \frac{15000 \times 30}{(30+15)} = \text{Rs. } 10000$$

(iii) Insurance $= \dfrac{2000 \times 30}{30+15} = \text{Rs. } 1333.33$

(iv) Depreciation = Rs. 5000

(v) Power = Rs. 2000

∴ Total overheads = Rs. 21666.66

$$\therefore \text{ Machine hour rate for lathes} = \frac{21666.66}{25000} = \text{Rs. } 0.87$$

(b) Shaper section

Total overhead for the shaper section will be as follows

(i) Building rent and depreciation $= \dfrac{5000 \times 15}{(30+15)} = \text{Rs. } 1666.66$

(ii) Indirect labour and material $= \dfrac{15000 \times 15}{30+15} = \text{Rs.} 5000$

(iii) Insurance $= \dfrac{2000 \times 15}{(30+15)} = \text{Rs. } 666.66$

(iv) Power consumption = Rs. 1000.00

(v) Depreciation = Rs. 3000.00

Total overheads = Rs. 11332.32

$$\therefore \text{ Machine hour rate for shapers} = \frac{11332.32}{8000}$$

$$= \text{Rs. } 1.42$$

5.4.6 Combination of Man-Hour and Machine-Hour Method

As the name indicates, this method is simply a combination of man-hour rate and machine-hour rate methods. The man-hour rate method is suitable only where work is done by hand, for example, in fitting and assembly shops etc. Similarly, machine hour rate method is suitable where almost all the work is done by machines. Thus, in this way, both the methods can be applied in one factory. This method is combination of man-hour and machine-hour rate method of allocation.

5.4.7 Unit Rate Method

This is also known as production unit basis method. In this, on-cost is allocated on the basis of unit of production. Unit of production is generally piece, kilogram, tonne, litres, metre, etc. This method is mostly used where only one type of production is carried out. This method cannot be used in factories, where different kinds of products are manufactured. Unit rate is the overheads for one unit. It can be calculated as the ratio of total overheads to the quantity of production during a particular period.

$$\text{Overhead/Unit} = \frac{\text{Total overheads}}{\text{Quantity of production}}$$

This will be more clear by the following solved example.

Example 5.27

A company produces 500000 components per year, if the overheads during that year are Rs. 80 lacs, calculate the overhead cost on each component.

Solution

$$\text{Overhead/Unit} = \frac{\text{Total overhead}}{\text{Quantity of production}}$$

$$= \frac{80,00,000}{5,00,000} = \text{Rs. } 16$$

$\therefore$ Overhead on each components = Rs. 16

5.4.8 Space Rate Method

The amount of space occupied by a machine has a relationship to certain overhead expenses. For example, building expense, heat, light, ventilation and service equipment such as cranes and conveyors.

Space rate/m^2 for a department is

$$\text{Rs.} = \frac{\text{Total overhead assigned to a department}}{\text{Total area of the production department in square metre}}$$

$\therefore$ Space charges to the individual machine for the defined period of time = Space rate × Total area with which the machine should be charged.

5.5 ESTIMATION OF DIFFERENT TYPES OF JOBS

5.5.1 Estimation of Forging Shop

5.5.1.1 Losses in Forging

It is well known that some metal is always lost in the different operations of forging and this lost metal must be added to the net weight before calculating the material cost. The different losses to be considered are:

(i) Scale loss.

(ii) Flash loss.

(iii) Tonghold loss.

(iv) Sprue loss.

(v) Shear loss.

(i) Scale loss

This is the material lost because of the surface oxidaton in heating and forging the piece. When iron is heated at a high temperature in atmospheric conditions a thin of iron oxide is formed all round the surface of the heated metal which goes as a waste. The iron oxide film is known as scale and it falls from the surface of the metal on being beaten up by the hammer. Scale loss depends upon the surface area, heating time and the type of material. For forgings under 5 kg loss is 7.5 per cent of the net weight, and for forgings from 5 to 12.5 kg and over an addition of 6 per cent and 5 per cent of the net weight is necessary for scale loss.

(ii) Flash loss

There is a certain quantity of metal which comes between the flat surfaces of the two dies after the die cavity has been filled in. This material equal to the area of the flat surface is a wastage. For finding the flash loss, the circumference is determined which multiplied by cross-sectional area of flash will give the volume of the flash. The volume multiplied by material density gives the flash loss. Generally, it is taken as 3 mm thick and 2 mm wide all round the circumference.

(iii) Tonghold loss

This is the loss of material due to a projection at one end of the forging to be used for holding it with a pair of tongs and turning it round and round to give the required cross section in drop forging. About 1.25 cm and 2.5 cm of the size of the bar is used for tonghold. The tonghold loss is equal to the volume of the protections. For example, the tonghold loss for a bar of 2 cm diameter will be

$$= \frac{\pi}{4}(2)^2 \times 1.25 \text{ cu.cm}$$

(iv) Sprue loss

The connection between the forging and tonghold is called the sprue or runner. The material loss due to this portion of the metal used as a contact is called sprue loss. The sprue must be heavy enough to permit lifting the workpiece out of the impression die without bending. The sprue loss is generally 7.5 per cent of the net weight.

(v) Shear loss

In forging, the long bars or billets are cut into required length by means of a sawing machine. The material consumed in the form of saw-dust or pieces of smaller dimensions left as defective pieces is called shear loss. This is usually taken as 5% of the net weight.

From above we see that nearly 15 to 20% of the net weight of metal is lost during forging. And as already said these losses must be added to the net weight to get the gross weight of the material.

5.5.1.2 Forging Cost

The cost of a forged component consists of following elements:

(i) Cost of direct materials.

(ii) Cost of direct labour.

(iii) Direct expenses such as due to cost of die and cost of press.

(iv) Overheads.

(I) Direct material cost

Cost of direct materials used in the manufacture of a forged component are calculated as follows:

(i) The net weight of forging

Net weight of the forged component is calculated from the drawings by first calculating the volume and then multiplying it by the density of the metal used.

$$\text{Net weight} = \text{Volume of forging} \times \text{Density of metal.}$$

(ii) Gross weight

Gross weight is the weight of forging stone required to make the forged component. Gross weight is calculated by adding material cost due to various factors discussed above, to the net weight.

$$\text{Gross weight} = \text{Net weight} + \text{Material loss in the process.}$$

In case of smith or hand forging, only scale loss and shear loss are to be added to net weight but in case of die forging all the losses are taken into account and added to net weight.

(iii) Diameter and length of stock

The greatest section of forging gives the diameter of stock to be used and

$$\text{Length of stock} = \frac{\text{Gross weight}}{\text{X – Sectional area of stock} \times \text{Density of material}}$$

(iv) The cost of direct metal is calculated by multiplying the gross weight by price of the raw material

$$\text{Direct material cost} = \text{Gross weight} \times \text{Price/kg.}$$

(II) Direct labour cost

Direct labour cost is estimated as follows:

$$\text{Direct labour cost} = t \times l$$

Where t = Time for forging per piece (in hrs)

l = Labour rate per hour

It is very difficult to estimate the exact time to forge a component. In practice the forging time per component is estimated based on the production of eight hours or a day.

(III) Direct expenses

Direct expenses include the expenditure incurred on dies and other equipment, cost of using machines and any other items, which can be directly identified with a particular product. The method of apportioning die cost and machine cost is illustrated below:

Apportioning of die cost

Let cost of die = Rs. x

No. of components than can be produced using.

This die (i.e., die life) = y components

Cost of die/component = Rs. x/y

Apportioning of machine (press) cost

Let cost of press = Rs. A

Life of press = B n year = n × 12 × 4 × 5 × 8 = 1920 n hours

(Assuming 8 hours of working per day, 5 days a week and 4 weeks a month in 12 months of year)

Hourly cost of production = A/B

No. of components produced per hour = N

$$\text{Cost of using press per component} = \frac{A}{BN} \text{ Rs.}$$

This excludes cost of power consumed and other consumables.

(IV) Overheads expenses

The overheads include supervisory charges, depreciation of plant and machinery, consumables, power and lighting charges, office expenses etc. The overheads are generally expressed as percentage of direct labour cost.

The total cost of forging is calculated by adding the direct material cost, direct labour cost, direct expenses and overhead.

5.5.1.3 Solved Problems

Estimation of forging cost

Example 5.28

Three hundred pieces of the bolt are to be made from 25 mm diameter rod. Find the length of each bolt before upsetting. What length of the rod is required if 4% of the length goes as scrap?

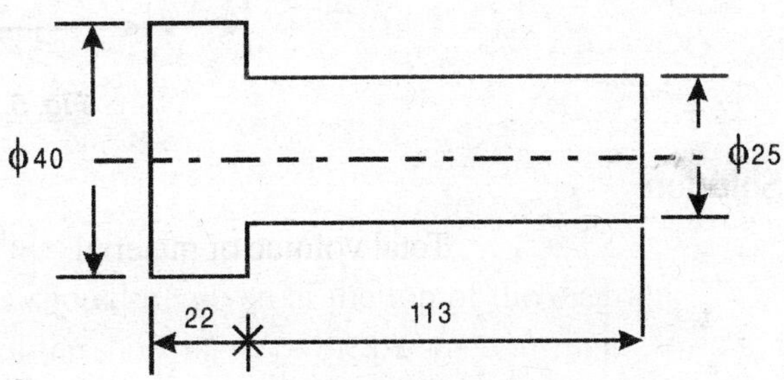

Fig. 5.16

Solution

$$\text{Volume of head of the bolt} = \frac{\pi}{d} D^2 \times L$$

$$D = 40$$

$$L = 22 \text{ mm}$$

$$= \frac{\pi}{4}(40)^2 \times 22 = 27{,}646 \text{ mm}^2$$

Length of material required for making the head

$$= \frac{\text{Volume}}{\text{Area}}$$

$$\text{Area} = \frac{\pi}{4} D_1^2 = \frac{\pi}{4}(25)^2 = 490.6 \text{ mm}^2$$

$$\therefore \quad \text{Length of bar} = \frac{27{,}632}{490.6} = 56.35 \text{ mm}$$

$$\text{Total length required for forming} = 56.35 + 113 = 169.35 \text{ mm}$$

$$\text{Length of rod required for making 300 bolts} = \frac{169.35 \times 300}{1000} = 50.8 \text{ metre}$$

Considering loss 4%,

$$\text{Total length required} = 50.8 + .4 \times 50.8 = 71.12 \text{ metre}$$

Example 5.29

Two hundred components as in figure 5.17 are to be made by upsetting a 20 mm diameter bar. Find the net weight, gross weight and length of bar required, density of material = 7.88 gms/cc.

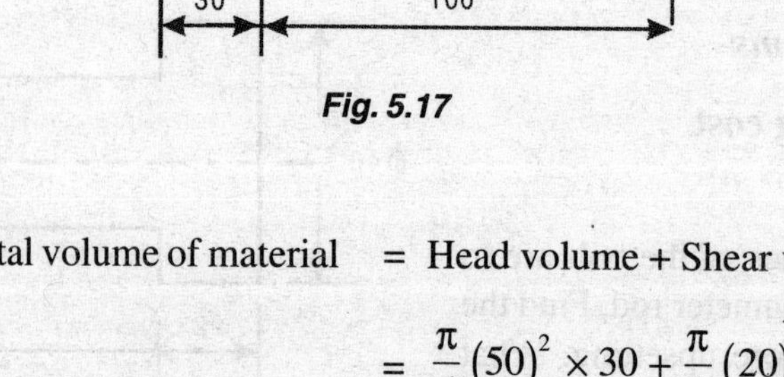

Fig. 5.17

Solution

$$\text{Total volume of material} = \text{Head volume} + \text{Shear volume}$$

$$= \frac{\pi}{d}(50)^2 \times 30 + \frac{\pi}{4}(20)^2 \times 100$$

$$= 58{,}875 + 31{,}400$$

$$= 90{,}275 \text{ mm}^3 = 90.275 \text{ cm}^3$$

Net weight per unit $= 90.275 \times 7.88$

$= 711.4$ grams

$\therefore$ Net weight for 200 units $= 711.4 \times 200$

$= 1{,}42{,}280$ gms $= 142.28$ kg

Considering losses

Shear loss $=$ 5% of net weight

$$= \frac{5}{100} \times 711.4 = 35.57 \text{ gms}$$

Scale loss $=$ 6% of net weight

$= 0.06 \times 711.4 = 42.684$ gms

Gross weight for 200 units $= 711.4 + 35.57 + 42.68 = 789.65$ gms

Gross weight for 200 units $= 200 \times 789.65 = 157.93$ kg

Length of 20 mm diameter bar required

$$= \text{Density} = \frac{\text{Mass}}{\text{Volume}} = \frac{\text{Mass}}{\text{Area} \times \text{Length}}$$

$$= \text{Length} = \frac{\text{Mass}}{\text{Area} \times \text{Density}}$$

$$= \frac{157930}{\frac{\pi}{4}(2)^2 \times 7.88}$$

$= 6393.9$ cm $= 63.93$ meters.

Example 5.30

A square bar of 3 cm side and 25 cm length is to be converted by hand forging into a bar of hexagonal section having each side equal to 1.5 cm. Calculate the length of thc hcxagonal bar produced, considering a scale loss of 6% of total volume. What would have been the length of a rod with diameter of 3 cm if the same hexagonal bar was to be forged from the rod?

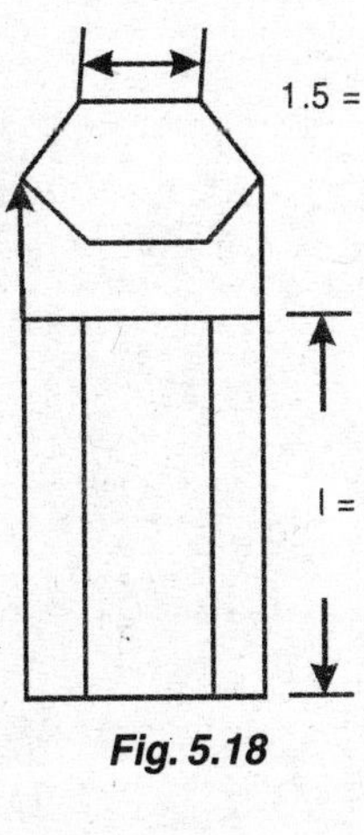

Fig. 5.18

Solution

1. Volume of square bar $= (a \times a)\, h$

a = Side length = 3 cm

h = Height of bar = 25 cm

$\therefore$ Volume $= 3 \times 3 \times 25 = 225 \text{ cm}^3$

2. Taking 6% scale losses,

$$\text{Volume of bar} = 225 - 0.06 \times 225 = 211.5 \text{ cm}^3$$

3. Cross sectional area of hexagonal bar $= \dfrac{3\sqrt{3}}{2} S^2$

$$= \frac{3\sqrt{3}}{2} \times (1.5)^2 = 5.85 \text{ cm}^2$$

$\therefore$ Length of hexagonal bar produced $= \dfrac{\text{Volume}}{\text{Area}}$

$$= \frac{211.5}{5.858}$$

$$= 36.1 \text{ cm} = 0.361 \text{ meter}$$

Second section

$$\text{Volume of rod} = \text{Volume of the square rod}$$

$$= \frac{\pi}{4} d^2 L = 225 \text{ cm}^3$$

$\therefore$ Length of rod 'L' $= \dfrac{225}{\frac{\pi}{4}(3)^2} = 31.83$ cm

Example 5.31

Find the number of mild steel rivets as in figure 5.19 can be produced from 19 kg of mild steel, assume a scale loss of 10% volume. The density of mild steel (ρ) is 7.92 g/cm³.

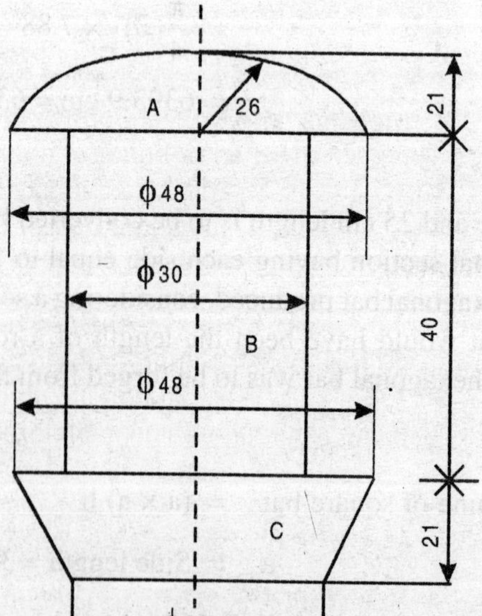

Fig. 5.19

Solution

$$\text{Volume of snap head (A)} = \frac{\pi}{3} h^3 (3R - h)$$

$$= \frac{\pi}{3} (2.1)^2 \times (3 \times 2.8 - 2.1) = 29.09 \text{ cm}^3$$

$$\text{Volume of stem (B)} = \frac{\pi}{4} d^2 h = \frac{\pi}{4} (3)^2 \times 4 = 28.27 \text{ cm}^3$$

$$\text{Volume of pan head (C)} = \frac{\pi}{12} h \left(D^2 + d^2 + Dd\right)$$

$$= \frac{\pi}{12} \times 2.1 \left(4.8^2 + 3^2 + 4.8 \times 3\right) = 25.55 \text{ cm}^3$$

$$\therefore \quad \text{Total volume of one rivet} = a + b + c$$

$$= 29.09 + 28.27 + 25.55 = 82.91 \text{ cm}^3$$

Considering 10% scale loss on total volume of one rivet,

$$\text{Volume required} = 82.91 \times \frac{110}{106} = 91.2 \text{ cm}^3$$

$$\therefore \quad \text{Weight of material required for one rivet} = 91.2 \times 7.92$$

$$= 722.3 \text{ gms} = 0.722 \text{ kg}$$

∴ Number of rivets than can be produced from 19 kg of H.S.

$$= \frac{19}{0.7223} = 26.3 \simeq 27 = 27 \text{ Numbers.}$$

Example 5.32

A hexagonal bolt with a finished diameter of 25 mm, shank length 110 mm and bolt head height of 25 mm is to be forged. What would be the size of the stock and its length, if forging loss is 3%? Find the total length of stock for 300 bolts, if scrap loss is 4%.

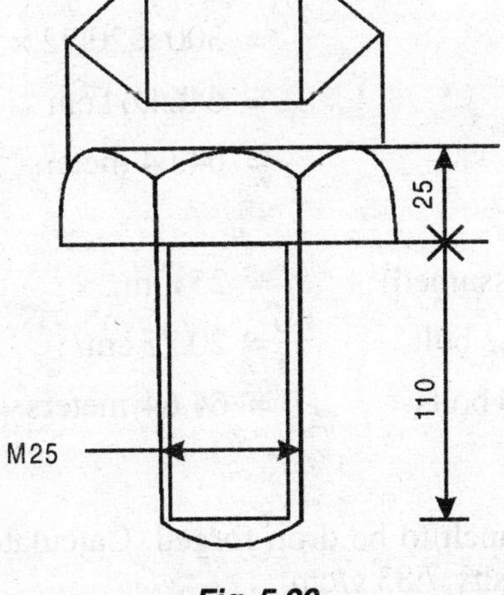

Fig. 5.20

Solution

$$\text{Volume of hexagonal head} = \frac{3\sqrt{3}}{2} S^2 \times h$$

$$= \frac{3\sqrt{3}}{2} \times (25)^2 \times 25 = 40.593 \text{ mm}^3$$

$$\text{Head volume} = 40.593 \text{ cm}^3$$

$$\text{Volume of shank} = \frac{\pi}{4} d^2 \times l$$

$$= \frac{\pi}{4} (25)^2 \times 110 = 53{,}968 \text{ mm}^3$$

$$\text{Shank volume} = 53.968 \text{ cm}^3$$

$$\text{Total volume} = \text{Head volume} + \text{Shank volume}$$

$$= 40.593 + 53.968$$

$$\text{Total volume of one bolt} = 94.561 \text{ cm}^3$$

$$\text{Diameter of stock taken} = 25 \text{ mm}$$

Considering 3% forging loss, loss, volume of material required for one bolt.

$$= 94.561 \times 1.03 = 97.398 \text{ cm}^3$$

Taking diameter of bar stock equal to the diameter of bolt shank, length of bar shock for each bolt is

$$= \frac{97.398}{\frac{\pi}{4}(2-5)^2}$$

$$\text{Length of bar stock/bolt} = 20.72 \text{ cm}$$

Now, considering 4% scrap loss, total length of stock required for 300 bolts.

$$= 300 \times 20.72 \times 1.04$$

$$= 6464.64 \text{ cm}$$

$$= 64.64 \text{ meters}$$

Ans.

(i) Diameter of stock (Assumed) = 25 mm

(ii) Length of stock for one bolt = 20.75 cm

(iii) Length of stock for 30 bolts = 64.64 meters.

Example 5.33

The figure shows a centre punch to be drop-forged. Calculate net weight, gross weight and length of M.S. bar. Mild steel density 7.83 g/cm^3.

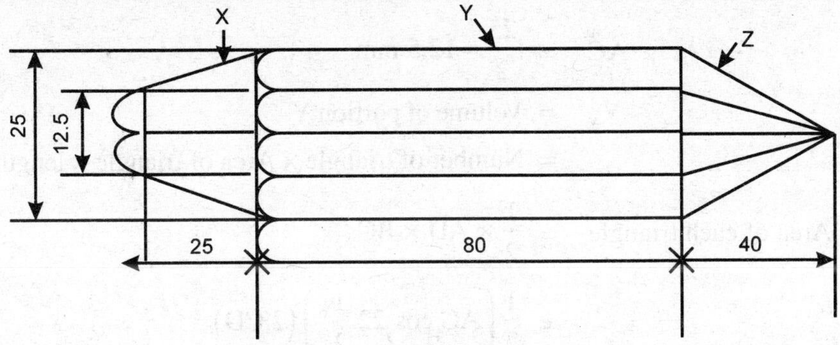

Fig. 5.21

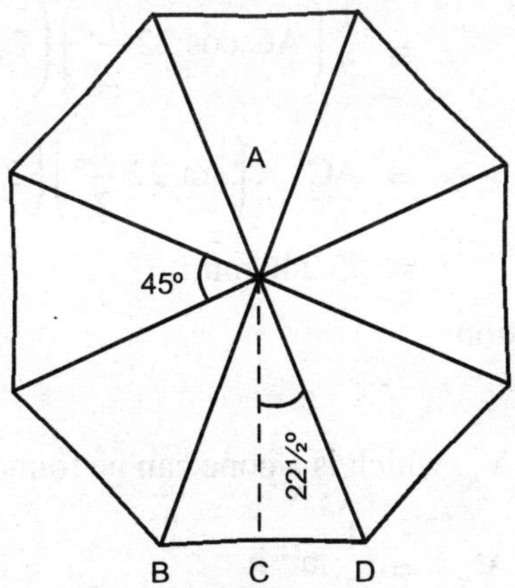

Fig. 5.22

Solution

Section Z

Volume of portion Z, can be calculated as follows. It is being a frustum of cone.

$$V_Z = \frac{\pi}{3} h\left[R^2 + r^2 + Rr\right]$$

Where

$$R = \text{Outer radius of punch } \frac{25}{2} = 12.5 \text{ mm}$$

$$r = \text{Convergent radius of punch}$$

$$= \frac{12.5}{2} = 6.25 \text{ mm, } h = 25 \text{ mm}$$

$$V_Z = \text{Volume of portion Z}$$

$$= \frac{\pi}{3}(25)\left[(12.5)^2 + (6.25)^2 + (12.5 \times 6.25)\right]$$

$$= 7154.88 \text{ mm}^3$$

Section Y

The holding portion Y consists of 8 triangles as in figure.

$$AC = \frac{25}{2} = 12.5 \text{ mm}$$

$$V_Y = \text{Volume of portion Y}$$

$$= \text{Number of triangle} \times \text{Area of triangle} \times \text{length}$$

$$\text{Area of each triangle} = \frac{1}{2} \times AD \times BC$$

$$= \frac{1}{2}\left(AC \cos 22\frac{1}{2}^\circ\right)(2\,CD)$$

$$= \frac{1}{2}\left(AC \cos 22\frac{1}{2}^\circ\right)\left(2\,AC \sin 22\frac{1}{2}^\circ\right)$$

$$= AC^2 \times \left(\sin 22\frac{1}{2}^\circ\right)\left(2A \sin 22\frac{1}{2}^\circ\right)$$

$$= 55.246 \text{ mm}^2$$

∴ Volume of Y portion

Section X

The cutting portion volume V_X, which is a cone can be found as follows.

$$V_X = \frac{1}{3}\pi r^2 h$$

Where $r = 12.5$ mm

$h = 40$ mm

$$V_X = \frac{\pi}{3}(12.5)^2(40) = 6541.6 \text{ mm}^3$$

Total volume

∴ Total volume of punch $V = V_Z + V_Y + V_X$

$= 7154.88 + 44,196.8 + 6541.6$

$= 57,893.28 \text{ mm}^3 = 57.8 \text{ cm}^3$

∴ Net weight of punch $=$ Volume × Density

$= 57.8 \times 7.83 = 452.57$ gms

Drop forging losses

(a) Shear loss $=$ 5% of net weight

$$= \frac{5}{100} \times 452.57 = 22.6 \text{ gms}$$

(b) Tong hold loss $=$ 25 mm long and equal to diameter of stock

$\therefore$ Tong hold volume = $\frac{\pi}{4} d^2 \times l$

$$d = \text{Stock diameter} = 25 \text{ mm}$$

$$l = \text{Tong hold length} = 25 \text{ mm}$$

$$= \frac{\pi}{4} (25)^2 \times 25$$

$$= 12{,}265.6 \text{ mm}^3$$

$\therefore$ Tong hold loss = Density × Tong hold volume

$$= 7.83 \times 12.265 = 96 \text{ gms}$$

(c) Scale loss 6% of the net weight

$$= \frac{6}{100} \times 452.57 = 27.15 \text{ gms}$$

(d) Flash loss

It depends upon the periphery of forging (P_L)

$$P_L = 12.5 + 2\,(25 + 100 + 40) = 342.5 \text{ mm}$$

$$P_L = 34.25 \text{ cm}$$

For flash loss 20 mm wide and 4 mm thick all around the periphery

$$\text{Wide} = w = 20 \text{ mm} = 2 \text{ cm}$$

$$\text{Thickness} = t = 4 \text{ mm} = 0.04 \text{ cm}$$

$$\text{Flash loss} = w \times t \times P_L \times e$$

$$= 2 \times .3 \times 34.25 \times 7.83 = 214.54 \text{ gm}$$

(e) Sprue loss: 7% of net weight

$$= \frac{7}{100} \times 452.57 = 31.68 \text{ gms}$$

$\therefore$ Total material loss during forging

$$= \text{(i)} + \text{(ii)} + \text{(iii)} + \text{(iv)} + \text{(v)}$$

$$= 22.6 + 96 + 27.15 + 214.54 + 31.68$$

$$= 391.97 \text{ gms}$$

$$\text{Gross weight} = \text{Net weight} + \text{losses}$$

$$= 452.57 + 391.97 = 844.54 \text{ gms.}$$

Length of bar required for forging the centre punch,

$$L = \frac{\text{Gross weight}}{\text{Area of cross section of stock} \times \rho}$$

Area of cross section of stuck $= \frac{\pi}{4}d^2 = \frac{\pi}{4}(2.5)^2 = 4.9 \text{ cm}^2$

$$\therefore \quad L = \frac{844.54}{4.9 \times 7.83}$$

Length of bar required $= 21.99 \text{ cm} \simeq 22 \text{ cm}.$

5.5.2 Estimation of Welding Shop

5.5.2.1 Welding Cost

Cost procedure

In estimation welding cost of a job, the different items which are to the taken into account are material, labour and tooling cost.

Material cost

In this, costs of all materials are included used in fabrication progress like metallic sheet or plate stock costing stampings, forging etc. Another major item is the consumable electrode or weld wire used to provide for the additional metal in the weld groove. This quantity is determined by the cross-sectional area, length and the particular welding process. In case of gas welding cost of gases like oxygen and acetylene consumed are taken into consideration.

Table 5.1

Plate thickness in mm	*Welding technique*	*Filler rod dia in mm*	*O_2 Consumption in cu m/hr*	*Acetylene consumption in cu m/hr*	*Welding time per metre in min*	*Length of filler rod required/m of welding in metre*
1	Leftward	1.00	0.04	0.02	9 to 11	1.0
2	Leftward	2.0	0.10	0.04	10 to 12	1.5
3	Leftward	2.5	0.2	0.07	12 to 13	1.6
4	Leftward	3.0	0.15	0.10	13 to 15	2.6
5	Leftward	3 to 4	0.21	0.14	15 to 17	4.0 to 1.8
5	Rightward	2.5	0.3	0.20	16 to 18	3.3
6	Rightward	3.0	0.4	0.25	18 to 20	3.4
8	Rightward	4.0	0.5	0.30	20 to 28	3.6
10	Rightward	5.0	0.7	0.50	30 to 35	4.5
15	Rightward	6.0	1.0	0.60	45 to 50	6.8
20	Rightward	6.0	1.2	0.80	60 to 67	10.0
25	Rightward	6.0	1.6	0.90	85 to 100	16.0

Labour cost

Under this category, costs of all persons are directly related to the making of weldment. First of all welding times are calculated and from that the labour cost is calculated. The labour cost is sub-divided into following groups:

(i) Preparation

The cost of preparing raw materials for welding would include preparing of edges according to requirements machining of welded joints to shape, and the cleaning of the foreign material from the surface to be welded.

(ii) Set-up

This includes assembling the parts in the welding fixture, heating prior to welding etc.

Table 5.2

Plate thick-ness in mm	*Nozzle dia in mm*	*O_2 pressure, kg/cm²*		*Consumption, m³/hr*				*Cutting speed m/hr*	
				O_2		*C_2H_2*			
		Hand	*Machine*	*Hand*	*Machine*	*Hand*	*Machine*	*Hand*	*Machine*
3	0.8 to	11.0-1.65	1.0-2.0	1.3-1.4	1.2-1.4	0.20-0.25	0.18-0.25	30-45	30-50
5	1	0.75-1.50	0.75-2.0	1.8-2.0	0.8-2.0	0.15-0.20	0.12-0.20	20-30	18-32
10	1 or 15	1.5-2.0	1.5-3.5	1.2-2.4	1.0-2.4	0.20-0.25	0.15-0.25	15-30	15-30
15	1.5	1.7-2.5	1.5-3.5	3.4-4.5	3.4-4.5	0.30-0.45	0.33-0.42	18-27	18-30
5	1.5	3.1-2.8	2.0-2.8	3.6-5.0	3.6-5.0	0.36-0.47	0.35-0.47	18-28	18-30

(iii) Material deposition

This is determined by the rate of weld deposit, weld joint preparation, number of passes required for the weld.

(iv) Post welding operation

This includes the cost for the removal of excess of weld metal, slag, rough or finish machining to weldment dimensions.

Cost of heat treatment operations after welding such as annealing, normalising, hardening etc., are also including under this.

(v) Finishing

Cost of cleaning welded portion for surface finish is considered under finishing cost.

Tooling cost

Under this item would be the costs of welding fixtures, machining fixtures and machining template.

5.5.2.2 Solved Problems

Example 5.34

Estimate the time required for making an open tank size 50 × 50 × 50 cm by gas welding size of sheets used is 50 × 40 × 0.3 cm. Welding to be done on inner surface only. Assume fatigue allowances to be 5%.

Solution

Length of portion where welding is required to be done, which is clear in figure 5.23.

$$= AB + BC + CD + DA + AE + BF + CG + DH$$

$$= 50 \times 8 = 400 \text{ cm} = 4 \text{ m}$$

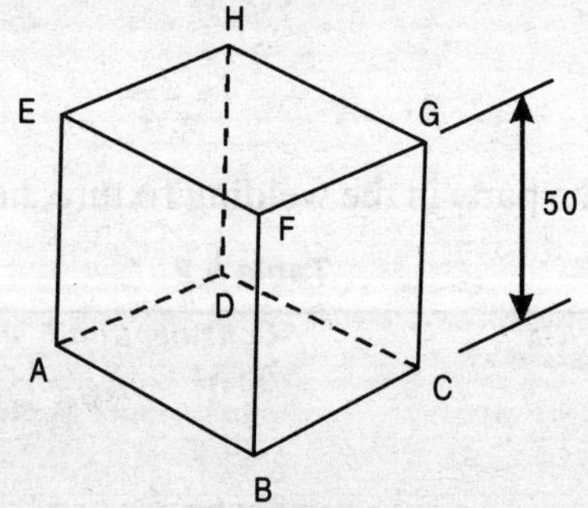

Fig. 5.23

As we are required to weld plates of 3 mm thickness which is less than 5 mm thickness hence we shall adopt left ward welding technique.

From table, welding speed is 12 min/m for 3 mm thick plates.

Time required for making one tank 12×4 = 48 min

Considering fatigue allowance = 5%

Actual time taken by welder for wedling one tank = $48 \times 1.05 = 50.4$ min

Example 5.35

Estimate the material cost for welding 2-flat pieces of ms $15 \times 6 \times 1$ cm size at an angle of 90° by gas welding. Neglect preparation cost and assume

Cost of O_2 = Rs. 12/m^3 Cost of C_2H_2 = Rs. 70/m^3

Of filler metal = Rs. 15/kg Cost of filler metal = Rs. 12/kg

Solution

As the thickness of the plates to be welded is more than therefore right ward welding method is adopted.

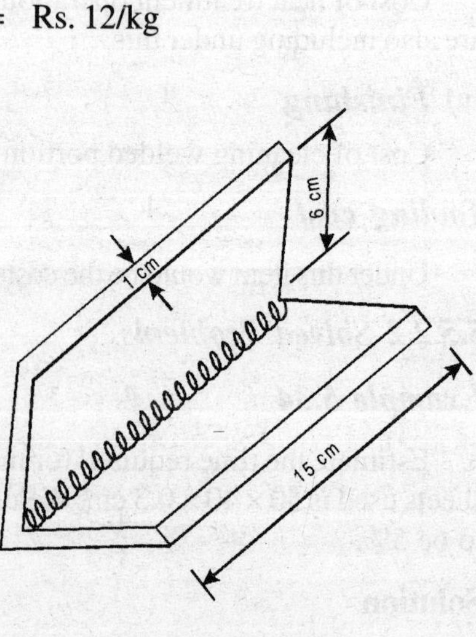

Fig. 5.24

From table, for 10 mm thick plates.

O_2 consumption = 0.7 cu m/hr

C_2H_2 consumption = 0.5 cu m/hr

Length of filler rod required 4.5 m/m of welding

Filler rod dia = 5 mm

Welding time = 30 min/m of welding

Time required to weld 15 cm length

$$= \frac{15}{100} \times 30 = 4.5 \text{ min}$$

(i) Amount of oxygen consumed at 0.7 cu m/hr $= \frac{4.5}{60} \times 0.7 = 0.053$ cu.m

Cost of oxygen at Rs. 12/cu.m = $0.053 \times 12 =$ Rs. 0.636/-

(ii) Now amount C_2H_2 consumed in 4.5 min

@ 0.5 cu m/hr $= 0.5 \times \frac{4.5}{60}$ = 0.0375 cu.m

Cost of C_2H_2 at Rs. 70/m³ = $0.0375 \times 70 =$ Rs. 2.63

(iii) Length of filler rod required for 15 cm job at 4.5 m/metre welding $= 0.15 \times 4.5$ $= 0.675$ m. But for 10 mm thick plates; filler rod dia = 5 mm.

Weight of fuller rod consumed = Volume × Density

$\frac{\pi}{4} \times 0.5^2 \times 67.5 \times 7$ gm = 0.0928 kg

Cost of filler rod at Rs. 15/kg = $15 \times 0.0928 =$ Rs. 1.392

Total material cost = $0.636 + 2.63 + 1.39$

= Rs. 4.658.

Example 5.36

Two 1 m long M.S plates of 10 mm thickness are to be welded by a lap joint with a 8 mm electrode. Calculate the cost of welding. Assume the following data.

(i)	Current used	=	30 amperes
(ii)	Voltage	=	300 V
(iii)	Welding speed	=	10 m/hr
(iv)	Electrode used	=	0.1 kg/m of welding
(v)	Labour charges	=	Rs. 4.00/hr
(vi)	Power charges	=	Rs. 0.2/kWh
(vii)	Cost of electrode	=	Rs. 40.00/kg
(viii)	Efficiency of machine	=	70%

Solution

(a) Cost of electrode required for 1 m length of welding = 0.1 kg

Cost of electrode as Rs. 40/kg = $40 \times 0.1 =$ Rs. 4.

(b) Labour cost

Time required for welding 1 m length

$= \frac{1}{10}$ hr

Labour charge $= \frac{1}{10} \times 4 =$ Rs. 0.4

(*c*) Power charges, as power consumed

$$= \frac{V \times I}{\text{Efficiency of the machine}}$$

$$= \frac{300 \times 30}{0.7} = 12.85 \text{ kW}$$

Energy consumed for welding 1 m length

$$= 12.85 \times \frac{1}{10} = 1.285 \text{ kWh}$$

Power charges at Rs. 0.1/kWh $= 1.28 \times 0.4$

$= \text{Rs. } 0.512$

Total welding cost = Cost of electrode + Labour charges + Power charges

$= 4 + 0.4 + 0.512 = \text{Rs. } 4.912.$

Example 5.37

A lap joint is to be prepared from 9.5 mm ms using flat welding position and 6 mm electrode. Current used is 250 amps and voltage 40 volts, welding speed is 14 m/hr and 0.4 kg of metal is deposite/metre length of joints.

Labour cost Rs. 3.5/hr, Power Rs. 0.4/kWh and electrode Rs. 45/kg. Efficiency of machine 60% and operation factor is 70%. Calculate cost of labour power and electrode power and electrode per metre of weld.

Solution

(*a*) Cost of electroded/metre of weld $= 45 \times 0.4$

$= \text{Rs.}18$

(*b*) Labour cost/meter of weld,

$$= 2.5 \times \frac{1}{14} \times \frac{1}{\text{Operation factor}}$$

$$= 2.5 \times \frac{1}{14} \times \frac{1}{0.7} = \text{Rs. } 0.255$$

(*c*) Power charges: Power consumed $= \dfrac{V \times I}{\text{Efficiency of machine}}$

$$= \frac{250 \times 40}{0.6} = 16.67 \text{ kW}$$

Power consumed/m of weld $= 16.7 \times \frac{1}{14}$ kWh

Cost of power/m of weld $= 16.7 \times \frac{1}{14} \times 0.4 = \text{Rs. } 0.477.$

Example 5.38

A cylindrical boiler drum $2\frac{1}{2}$ m × 1 mϕ is to be made from 15 mm thick ms plates. Both the ends are closed by welding circular plates to the drum. Cylindrical portion is welded along the longitudinal seam. Welding is done both on inner and outer sides. Calculate electric welding cost using the following data:

(i)	Rate of welding	=	2 m/hr on inner side. 2.5 m/hr on outer side
(ii)	Length of electrode required	=	1.5 m/m of welding
(iii)	Cost of electrodes	=	Rs. 8.7/m
(iv)	Power consumption	=	4 kWh/m of weld
(v)	Power charges	=	30 paise/kWh
(vi)	Labour charges	=	Rs. 5/hr
(vii)	Other overhead charges	=	100% of prime cost
(viii)	Discarded electrodes	=	10%
(ix)	Fatigue and setting up time	=	10% of welding time

Solution

Total length of weld on outer side = Length of weld on inner side = Length for welding on circular plates + Length for seam welding = 2(π) + 2.5 = 8.78 m.

(i) Labour charges

$$\text{On outer side} = \frac{8.78}{2.5} \text{ hr} = 3.51 \text{ hr}$$

$$\text{On inner side} = \frac{8.78}{2} \text{ hr} = 4.39 \text{ hr}$$

$$\text{Total time required} = 3.51 + 4.39$$

$$= 7.9 \text{ hrs}$$

Labour charges at Rs. 5/hr

$$= 7.9 \times 5 \;\; = \text{Rs. } 36.9$$

$$\text{Actual labour charges} = 39.5 \times 1.10$$

$$= \text{Rs. } 43.5$$

(ii) Cost of electrodes

Length of electrode required at 1.5 m/m of welding

$$= 1.5\,(2 \times 8.78) = 26.34 \text{ mm}$$

∴ Cost of electrode Rs. 3.7/m

$$= 28.97 \times 3.7 = \text{Rs. } 107.204$$

(iii) Cost of power

Power consumption for 17.56 of welding

$$4 \times 17.56 = 70.24 \text{ kWh}$$

Cost of power at 30 paise/kWh

$$= 70.24 \times 0.3 = \text{Rs. } 21.072$$

Overhead charges

$$\text{Prime cost} = \text{Direct labour cost + Direct material cost}$$

$$= 43.5 + 107.2 = \text{Rs. } 150.7$$

$$\text{Overhead} = 10\% \text{ of prime cost} = \text{Rs. } 150.7$$

$$\text{Total welding cost} = 150.7 + 21.072 + 150.7$$

$$= \text{Rs. } 322.5$$

Example 5.39

Find the welding material cost for making a rectangular frame for a gate of 2 m × 1 m from angle iron of size 30 mm × 30 mm × 5mm

(a) Oxygen consumption = 0.6 cu m/hr which is available at Rs. 50/cu.m

(b) Acetylene consumption = 0.6 cu m/hr. which is available at Rs. 60/cu.m

(c) Welding speed = 5 m/hr

(d) Length of filler rod of ϕ 2.5 mm = 4.5 m/m welding

(e) Fill rod material cost = Rs. 13/kg

(f) Welding is to be done at both ends.

Solution

$$\text{Length AB} = \frac{30}{\sin 45} = 30\sqrt{2} = 41.4 \text{ mm}$$

$$\text{Length AC} = 30 \text{ mm}$$

Length of welding on one corner on one side

$$42.4 + 30 = 72.4 \text{ cm}$$

Length of welding on all the 4 corner on one side

$$42.4 + 30 = 72.4 \text{ mm} = 7.24 \text{ cm}$$

Length of welding on all the 4 corner and on both ends = 7.24 × 8 = 57.92 cm

$$\text{Time required for welding} = 0.58 \text{ m}$$

$$= \frac{60}{5} \times 0.58 = 6.96 \text{ min}$$

(i) Oxygen consumption at 0.6 cu.m/hr.

$$= \frac{6.96}{60} \times 0.6 = 0.0696$$

Cost of oxygen at Rs. 50/cu. m/hr

$$= 0.0696 \times 50 = \text{Rs. } 3.48$$

(ii) Acetylene consumption at 0.6 cu. m/hr

$$\frac{6.96}{60} \times 0.6 = 0.0696 \text{ cu.m}$$

Cost of acetylene at Rs. 60/cu. m

$$= 0.0696 \times 60 = \text{Rs. } 4.176$$

Length of filler rod required at 4.5 cu. m/m of welding

$$= 4.5 \times 0.696 = 3.132 \text{ m}$$

wt. of filler rod (p = 7 gm/cc)

$$= \frac{\pi}{4} \times 0.25^2 \times 313.2 \times 7$$

$$= 107.62 \text{ gm} = 0.107 \text{ kg}$$

Cost of filler rod at Rs. 13/kg $= 0.107 \times 13 = \text{Rs. } 1.391$

Total welding material cost $= 3.48 + 4.18 + 1.391 = \text{Rs. } 9.051$

Example 5.40

Estimate the time required for the fabrication of an open tank of size 50 × 50 × 50 cm by gas welding, done on inner sides only. Assume fatigue allowance to be 6%. It is fabricated from sheets of size 50 × 50 × 0.3 cm.

(Speed of gas welding on 0.3 cm sheets is 12 min/m length).

Material cost—Not given

Cost of preparation, cutting and fixing in position—Not given

Actual welding time alone is to be determined

Solution

Total length of weld $= 8 \times 50 = 4.0 \text{ m}$

Rate of welding $= 12 \text{ min/m}$

Time required to weld 3.2 m giving

6% fatigue allowance $= 3.2 \times 12 = 38.4 \text{ min}$

Time required to weld $= 38.4 \times 1.06 = 40.7 \text{ min}$

Total time taken to weld a tank $= 40.7 \text{ min} \simeq 41 \text{ min.}$

Example 5.41

A cylindrical boiler drum 2.5 m × 1 m f is to be made from a 15 mm thick ms plate. The ends are closed by welding circular plates to the drum. The cylindrical portion is welded along the longitudinal seam. Welding is done on both inner and outer sides. Calculate the electric welding cost using the following data.

Rate of welding	= 3 m/m on inner side and 3.5 m/m on outer side
Cost of electrodes	= Rs. 0.80/m
Length of electrodes required	= 1.5 m/m weld
Power	= 4 kW/h/m of weld
Power charges	= 20 paise/kWh
Labour charges	= 90 paise/m
Other overhead costs	= 150% the prime cost
Discord electrodes	= 7%
Fatigue and setting up time	= 7% of welding time

Solution

(*i*) Total length $= [3(\pi + 3.5)] = 12.92$ m

Labour charges,

Welding time for outer welding $= \dfrac{12.92}{3.5} = 3.693$ hr

Welding time for inner side $= \dfrac{12.92}{3} = 4.306$ hr

Total welding time $= 4.31 + 3.69$

$= 7.99$ h

Total labour charge $= 7.99 \times 0.9$

$=$ Rs. 7.197

Fatigue and set up charges at 7%

$7.197 \times 1.07 =$ Rs. 7.7

Cost of electrodes

Length of electrodes required $= 12.92 \times 1.5$ m

$= 19.38$ m

Cost of electrodes considering 7% discard $= 19.38 \times 1.07 \times 0.8$

$=$ Rs. 21.25

Cost of power

At Rs. 4.00 kNh/m and at 20 paise/kWh

$= 4.00 \times 25.84 \times 0.2$

$=$ Rs. 20.672 (Indicated 2 side)

$[2 \times 12.92 = 25.84]$

Overheads

$$\text{Prime cost} = \text{Direct labour cost} + \text{Direct material cost}$$
$$= 7.7 \times 21.25 = \text{Rs. } 28.95$$
$$\text{Overhead cost} = 150\% \text{ of prime cost}$$
$$= 1.5 \times 28.95 = \text{Rs. } 43.43$$
$$\text{Total cost} = \text{Prime cost} + \text{Power cost} + \text{Overhead cost}$$
$$= 43.43 + 20.67 + 43.43$$
$$= \text{Rs. } 107.52 \simeq 108 \text{ Rs.}$$

Example 5.42

Calculate a) Cost of cutting a V-groove with gas, b) Welding cost for welding two 1 m long ms pieces of 8 mm thickness. If cost of O_2 Rs. 10.00 m³; cost of C_2H_2 Rs. 50 m³; cost of filler rod Rs. 14/kg; labour charges are Rs. 1.80/hr and 60° V groove is prepared for welding.

Solution

(a) Groove cutting

$$\text{Length of cut AB} = \frac{10}{\sin 70^\circ} = 10.64 = 10 \text{ (say)}$$

$$\text{From table, cutting speed} = 20 \text{ m/hr}$$
$$\text{Oxygen consumption} = 2 \text{ cu. m/hr}$$
$$\text{Acetylene consumption} = 0.2 \text{ cu. m/hr}$$

∴ Time required to cut piece of 1 m length

$$= \frac{1}{20} \text{ hr} = 3 \text{ min}$$

Time required to cut both pieces each of 1 m

$$= 2 \times 3 = 6 \text{ min}$$

(i) Amount of oxygen required $= 6 \times \dfrac{2}{60} = 0.2$ cu. m

Cost of oxygen at Rs. 10.00/cu. m $= 0.2 \times 10 = $ Rs. 2

(ii) Amount of acetylene required $= 6 \times \dfrac{0.2}{60} = 0.2$ cu. cm

Cost of acetylene at Rs. 50/cu. m $= 0.02 \times 50 = $ Rs. 1.0

(iii) Labour cost of cutting at Rs. 1.8/hr $= 1.8 \times \dfrac{6}{60} = $ Rs. 0.18

Total cutting cost $= 2.0 + 1 + 0.18 = $ Rs. 3.18

(b) Welding cost

For 8 mm thick plate,

$$\text{Filler rod dia} = 4 \text{ mm}$$

$$\text{Oxygen consumption} = 0.5 \text{ cu. m/hr}$$

$$\text{Acetylene consumption} = 0.3 \text{ cu. m/hr}$$

$$\text{Welding time/m. length} = 25 \text{ min}$$

$$\text{Length of filler rod used/m of welding} = 3.6 \text{ m}$$

The length of portion to be welded is 1 m

$$\text{Time required for welding} = 25 \times 1 = 25 \text{ min}$$

(i)

$$\text{Oxygen consumed} = 0.5 \times \frac{25}{60} \Rightarrow 0.209 \text{ cu. m}$$

$$\text{Cost of oxygen at Rs. } 10.00/\text{m}^3 = 0.209 \times 10 \Rightarrow \text{Rs. } 2.09$$

(ii)

$$\text{Acetylene consumed} = 0.3 \times \frac{25}{60} = 0.125 \text{ cu. m}$$

Cost of acetylene consumed Rs. 50/cu. m

$$= 0.125 \times 50 = \text{Rs. } 6.25$$

(iii) Length of filler rod used for 1 m welding = 3.6 m

$$\text{Weight of filler rod} = \frac{\pi}{4}(0.4)^2 \times 360 \times 7 \text{ gm}$$

$$= 316.8 \text{ gm} = 0.3168 \text{ kg}$$

$$\text{Cost of filler rod at Rs. } 14/\text{kg} = 14 \times 0.3168 = \text{Rs. } 4.4352$$

(iv) Labour charges of welding at 1.80/hr for 25 min

$$= \frac{25}{60} \times 1.8 = \text{Rs. } 0.75$$

Total cost of welding

$$2.09 + 6.25 + 4.4352 + 0.75 = \text{Rs. } 13.5252$$

Hence,

$$\text{Cost of cutting} = \text{Rs. } 3.18$$

$$\text{Cost of welding} = \text{Rs. } 12.19$$

Example 5.43

Calculate the cost of welding two plates 200 × 100 × 8 mm thick to obtain a piece 200 × 200 × 8 mm approximately using right ward welding technique.

(i) Cost of filler material = Rs. 7/kg

(ii) Cost of oxygen = Rs. 80 per 100 cu. meter

(iii) Cost of acetylene = Rs. 800 per 100 cu. meters

(iv) Consumption of oxygen = 0.8 cu. m

(v) Consumption of acetylene = 0.8/cu. m

(vi) Diameter of filler rod = 4 mm

(vii) Density of filler material = 7.3 gms/cc

(viii) Filler rod used/m of weld = 350 cms

(ix) Speed of welding = 2.5 m/hr

Solution

Labour is paid Rs. 2/hr and overheads may be taken as 100% of labour cost.

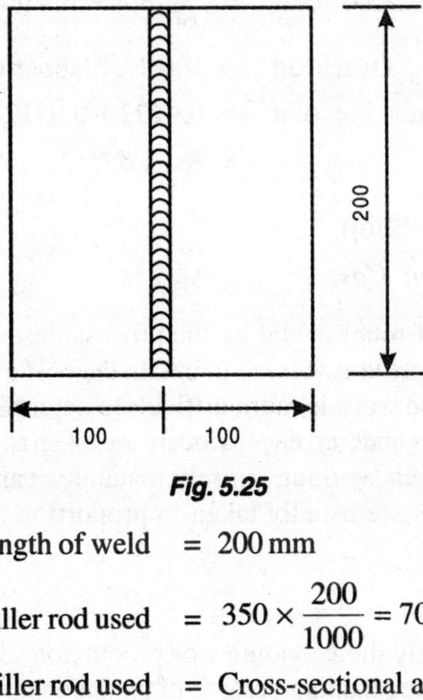

Fig. 5.25

Total length of weld = 200 mm

$$\text{Filler rod used} = 350 \times \frac{200}{1000} = 70 \text{ cms}$$

Volume of filler rod used = Cross-sectional area of rod × Length of rod

$$= \frac{\pi}{4} \times 0.4^2 \times 70 = 8.79 \text{ cm}^3$$

Weight of filler rod = 8.79 × 7.3 = 64.17 gms

$$\text{Cost of filler material} = 64.17 \times \frac{7}{1000} = \text{Rs.}0.4492$$

$$\text{Time to weld 200 mm length} = \frac{200}{1000 \times 2.5} = 0.08 \text{ hrs}$$

Oxygen consumed = 0.08 × 0.8 = 0.064 cu. m

Acetylene consumed = 0.08 × 0.8 = 0.064 cu. m

$$\text{Cost of oxygen consumed} = 0.064 \times \frac{80}{100} = \text{Rs. } 0.0512$$

$$\text{Cost of acetylene consumed} = 0.064 \times \frac{700}{100}$$

$$= \text{Rs. } 0.448$$

$$\text{Time to weld} = \frac{1}{12} \text{ hrs} = 5 \text{ min}$$

Add 4 min (80% of time to weld) for edge preparation and finishing and handling time.

$$5 + 4 = 9 \text{ min}$$

$$\text{Labour cost} = \frac{9}{60} \times 2 = \text{Rs. } 0.3$$

$$\text{Overhead} = 100\% \text{ of labour cost} = \text{Rs. } 0.3$$

$$\text{Cost of making joint} = 0.4492 + 0.0512 + 0.448 + 0.3 + 0.3$$

$$= \text{Rs. } 1.55.$$

5.5.3 Estimation of Foundry Shop

5.5.3.1 Estimation of Pattern Cost

After finding the volume of rough wood by the process described in the previous article, it is multiplied by the existing price per unit volume to obtain the cost of wood required for the pattern of furniture. The labour cost for the work is more difficult to determine, since the process in values a lot of manual work. Similar works undertaken previously are taken as guides in this respect. Experience tells us that a good pattern-maker, working entirely manually, can finish the work on 0.025 m^3 of wood in 8 hours. Other charges are usually taken in proportion to either the material cost or the labour cost.

5.5.3.2 Foundry Losses

- Losses influence strongly the economies of production of castings.
- Losses occur mainly during melting because of oxidation or volatilization of alloying elements and the entrapment of molten metal in the dross or slag removed from the furnace or crucible.
- Melting losses are most serious when they occur in costly alloys.
- Melting losses vary with the type of foundary and its conditions such as raw material, melting practice, composition of alloy etc.
- Highest melting losses occur when the surface area to volume ratio of the charge is more i.e., in a scrap charge containing large proportion of turnings, swarf and fines (and that too heavily contaminated).
- Furnace type and design also affect melting losses.
- Rotary and reverberatory furnaces, owing to more pronounced contact of melt with furnace atmosphere and constant renewal of metal surface are susceptible to higher losses than a crucible furnace with a small bath area.
- Losses in the melting of cast iron in cupola are lesser than obtained in air furnace.
- In the melting of steel, cupola converter practice produces highest losses of the order of 12.5% whereas they are only 3 to 5% in electric are furnace and about 1% in high frequency induction heating furnace.

- Melting losses depend upon the time of exposure of molten metal to the furnace atmosphered.
- Melting losses and gas contamination can be minimized by carrying out melting at a fast rate and with minimum of disturbance.
- Melting losses can also be reduced by avoiding, excessive liquid metal temperatures and too many liquid metal transfers.
- In brief, a proper care and close control of melting conditions will definitely help in lowering melting losses.

5.5.3.3 Steps for Finding Costing Cost

1. Calculate the volume of the casting from the past drawing, as explained earlier.
2. Multiply the volume by the density of the part material in order to arrive at net weight of the casting.
3. Calculate the weight of metal lost in oxidation in the furnace and as sprues, gates, risers etc. This metal loss is roughly 10% of the net weight of the casting.
4. Calculate the weight of foundry process scrap.
5. Add (2), (3) and (4) above to get total weight.
6. Calculate cost of metal by multiplying the total weight with the cost per unit weight of the metal.
7. Calculate process scrap return value and deduct it from the cost of metal in order to arrive at Net direct material cost.
8. Calculate indirect material cost by estimating the amount of coke, flux, etc., required to melt and cleanse the molten metal for casting.
9. Calculate direct and indirect labour costs.
   - *(a)* Cost of making moulds.
   - *(b)* Cost of making and baking cores.
   - *(c)* Cost of firing the furnace
   - *(d)* Cost of melting metal.
   - *(e)* Cost of pouring molten metal into the moulds.
   - *(f)* Cost of removing solidified castings from the moulds.
   - *(g)* Cost of fettling and finishing of castings.
   - *(h)* Cost of heat-treatment, if any.
10. Cost of inspection.

5.5.3.4 Solved Problems

Example 5.44

What will be the cost of manufacturing one set of fast and loose pulleys as given in figure. The pulleys are to be machined on the top (belt surface) sides and bore and a machining allowance of 3 mm is provided on a casting for machining, other particulars:

CI castings cost Rs. 85 per quintal and brass casting Rs. 5 per kg.

Boring, turning and side cutting will roughly take 9 h for each pulley at 60 paises per/hr cutting key-way 30 paise per cm of keyway. Overhead charges are 10% on labour profits are 5% on total cost.

CI weights 0.0073 kg/cm³. Brass weighs kg/cm³ missing dimensions in the drawing and other data, if required, may be assumed.

Reference sketch	***Formulae and Calculation***	***Volume cm³***	***Remarks***
Fast pulley 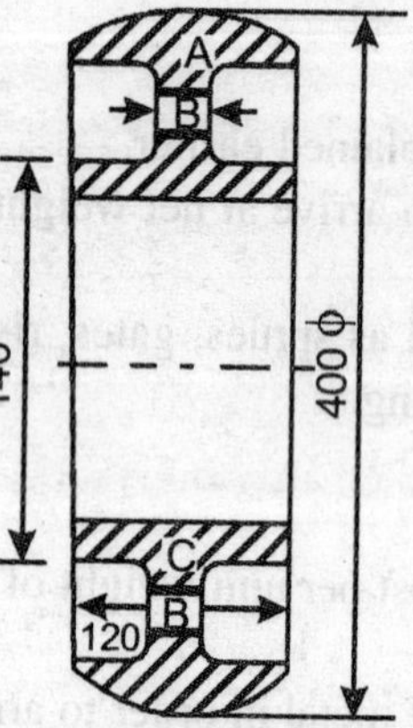 ***Fig. 5.26***	Volume of part A $= \frac{\pi}{4}\left[\begin{matrix}(40+2\times0.3)^2 \\ -(40-2\times1.5)^2\end{matrix}\right] \times (15 + 2\,(0.3))$ $= 3422.78$ cm³	3422.78	Belt surface (top), sides and bore of CI pulley are to be machined [3 mm m/c allowance]
	Volume of part B $= \frac{\pi}{4}\left[(40-2\times1.5)^2 - 14^2\right]\times1.5 - 4\times\frac{\pi}{4}\times8^2\times1.5$ $= 1145.04$ cm³	1145.04	
	Volume of part C		
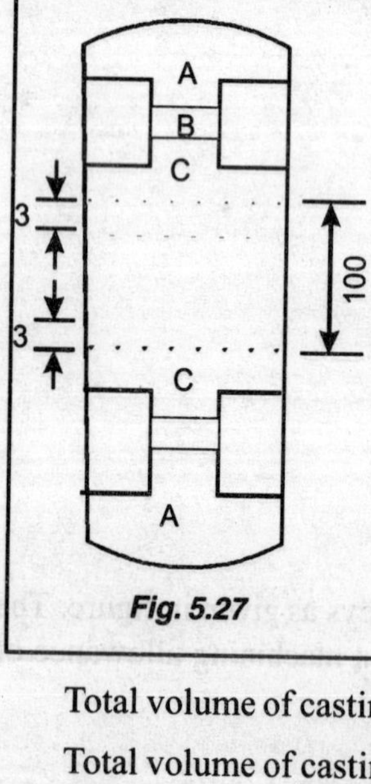 ***Fig. 5.27***	$= \frac{\pi}{4}\left[\left(14^2-(8-2\times0.3)^2\right)\right]\times$ $12 + 2(0.3) = 1397.8$ cm³	1397.8	
	Volume of part A	3422.8	
	Volume of part B	1145.04	
	Volume of part C $\therefore\ \frac{\pi}{4}\left[\left(14^2-(10-2\times0.3)^2\right)\right]\times$ $(12 + 2\times0.3)$ $= 1065.3$ cm³	1065.3	

Total volume of casting of the loose pulley = 5633.14 cm³

Total volume of casting of the fast pulley = 5965.62 cm³

Grand total of CI casting volume for both pulley = 11598.76 cm³

Grand total of CI casting wt for both pulley = 84.67 kg

Brass casting brass bush	Volume of rough casting for the brass bush $\frac{\pi}{4}\left[10+(2\times0.3)\right]^2$ $[(8-2\times0.3)^2]\times(12.6)$	Volume 570 cm^3	m/c allowance of 3 mm all over for the brass bush

Weight of brass casting at 0.0078 kg/cm^3 = 570 × 0.0078 = 4.44 kg

Description	*Calculation*	*Cost*
1. Cost of castings		
(a) CI at Rs. 85 per quintal	$\frac{85}{100}\times84.67$	71.96
(b) Brass at Rs. 5 per kg	5 × 4.44	22.2
2. Boring, Turning, side cutting 9 hr on each pulley at 60 paise/hr	0.6 × 9 × 2	10.8
3. Key way cutting at 30 paise per cm	0.3 × 10	3
4. Overhead charges at 100% on labour	$10\times\frac{100}{100}$	10.00

Example 5.45

Figure represents a face chuck and the dimensions shown are finished dimensions. You are required to find out the esteemed cost of manufacturing and the selling price of the face chuck on the basis of the data supplied below.

Solution

CI casting = Rs. 70 per 120 kg
Fettling = 90 paise/piece
Turning and facing at 7 paise per cm^3 of material removed.
Reaming and boring at 7 paise/mm depth of hole.
Overhead charges at 100% on labour cost.
Profit at 15% on total cost.
Double arrows in the figure indicate machined surface.
Sketch

Formulae and calculation
Volume of part A

$$\frac{\pi}{4}\left[(350+2\times3)^2-(70-2\times3)^2\right]\times(20+3)=2215.4\text{ cm}^3$$

Volume of part B

$$\frac{\pi}{4}\left[100^2 - (70 - 2\times 3)^2\right] \times 70 \text{ mm}^3 = 324.6 \text{ cm}^3$$

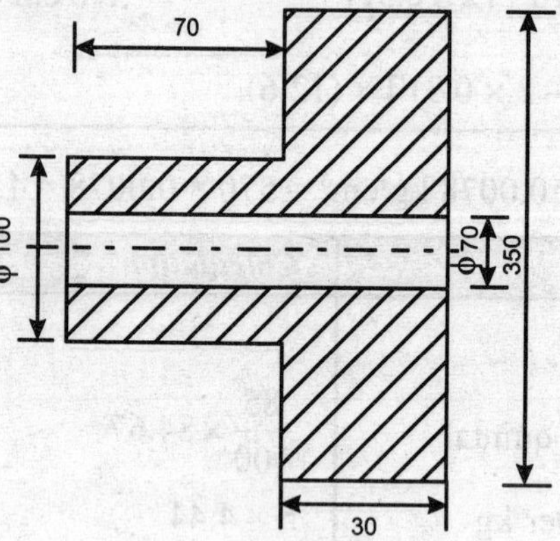

Fig. 5.28

By turning $\quad \text{Vol.} = \frac{\pi}{4}\left[\left(356^2 - 350\right)^2\right] \times 23 = 76.52 \text{ cm}^3$

By facing $\quad \text{Vol.} = \frac{\pi}{4}\left[\left(350^2 - (70-6)^2\right)\right] \times 3 \text{ mm}^3 = 278.9 \text{ cm}^3$

Total volume of material removed by turning and facing only

$= 355.5 \text{ cm}^3$

Total volume of CI casting $= 2539.9 \text{ cm}^3$

Costing

Costing, wt of CI casting $= 2539.9 \times 7.3$ g

$= 18541.3 = 18.54$ kg

(Sp. wt of CI $= 7.3$ g)

1. Cost of costing at Rs. 70 per 120 kg $\quad \frac{70}{100} \times 18.54 = 12.98$
2. Fettling charge at 90 paise per piece $\quad 0.9 \times 1 = 0.9$
3. Turning and facing at 7 paise per cm^3 of material removed $\quad 0.07 \times 355.5 = 24.89$
4. Reaming and boring at 7 paise per mm depth $\quad 0.07\ (50 + 15) = 4.55$
5. Overhead charge at 100% on labour $\quad 0.09 + 4.55 + 24.89 = 30.34$

Cost of manufacturing one face chuck $= 73.66 =$ (Total cost here)

Now profit at 15 paise on total cost $=$ Rs. 11.05

Selling price of face chuck $=$ Rs. 84.71.

Example 5.46

What will be the cost of manufacturing one solid bearing as shown in figure? Select the surfaces to be machined and provide for proper machining allowances on such surface. CI weighs 0.0073 kg/cc.

Other casting at 95 paise/kg
CI casting at 95 paise/kg
Boring at 25 paise/cm length of bore
Facing at 1.25 paise/sq. cm of surface faced
Drilling at 25 paise per drilled hole
Overhead charges at 100% on labour charges.

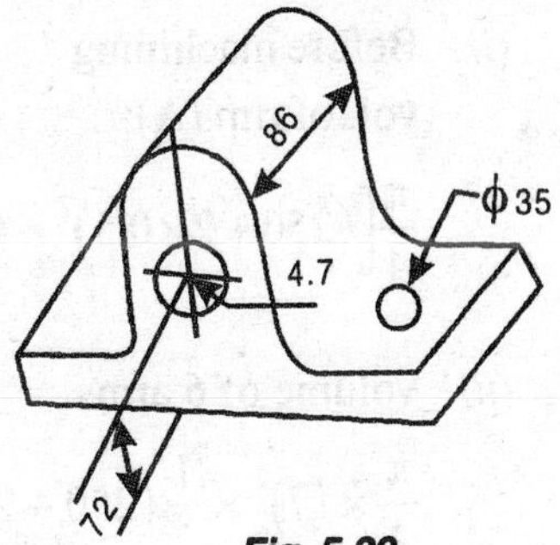

Fig. 5.29

Solution

Formula and calculation volume of half cylinder considered solid. (A)

$$= \frac{1}{2} \times \frac{\pi}{4} (7.2 \times 2)^2 \times 8.6 \text{ cm}^3 = 200.3 \text{ cm}^3$$

Volume of rectangular section considered section B

$$2 \times 7.2 \, (7.2 - 3.5) \times 8.6 \quad = 458.21 \text{ cm}^3$$

Volume of shaft hole with 3 mm machine allowance (C)

$$\frac{\pi}{4} (2 \times 4.7 - 2 \times 0.3)^2 \times 8.6 \quad = 523.1 \text{ cm}^3$$

Volume of part D with 3 mm m/c at bottom

$$35 \, (35 + 0.3) \times 8.6 \quad = 10625.3$$

$$= 700.3 + 458.1 - 523.1 + 10625.3$$

$$= 11260.6 \text{ cm}^3$$

$$\text{Weight of casting} \quad = 12.98 \text{ kg}$$

$$\text{Area of surface to be faced} \quad = 35 + 8.6 \text{ sq cm.} = 301 \text{ sq. cm}$$

Costing

(i)	Cost of CI casting at 95 paise/kg	0.95×12.98	=	Rs. 12.331
(ii)	Cost of boring at 25 paise/cm length of bore	0.25×8.6	=	Rs. 2.15
(iii)	Cost of facing at 1.25/sq.cm of surface faced	0.0125×301	=	Rs. 3.76
(iv)	Drilling at 25 paise/drilled hole	0.15×2	=	0.3
(v)	Overhead charges at 100% on labour	Rs. 6.21		
	Cost of manufacturing one solid bearing		=	Rs. 24.75

Example 5.47

Calculate the weight of rough casting of a fly wheel with a machining allowances of 5 mm on the surfaces to be machined. How much material has to be removed during machining?

Solution

CI weight 0.0073 kg/cm³.

Formulae and calculation **Vol.**

(i) Before machining

vol. of rim (A)

$$\frac{\pi}{4}\left[(250+2\times0.5)^2-(250-2\times10)^2\right] \times (25+2\times0.5) \qquad 7933.306\ \text{cm}^3$$

(ii) Volume of 6 arms

$$\frac{\pi}{4}\times(7)^2\times\frac{1}{2}(250-2\times10-35)\times6 \qquad 22513.44\ \text{cm}^3$$

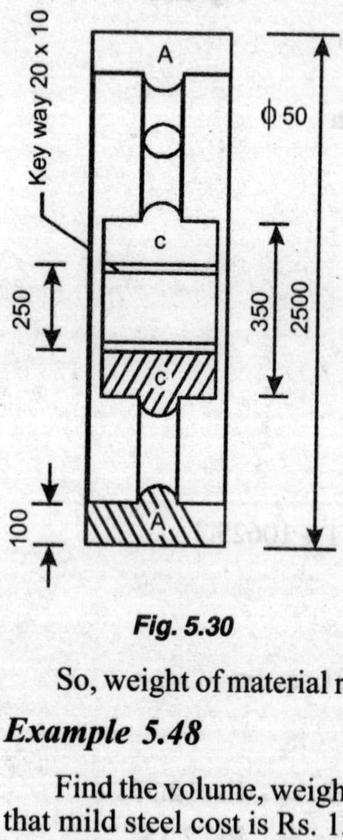

Fig. 5.30

(iii) Volume of box (part C)

$$\frac{\pi}{4}\left[\left(35^2-(25-2\times0.5)^2\right)\right]\times(15+2\times0.5) = 8155.6\ \text{cm}^3$$

Total volume of rough casting $= 38602.34\ \text{cm}^3$

wt of rough casting $= 1729.6$ kg

After machining

vol. of rim

$$\frac{\pi}{4}\left[\left(250^2-(250-2\times15)^2\right)\right]\times25 = 27682.8\ \text{cm}^3$$

Volume of 6 arms same as before, $= 22513.4\ \text{cm}^3$

vol. of box, $= 7061.1\ \text{cm}^3$

$$\frac{\pi}{4}(35^2-25^2)\times15-15\times2\times1$$

Total volume of finish casting $= 306427\ \text{cm}^3$

Weight of finish casting $= 2236.9$ kg

So, weight of material removed during machining $= 507$ kg

Example 5.48

Find the volume, weight and cost of the material required for making a mild steel shaft. Assume that mild steel cost is Rs. 13 per kg.

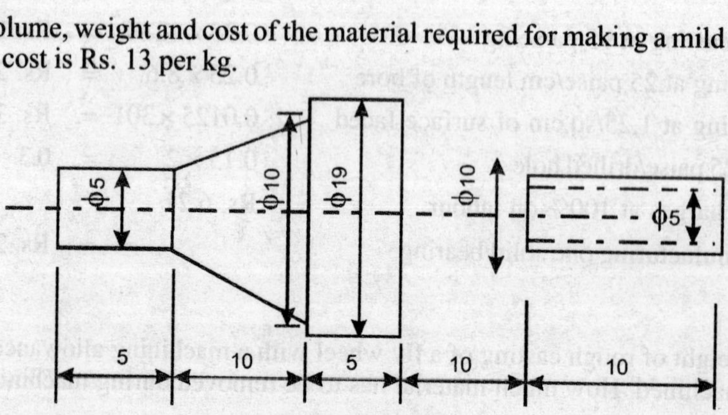

Fig. 5.31

Solution

$$\text{Volume of portion A} = \frac{\pi}{4} \times 5^2 \times 5 = 98.12 \text{ mm}^3$$

Volume of portion B which is frustum of cone

$$V_B = \frac{\pi \times 10}{3}\left[5^2 + 10^2 + 50\right] = 1831.66 \text{ mm}^3$$

$$\text{Volume of portion C} = \frac{\pi}{4} \times 17^2 \times 5 = 1134.9 \text{ mm}^3$$

$$\text{Volume of portion D} = \frac{\pi}{4} \times 10^2 \times 10 = 785.4 \text{ mm}^3$$

$$\text{Volume of portion E} = \frac{\pi}{4}\left(6^2 - 5^2\right) \times 10 = 86.39 \text{ mm}^3$$

$$\text{Total volume} = V_A + V_B + V_C + V_D + V_E = 3.94 \text{ cm}^3$$

$$\text{Weight of the product} = 30.90 \text{ g}$$

$$\text{Hence, cost of the material} = 30.9 \times \frac{12}{1000} = \text{Rs. } 0.371$$

Example 5.49

Estimate the cost of production of the job.

Material - CI casting 70 mm $\phi \times$ 150 mm long

Weight of material (CI) = 0.0075 kg/cm^3

Cost of CI Rs. 500/kg.

Turning at Rs. 0.85/cm^3 of metal removed

Facing at Rs. 0.85/cm^3 of metal removed.

Drilling and boring Rs. 2.00/cm^3 of metal removed.

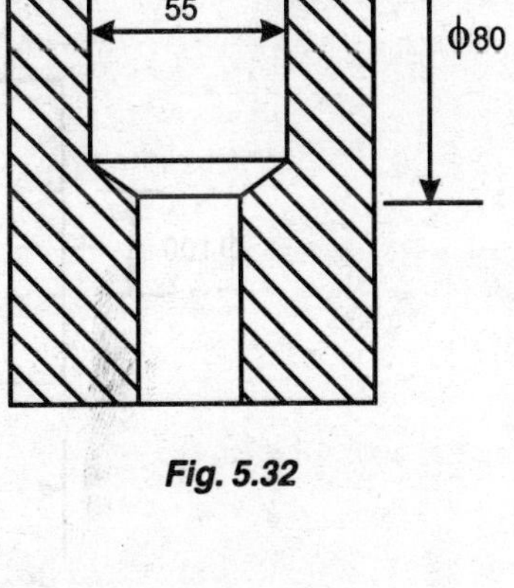

Fig. 5.32

Solution

Formulae,

Volume of 40 ϕ hole

$$\frac{\pi}{4}(4)^2 \times 5 \text{ cm}^3 = 62.83 \text{ cm}^3$$

Volume of taper hole

$$\frac{\pi \times 0.85}{12}\left[4^2 + (5.5)^2 + 4 \times 5.5\right] = 15.19 \text{ cm}^3$$

Volume of 55 ϕ hole (E)

$$= \frac{\pi}{4} \times 5.5^2 \times (8 - 2 \times 0.85) = 149.67 \text{ cm}^3$$

Total volume of the hole = Volume of material removed in drilling and boring

1. Volume of rough casting $V_1 = \frac{\pi}{4} \times 7^2 \times 15 = 577.3 \text{ cm}^3$

2. Volume of the solid job after turning and facing i.e., before drilling and boring

$$V_2 = \frac{\pi}{4} \times (6)^2 \times (4 + 6 + 4) = 395.84 \text{ cm}^3$$

$$= 395.84 \text{ cm}^3$$

3. Volume of material removed in turning and facing

$$= V_1 - V_2 = 181.43 \text{ cm}^3$$

4. Weight of rough casting = 4.33 kg

Costing

Cost of CI at Rs. 5 per kg labour charges

$$= 5 \times 4.329 = \text{Rs. } 21.65$$

(a) Turning and facing Rs. 0.85/cm³ of metal removed

$$= 0.75 \times 181.43 = \text{Rs. } 136.07$$

(b) For drilling and boring Rs. 1/cm³ of metal removed

$$= 1 \times 227.69 = \text{Rs. } 227.69$$

Cost of production of the job = Rs. 385.41.

Example 5.50

Figure shows a bevel gear blank made up of ms. Find the weight and cost of material required for it. Assume the density of ms = 7.85 gm/cm³ and its cost as Rs. 12/kg.

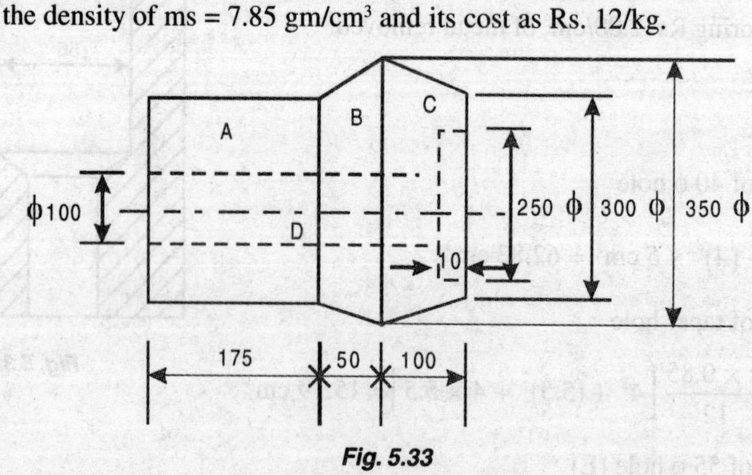

Fig. 5.33

$$\text{Volume of portion A} = \frac{\pi}{4} \times 250^2 \times 175$$

$$= 8585937.5 \text{ mm}^3$$

$$\text{Volume of portion B} = \frac{\pi}{3} \times 150\left[175^2 + 125^2 + (175 \times 125)\right]$$

$$= 3565208.3 \text{ mm}^3$$

$$\text{Volume of portion C} = \frac{\pi}{3} \times 100\left[175^2 + 150^2 + (175 \times 150)\right]$$

$$= 8303916.6 \text{ mm}^3$$

$$\text{Volume of portion D} = \frac{\pi}{4} \times 100^2 \times 315 + \frac{\pi}{4} \times 250^2 \times 10$$

$$= 2963375 \text{ mm}^3$$

$$\text{Total volume of bevel gear} = V_A + V_B\ V_C - V_D = 17495.67 \text{ cm}^3$$

$$\text{The weight of the bevel gear} = 17495.67 \times \frac{7.85}{1000} = 137.34 \text{ kg}$$

Hence, the cost of material of the bevel gear

$$137.34 \times 12 = \text{Rs. } 1648.$$

Example 5.51

Find the weight of the material and material cost of the brass component as shown in figure. Assume density of brass as 85 gm/cm^3. Cost of brass of Rs. 90/kg.

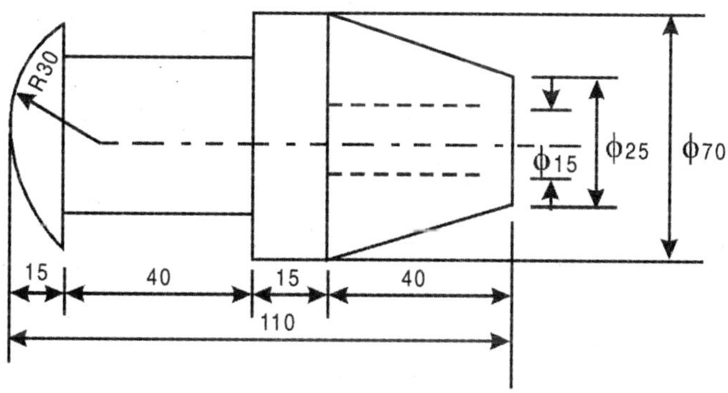

Fig. 5.34

Solution

$$\text{Volume of portion A} = \frac{\pi}{6} k^2 (3D - 2h)$$

Where $h = 15$ mm and $D = 2 \times 30 = 60$ mm

$$V_A = \frac{\pi}{6} \times 15^2 \,(3 \times 60 - 2\,15) = 17662.5 \text{ mm}^3$$

$$\text{Volume of portion B} = \frac{\pi}{4} \times 35^2 \times 40 = 38465 \text{ mm}^3$$

$$\text{Volume of portion C} = \frac{\pi}{4} \times 70^2 \times 15 = 57697.5 \text{ mm}^3$$

$$\text{Volume of portion D} = \frac{\pi}{3} \times 40 \left[35^2 + 12.5^2 + (35 \times 12.5)\right]$$

$$= 76145 \text{ mm}^3$$

$$\text{Volume of portion E} = \frac{\pi}{4} \times 15^2 \times 40 = 7065 \text{ mm}^3$$

$$\text{Volume of fillet F} = 0.215 \text{ R}^2 \times \text{Mean peripheral } \phi$$

$$= V_A + V_B + V_C + V_D - V_E + V_F$$

$$= 185444.68 \text{ mm}^3 = 185.4 \text{ cm}^3$$

$$\text{Total weight of the component} = \frac{185.44 \times 8.5}{1000} = 1.576 \text{ kg}$$

$$\text{Hence, the cost of material} = 1.576 \times 90 = \text{Rs. } 141.84$$

Example 5.52

Estimate the weight and cost of material required for manufacturing 10 CT wheels as shown in figure. Assume density of CI = 7.2 gm/cm³ and its cost Rs. 10/kg.

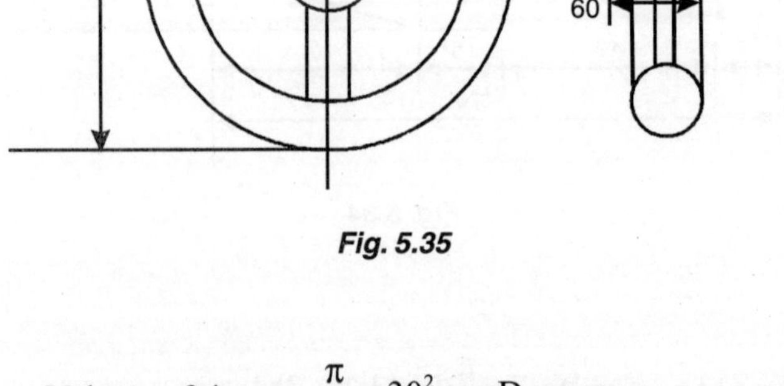

Fig. 5.35

Solution

$$\text{Volume of rim} = \frac{\pi}{4} \times 30^2 \times \pi \text{D mean}$$

$$= \frac{\pi}{4} \times 30^2 \times \pi \times 100$$

$$= 222066.1 \text{ mm}^3$$

$$\text{Volume of hub} = \frac{\pi}{4}\left(40^2 - 10^2\right) \times 60 = 70685.8 \text{ mm}^3$$

$$\text{Volume of 4 spokes } 4V_s = 4 \times \frac{\pi}{4}(5)^2 \times \frac{1}{2}(125 - 30 - 30 - 40)$$

$$= 981.74 \text{ mm}^3$$

$$\text{Total volume} = 293.73 \text{ mm}^3$$

$$\text{Weight} = 293.73 \times \frac{7.2}{1000}$$

$$\text{Weight of wheels} = 21.1 \text{ kg}$$

$$\text{Hence, the cost of material} = \text{Rs. } 211$$

Example 5.53

Estimate the weight and cost of the ms casting as shown in figure. Assume density of steel as 7.85 gm/cm³ and steel cost as Rs. 11/kg.

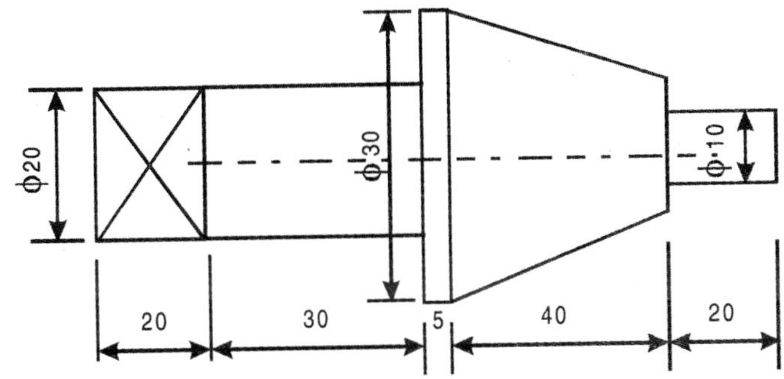

Fig. 5.36

Solution

$$\text{Volume of portion A} = 20 \times 20 \times 20 = 8000 \text{ mm}^3$$

$$\text{Volume of portion B} = \frac{\pi}{4} \times 20^2 \times 30 = 9420 \text{ mm}^3$$

$$\text{Volume of portion C} = \frac{\pi}{4} \times 30^2 \times 5 = 3532.5 \text{ mm}^3$$

$$\text{Volume of portion D} = \frac{\pi \times 40}{3}\left[15^2 + 10^2 + (150)\right]$$

$$= 19886.35 \text{ mm}^3$$

$$\text{Volume of portion E} = \frac{\pi}{4} \times 15^2 \times 20 = 3532.3 \text{ mm}^3$$

$$\text{Total volume of the part} = 44.37 \text{ cm}^3$$

The weight of the part $= 44.37 \times \frac{7.85}{1000} = 0.348$ kg

Hence, the cost of the part $= 0.348 \times 11 =$ Rs. 3.82.

5.5.4 Estimation of Machining Time

5.5.4.1 Introduction

In general all components or products manufactured in the workshop, required one or more machining operations to be done on them. Hence, the products have to travel through the machine shop to attain their final shape and size. The machining operations necessary for a job may be of different types, such as turning, shaping, planing, drilling, milling, boring and grinding.

In estimating the time requires to perform an operation on a work piece by any machine, the following factors must be considered.

1. Set up time.
2. Operation time.
3. Tear down time.
4. Personal allowance.
5. Fatigue allowance.
6. Checking allowance.
7. Miscellaneous allowance.

1. Set up time

This takes into account the time required to prepare the machine for doing the job, together, with the time taken to study the blueprint. The time to prepare the machine, in turn, includes the time to install and adjust the tools in the machine, as well as to make the machine ready to start the work.

2. Operation time

The sum of handling time and machining time for a job is called operation time. It is the duration of time that elapses between output of two consecutive units of production. It is also called cycle time.

3. Tear down time

Tear down time takes into account the time necessary to remove from the machine all tools and accessories, such as jigs and fixtures, gauges and instruments etc. The time required for clearing operational chips from the machine table and clearing of the machine itself are included on this. Tear down time is generally 10-15 minute per shift of 8 hrs.

4. Personal allowance

The time allowed for workers to meet their personal needs, such as going to the urinal, drinking water, smoking, washing their hands, etc., is known as personal allowance. It is generally 5 to 7% of the total working hours in a day.

5. Fatigue allowance

The long working hours and poor working conditions such as poor lighting, poor ventilation etc., cause fitigue and effect the efficiency of worker is fatigue decreases the worker capacity to work. The allowance for fatigue is taken depending upon the type of work.

5.5.4.2 Importance of Machine Time Calculation

To find the manufacturing cost of a particular job which requires one or more machining operations, the calculation of machining time is important. After determining the total time for machining, and knowing the machining cost per unit time, the total cost of machining can be worked out. Machining time is calculated by applying certain basic formulae, tables of variables and constants.

The basic formula used is

$$\text{Machining time} = \frac{\text{Travel of the tool necessary}}{\text{Feed} \times \text{rpm}}$$

1. Travel of the tool

This is determined from the dimensions in the actual drawing of the part to be manufactured. The necessary allowances for the tool approach and over-run for clearing the tool off the job are taken into account with the actual length of the work, to find the travel of the tool.

If actual length of the work $= l$

Amount of tool approach $= A$

Amount of tool over run $= O$

Then, travel of the tool L $= l + A + O$

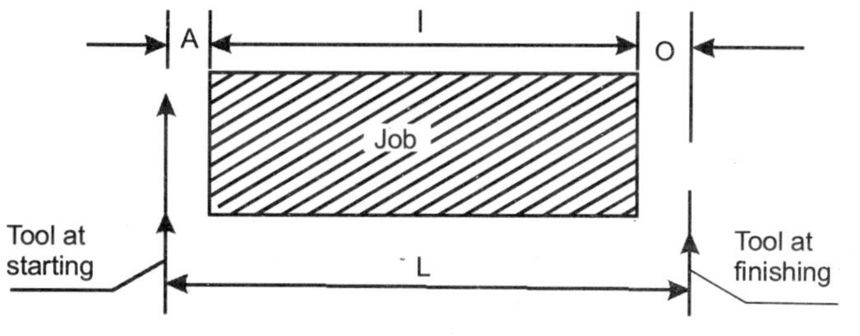

Fig. 5.37

2. Feed

Feed is the distance that the tool travels into the job in one revolution if the work or the distance that the table holding the work travels is one stroke of the tool. In metric units, feed is usually expressed in mm/revolution or mm/stoke. Feed depends on the depth of cut, fitness of the work desired, rpm of the job, etc.

3. Depth of cut

It is the penetration of the cutting tool into the job in a single cut. In metric units, the depth of cut is expressed in mm. The depth of cut depends upon the fitness of the job required, such as higher depth of cut for rough cut and smaller depth of cut for finish cut.

4. RPM

It represents the number of revolutions of the m/c spindle in one minute. Thus it is the number of revolutions per minute of the job or of tool.

5. Cutting speed

The cutting speed can be defined as the relative surface speed between the tool and the job. It is expressed in metres per minute (mpm).

For example, if a job of diameter D mm is revolving at a speed of N rpm, then

$$\text{Cutting speed } V = \frac{\pi DN}{1000} \text{ m/min}$$

5.5.4.3 Calculation of Machining Time for Different Lathe Operations

Turning

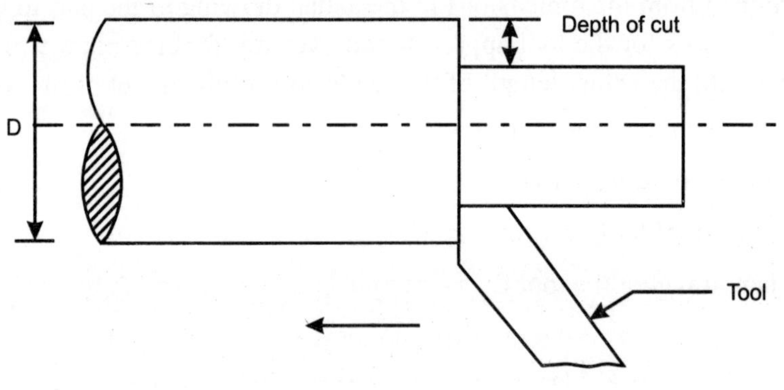

Fig. 5.38

$$\text{Time of turning,} \quad T_m = \frac{L + A + O}{N \times f}$$

Where, L = Tool distance

N = Number of revolution/minute

A = Tool approach mm

O = Tool over travel, mm

f = Feed/revolution, mm/rev.

$$\text{Number of cuts} = \frac{D - d}{2 \times \text{Depth of cut}}$$

Where D = Diameter of given blank,

d = Diameter of blank after turning

It turning operation, the depth of cut should not exceed 3 mm for rough cuts and 0.75 mm for finishing cuts.

Facing

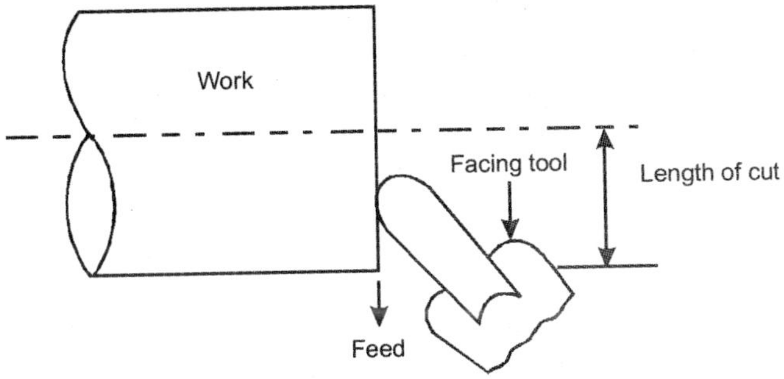

Fig. 5.39

$$T_m = \frac{1}{f \times N} \text{ min}$$

$$\text{Where} \quad N = \frac{1000 \times V}{\pi \times D_{av}}$$

$$\text{Here, of cut} = \frac{D}{2}$$

Other turning operation

For turning operation like chamfering, knurling, forming etc., the machining time formula is the same.

$$T_m = \frac{l}{f \times N} = \frac{\text{Length of cut}}{\text{Feed} \times \text{rpm}}$$

$$\text{Where} \quad N = \frac{1000 \times V}{\pi \times D}$$

5.5.4.4 Machining Time Calculation for Drilling Lathe and Boring

Drilling

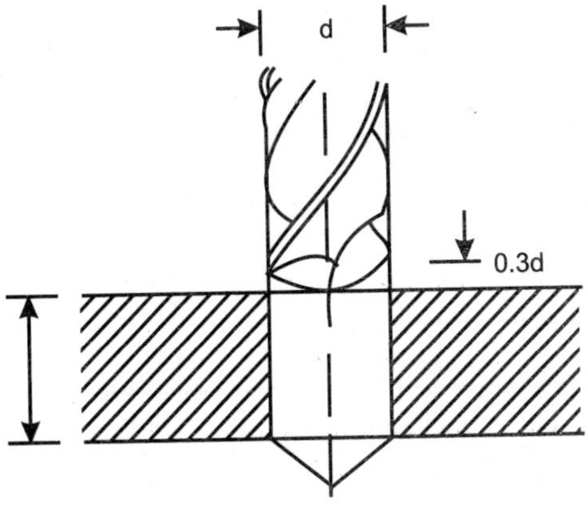

Fig. 5.40

Drilling is the operation of production a hole in an object by forcing a drill against it. The time taken to drill a hole depends upon the cutting speed and feed given to the tool. Due allowances must be made for the distance. The drill must travel before the cut commences. Some holes are drilled to a specified depth. Such holes are called blind holes.

$$\text{Time for drilling blind holes } T_m = \frac{l + 0.3d}{f + N}$$

$$\text{Time for drilling through holes } T_m = \frac{l + 0.5d}{f + N}$$

Where l = Depth of hole

f = Feed

d = Diameter

Boring

The finishing or enlarging of internal diameter of a hole, which has been previously drilled by a boring tool, is called the boring operation.

$$\text{Time taken for boring operation} = \frac{\text{Length of cut}}{\text{Feed} \times \text{rpm}}$$

5.5.4.5 Machining Time Calculation for Milling Operation

Depending upon the different requirements of the different jobs, various milling operations are adopted. But all operate on same principle.

$$N = \frac{1000 \times V}{\pi \times D}$$

$$\text{Time for one cut } T_m = \frac{\text{Total table travel}}{\frac{\text{Table feed}}{\text{min}}}$$

Where, Total tabel travel = Length of job + Added table travel

$$\frac{\text{Table feed min}}{\text{min}} = \text{Feed/tooth} \times \text{Number of teeth} \times \text{rpm}$$

The approach is the distance the cutter must be engaged before the full depth of cut is reached.

(a) When cutter diameter is less than the width of the work.

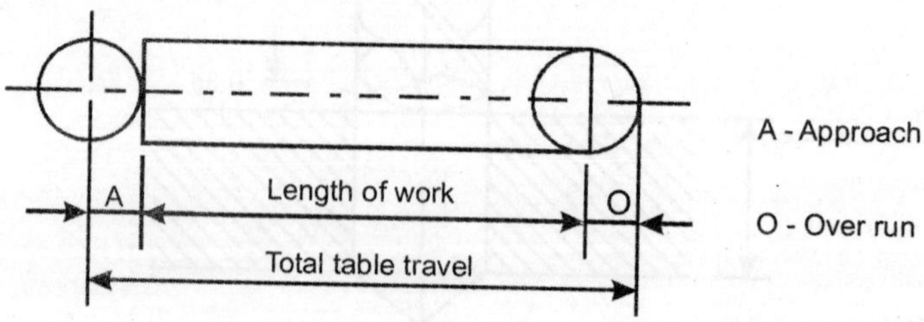

Fig. 5.41

$$\text{Approach} = 0.5\text{ d}$$

(b) When cutter diameter is greater than the width of the work.

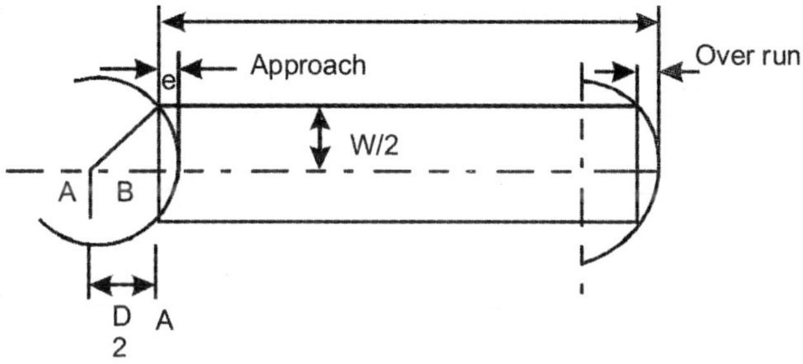

Fig. 5.42

$$\text{Approach A} = \text{AC} - \text{AB}$$

In ΔABC,

$$\text{AB} = \sqrt{\text{AC}^2 - \text{BC}^2}$$

$$\frac{\text{D}}{2} - \text{A} = \sqrt{\left(\frac{\text{D}}{2}\right)^2 - \left(\frac{\text{W}}{2}\right)^2}$$

$$\text{A} = \frac{\text{D}}{2} - \sqrt{\left(\frac{\text{D}}{2}\right)^2 - \left(\frac{\text{W}}{2}\right)^2}$$

$$\text{A} = \frac{1}{2}\left[\text{D} - \sqrt{\text{D}^2 - \text{W}^2}\right]$$

Slab milling operation

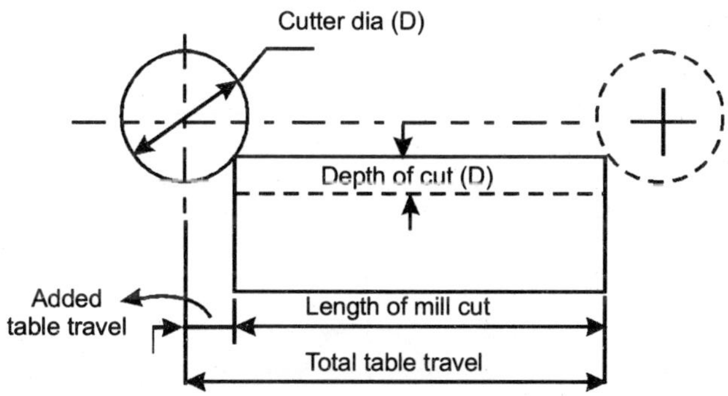

Fig. 5.43

$$\text{Added table travel} = \sqrt{\text{Dd} - \text{d}^2}$$

$$\text{when d} < \frac{\text{D}}{2}$$

Where $\quad d = \text{Depth of cut}$

$\quad D = \text{Diameter of the cutter}$

If the depth of cut equals or exceeds the cutter radius the added table travel will be equal to radius of the cutter.

$$\text{Added table travel} = \frac{D}{2}$$

For finishing pass, the cutter is permitted to travel beyond the end of the work piece, so the trailing edges give the same wiping action to the entire surface.

$$\text{when } d \geq \frac{D}{2}$$

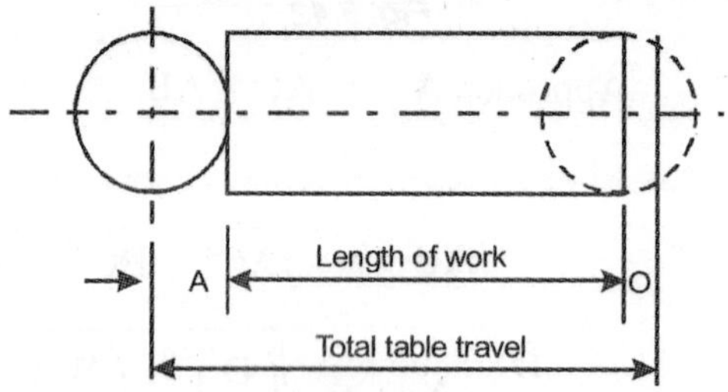

Fig. 5.44

$$\text{Added table travel} = A + O$$

$$= 2\sqrt{D \times d - d^2}$$

$$\text{when } d < \frac{D}{2}$$

$$= D \quad \text{when } d \geq \frac{D}{2}$$

(c) When cutting a flat across the round bar stock

Length of cut will be the length of chord

$$L = 2\sqrt{D_1 d - d^2}$$

$$\text{Added table travel} = \sqrt{D_2 d + D_1 d - d^2} - \sqrt{D_1 d - d^2}$$

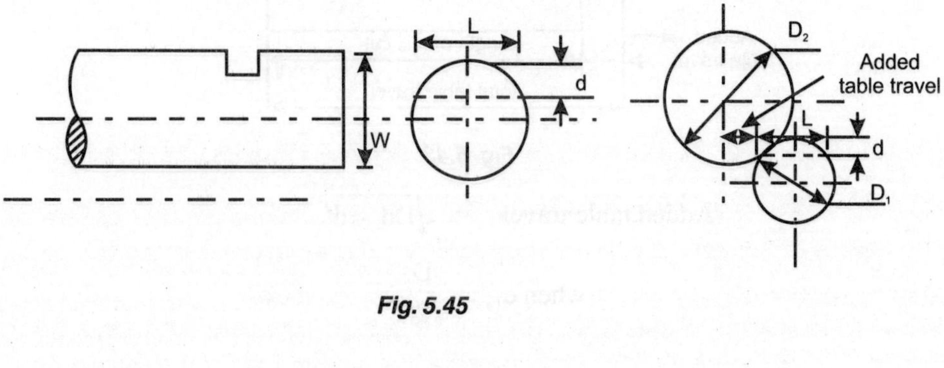

Fig. 5.45

5.5.4.6 Machining Time Calculation for Shaping and Planing

(a) Shaping

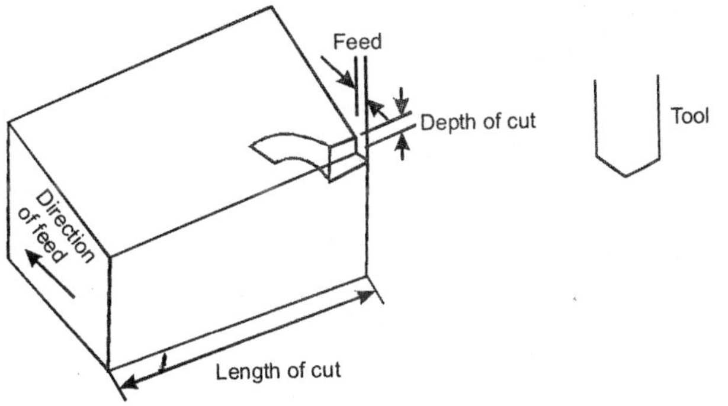

Fig. 5.46

Usually $\frac{\text{Return stroke}}{\text{Forward stroke}} = \frac{2}{3}$

$$\text{Time of forward stroke} = \frac{3}{5} \times \text{Total time}$$

L = Length of the work

S = Stroke length

It is generally taken as (L + 50) mm.

Similarly, if B is the width of the work, the width for calculation purpose is taken as (B + 25) mm

N = Number of stroke/min

f = Feed/stroke in mm

V = Cutting speed m/min

K = Return time/Cutting time

$$\text{Cutting stroke time} = \frac{L + 50}{1000 \times V}$$

$$\text{Return stroke time} = K \times \text{Cutting stroke time}$$

$$= K \times \frac{L + 50}{1000 \times V}$$

$$\text{Total time/cycle} = \frac{(L + 50)}{1000V} + \frac{K(L + 50)}{1000\ V}$$

$$= \frac{(L + 50)(1 + k)}{1000\ V}$$

Total number of cycles required to complete one cut on feed width (W) of job.

$$= \frac{(B + 25)}{f}$$

$$\text{Total time for one cut } T_m = \frac{(L + 50)(B + 25)(1 + k)}{1000\, V \times f}$$

Planing operation

For calculation purpose

$$\text{Stroke length} = L + 250$$

$$\text{Width} = B + 50$$

$$\text{Planing time } T_m = \frac{(L + 250)(B + 50)(1 + k)}{1000 \times v \times f}$$

5.5.4.7 Machining Time Calculation for Grinding

Grinding

Grinding is the operation of metal removal by abrasion. There are mainly two different grinding processes depending on the surface to be ground, viz., (i) Surface grinding, (ii) Cylindrical grinding.

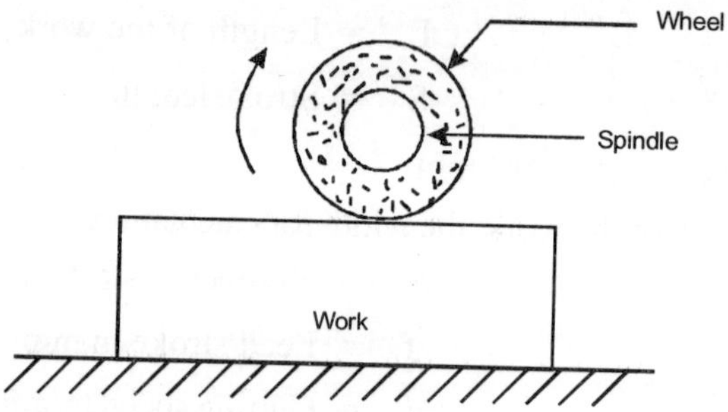

Fig. 5.47

$$\text{For grinding } T_m = \frac{L \times i}{f \times N}$$

$$T_m \text{ at every cycle with feed adjustment} = \frac{2 \times L \times i}{f \times N}$$

Where i → Number of cuts.

5.5.4.8 Solved Problems

Turning

Example 5.54

Calculate the machining time to turn the dimensions shown in figure starting from a ms bar of f 100 mm. The cutting speed with HSS tool 80 mpm and feed is 0.8 mm/rev., depth of cut is 3 mm per pass.

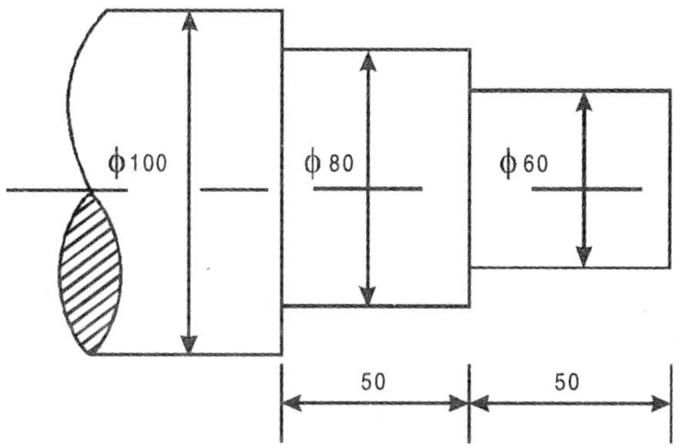

Fig. 5.48

Solution

$$V = 80 \text{ m/min}$$

$$f = 0.8 \text{ mm/rev}$$

The turning will be done in 2 steps. In first step a length of (50 + 50) = 10 mm will be reduced from 100 ϕ to 80 ϕ and in second step a length of 50 mm will be reduced from 80 ϕ to 60 ϕ.

Step 1

$$N = \frac{1000 \times V}{\pi \times D} = \frac{1000 \times 80}{\pi \times 100} = 255 \text{ rpm}$$

$$\text{Number of passes} = \frac{\text{Depth of material to be removed}}{\text{Depth of cut}}$$

$$= \frac{(100 - 80)}{2 \times 3} = 4$$

$$\text{Time required} = \frac{L}{f \times N} \times 4 = \frac{100}{0.8 \times 255} \times 4 = 1.96 \text{ min}$$

Step 2

To turn from ϕ 80 to ϕ 60 for 50 m long.

$$N = \frac{1000 \times V}{\pi \times D} = \frac{1000 \times 80}{\pi \times 80} = 318 \text{ rpm}$$

$$\text{Number of passes} = \frac{(80 - 60)}{2 \times 3} = 4$$

$$\text{Time} = \frac{L}{f \times N} \times 4 = \frac{50}{0.8 \times 318} \times 4 = 0.79 \text{ min}$$

$$\text{Total time} = 1.96 + 0.79 = 2.75 \text{ min.}$$

Example 5.55

A mild steel bar 100 mm long and 40 mm in diameter is turned to 38 mm diameter and was again turned to a diameter of 35 mm over a length of 40 mm as shown in figure. The bar was chamfered at both the ends to give a chamfer of 45° × 5 mm after facing. Calculate the m/cing time. Assume cutting speed of 60 m/min and feed 0.4 mm/rev. The depth of cut is not to exceed 3 mm in any operation.

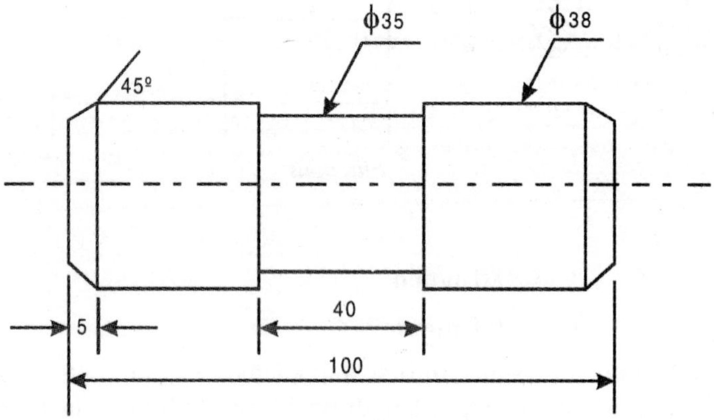

Fig. 5.49

Solution

$$V = 60\,\text{m/min}, \qquad f = 0.4\ \text{mm/rev}$$

Step 1

Turning from ϕ 40 to ϕ 38

$$N = \frac{1000 \times V}{\pi \times D} = \frac{1000 \times 60}{\pi \times 40} = 478\ \text{rpm}$$

$$\text{Time taken} = \frac{L}{f \times N} = \frac{100}{478 \times 0.4} = 0.52\ \text{min}$$

Step 2

$$\text{External relief} \quad N = \frac{1000 \times 60}{\pi \times 38} = 502\ \text{rpm}$$

$$\text{Time taken} = \frac{L}{f \times N} = \frac{40}{502 \times 0.4} = 0.19\ \text{min}$$

Step 3

$$L = \text{Length of cut} = \frac{38}{2} = 19\ \text{mm}$$

$$D = 38\ \text{m}; \quad V = 60\ \text{m/min}$$

$$N = \frac{1000 \times 60}{\pi \times 38} = 502\ \text{rpm}$$

$$\text{Time for facing} = \frac{L}{f \times N} = \frac{19}{0.4 \times 502} = 0.095\ \text{min}$$

Time for facing both ends $= 2 \times 0.095 = 0.19$ min

Step 4

Chamfering 45° × 5 mm; Length of cut = 5 mm, rpm N = 502

$$\text{Time for chamfering on one side} = \frac{5}{502 \times 0.4} = 0.025 \text{ min}$$

$$\text{Time for chamfering on both side} = 0.025 \times 2 = 0.05 \text{ min}$$

Step 5

$$\text{Machining time} = 0.52 + 0.19 + 0.19 + 0.05$$
$$= 0.95 \text{ min}$$

Example 5.56

An ms shaft shown in figure is to be turned from a 25 f bar. Speed is 60 m/min., feed is 0.2 mm/rev. Calculate the m/cing time feed for drilling is 0.08 mm/rev., feed for knurling is 0.3 mm/rev.

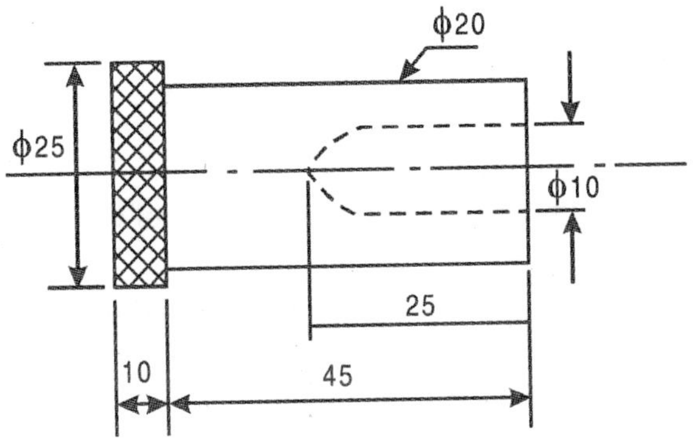

Fig. 5.50

Solution

$$V = 60 \text{ m/min}, \qquad f = 0.2 \text{ mm/rev}$$

Step 1

Facing 25 ϕ bar on both ends

$$\text{Length of cut} = 25/2 = 12.5 \text{ mm}$$

$$N = \frac{1000 \times 60}{25 \times \pi} = 764 \text{ rpm}$$

$$T_m = \frac{L}{f \times N} = \frac{12.5}{0.2 \times 764} = 0.082 \text{ min}$$

$$\text{Time to face on both ends} = 2 \times 0.082 = 0.164 \text{ min}$$

Step 2

Turn ϕ 20 from ϕ 25

$$T_m = 40 \frac{L}{f \times N} = \frac{45}{0.2 \times 764} = 0.29 \text{ min}$$

Step 3

Drilling of 8 mm ϕ hole

$$N = \frac{1000 \times 60}{10 \times \pi} = 1910 \text{ rpm}$$

$$T_m = \frac{L}{f \times N} = \frac{25}{0.08 \times 1910} = 0.16 \text{ min}$$

Step 4

Knurling

$$N = \frac{1000 \times 60}{\pi \times 25} = 764 \text{ rpm}$$

$$T_m = \frac{L}{f \times N} = \frac{10}{0.3 \times 764} = 0.04 \text{ min}$$

$$\text{Total machining time} = 0.164 + 0.29 + 0.16 + 0.04$$

$$= 0.65 \text{ min}$$

Example 5.57

Calculate the machining time required to produce one piece of w/p shown in figure starting from ϕ 25 mm.

For turning

V = 40 m/min

f = 0.4 mm/rev

d = 2.5 mm/pass

For thread cutting

V = 8 m/min

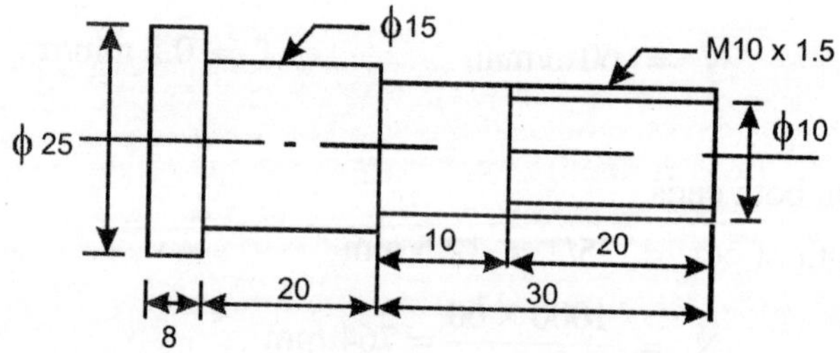

Fig. 5.51

Solution

Step 1

Time for turning to 15 mm ϕ from 25 mm ϕ

As depth of material to be removed is $\frac{(25-15)}{2} = 5$ mm it will be accomplished in 2 cuts.

$$\text{Average diameter} = D_{av} = \frac{25+15}{2} = 20 \text{ mm}$$

$$N = \frac{40 \times 1000}{20 \times \pi} = 637 \text{ rev/min}$$

$$T_m = \frac{L}{f \times N} = \frac{50}{637 \times 0.4} \times 2 = 0.4 \text{ min}$$

Step 2

Turning from 15 mm to 10 mm dia over a length of 30 mm in one pass.

$$N = \frac{40 \times 1000}{\pi \times 15} = 0.850 \text{ rev/min}$$

$$T_m = \frac{L}{f \times N} = \frac{30}{0.4 \times 850} = 0.09 \text{ min}$$

Step 3

$$\text{Threading} \quad N = \frac{8 \times 100}{\pi \times 10} = 255 \text{ rpm}$$

$$\text{Pitch} = 1.5 \text{ mm}$$

$$\text{Threads/cm} = \frac{10}{1.5} = \frac{100}{15}$$

$$\text{Number of cuts} = \frac{25}{\text{Thread/cm}} = \frac{25 \times 15}{100} = 4 \text{ cut}$$

$$\text{Time for one cut} = \frac{L}{f \times N} = \frac{20}{1.5 \times 225} = 0.05 \text{ min}$$

$$\text{Time for 4 cuts} = 0.05 \times 4 = 0.2 \text{ min}$$

Step 4

$$\text{Total m/cing time} = 0.4 + 0.09 + 0.2$$

$$= 0.69 \text{ min}$$

Example 5.58

A plug gauge as shown in figure is to be knurled. Estimate the knurling time. Take knurling speed as 15 m/min and a feed of 0.35 mm/rev.

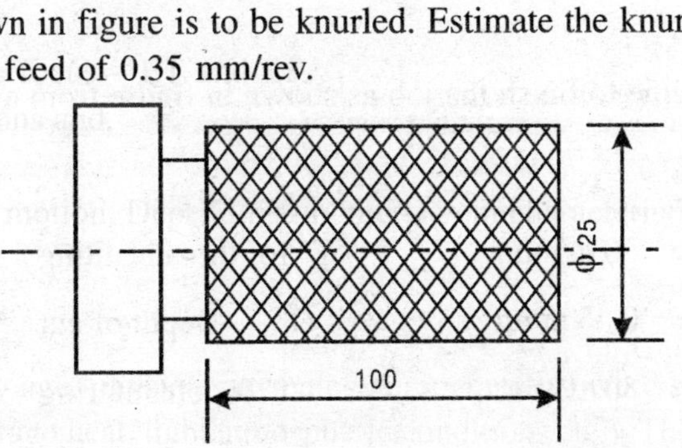

Fig. 5.52

Solution

$$V = 15 \text{ m/min}$$

$$f = 0.35 \text{ mm/rev}$$

$$N = \frac{1000 \times V}{\pi \times D} = \frac{1000 \times 15}{\pi \times 25} = 191 \text{ rpm}$$

$$T_m = \frac{L}{f \times N} = \frac{100}{0.36 \times 191} = 1.495 \text{ min}$$

Example 5.59

Calculate the time required for threading a 35 mm f steel bar for a length of 100 mm by a single point tool on lathe. Take that 3 threads per com are to be cut as a cutting speed of 10 m/min. Assume suitable approach and overtake for the tool.

Solution

$$N = \frac{1000 \times V}{\pi \times D} = \frac{1000 \times 10}{\pi \times 35} = 91 \text{ rpm}$$

$$\text{Time for threading} = \frac{\text{Length of cut + Tool approach + Tool overtake}}{\text{Pitch} \times N}$$

Assume tool approach as 5 mm and tool overtake also as 5 mm

$$\text{Now pitch} = \frac{1}{\text{Number of threads/mm}} = \frac{1}{0.3}$$

$$T_m = \frac{100 + 5 + 5}{\frac{1}{0.3} \times 91} = 0.363 \text{ min}$$

To obtain full depth for threading the number of cuts will be

$$\frac{25}{\text{Number of threads per cm}} = \frac{25}{3} = 8.33 \simeq 8$$

$$\text{Hence, total time required} = 0.363 \times 8 = 2.9 \text{ min}$$

Example 5.60

Find the machining time to finish the job as shown in figure from a 45 mm f and 95 mm long raw material.

Assume

'V' for turning = 30 m/min; 'V' for thread cutting = 10 mm/min

'f' for turning = 0.35 mm/rev; Depth of cut = 1.25 mm

'V' for drilling = 30 m/min; 'f' for chamfering = 0.25 mm/rev

'f' for drilling = 0.1 mm/rev

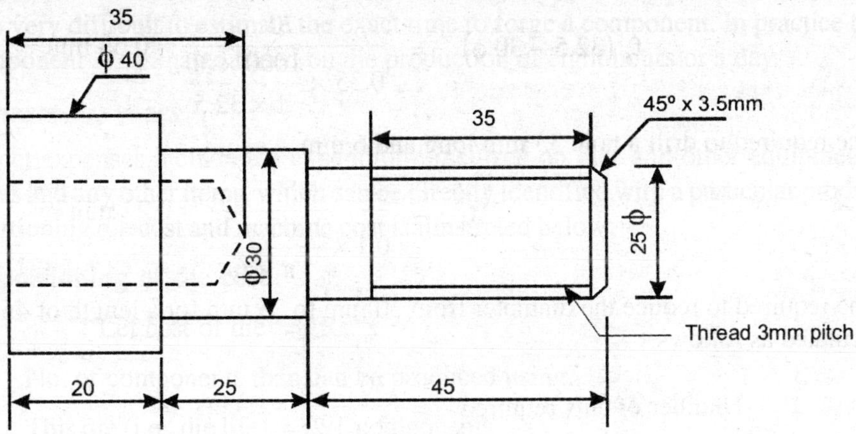

Fig. 5.53

Solution

(i) Number of cuts required to reduce 45.0 ϕ of workpiece to 40 ϕ

Time required for turning from 45 mm ϕ to 42.5 mm ϕ

$$t_1 = \frac{95}{0.35 \times \dfrac{1000 \times 0}{\pi \times 45}} = 1.275 \text{ min}$$

Time required for turning from 42.5 mm ϕ to 40 mm ϕ

$$t_2 = \frac{95}{0.35 \times \dfrac{1000 \times 30}{\pi \times 42.5}} = 1.207 \text{ min}$$

(ii) Time required to reduce diameter from 40 mm to 30 mm for a length of (25 + 45) = 70 mm can be calculated as following:

$$\text{Number of cuts required} = \frac{40 - 30}{2 \times 1.25} = 4 \text{ cuts}$$

$$\therefore \quad t_3\,(40 - 37.5\,\phi) = \frac{70}{0.35 \times \dfrac{1000 \times 30}{\pi \times 40}} = 0.837 \text{ min}$$

$$t_4\,(37.5 - 35\,\phi) = \frac{70}{0.35 \times \dfrac{1000 \times 30}{\pi \times 37.5}} = 0.785 \text{ min}$$

$$t_5\,(35 - 32.5\,\phi) = \frac{70}{0.35 \times \dfrac{1000 \times 30}{\pi \times 35}} = 0.732 \text{ min}$$

$$t_6\,(32.5 - 30\,\phi) = \frac{70}{0.35 \times \dfrac{1000 \times 30}{\pi \times 32.5}} = 0.68 \text{ min}$$

(iii) Time required to drill a hole 35 mm long and 6 mm

$$t_1 = \frac{35}{0.1 \times \dfrac{1000 \times 30}{\pi \times 6}} = 0.22 \text{ min}$$

(iv) Time required to reduce the diameter from 30 mm to 25 mm for a length of 45 mm can be calculated as follows:

$$\text{Number of cuts required} = \frac{30 - 25}{2 \times 1.25} = 2 \text{ cuts}$$

$$\therefore \quad t_8\,(30 - 25\,\phi) = \frac{45}{0.35 \times \dfrac{1000 \times 30}{\pi \times 27.5}} = 0.403 \text{ min}$$

$$\therefore \quad t_9\,(27.5 - 25\,\phi) = \frac{45}{0.35 \times \dfrac{1000 \times 30}{\pi \times 27.5}} = 0.370 \text{ min}$$

(v) Time required to cut threads for a length of 35 mm ϕ 25 mm and pitch 3 mm

$$t_{10} = \frac{45}{3 \times \dfrac{1000 \times 10}{\pi \times 25}} \times \text{Number of cuts } (8)$$

$$\text{Number of cuts} = \frac{25}{\text{Threads per cm}} \; \frac{25}{1/\text{pitch}} = \frac{25}{1/3}$$

$$= \frac{25}{1/0.3} = 25 \times 0.3 = 7.5 \approx 8 \text{ cuts}$$

$$t_{10} = 0.732 \text{ min}$$

(vi) Time required to champer 45°, 3.25 mm at 25 mm ϕ

$$t_{11} = \frac{3.25}{0.25 \times \dfrac{1000 \times 30}{\pi \times 25}} = 0.034 \text{ min}$$

Total time required for finishing the w/p,

$$T = t_1 + t_2 + \cdots + t_{11}$$

$$T = 1.278 \text{ min}$$

Example 5.61

Calculate the time required to turn the component as shown in figure. Assume cutting speed of 30 min. hand feed by compound rest 10.5 mm/rev., depth of cut 2.5 mm, and feed for turning 0.75 mm/rev.

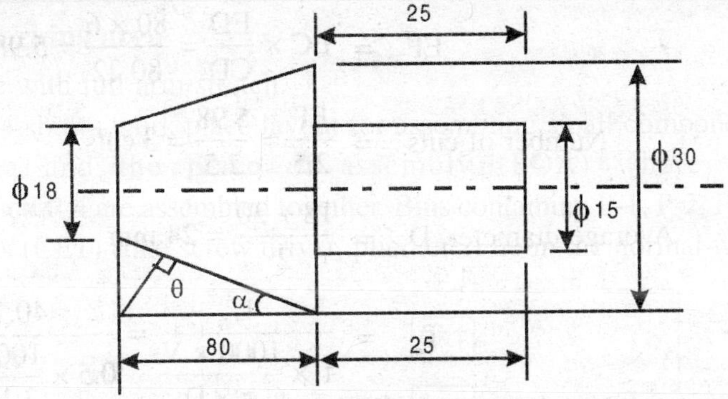

Fig. 5.54

Solution

(i) Time required to reduce from 30 mm dia to 15 mm dia for 25 mm length is calculated as follows:

$$\text{Number of cuts} = \frac{30-15}{2 \times 2.5} = 3 \text{ cuts}$$

$$t_1 = (30 - 25\phi) = \frac{25}{0.75 \times \dfrac{1000 \times 30}{\pi \times 30}} = 0.1046 \text{ min}$$

$$t_2 = (25 - 20\phi) = \frac{25}{0.75 \times \dfrac{1000 \times 30}{\pi \times 25}} = 0.087 \text{ min}$$

$$t_3 = (20 - 15\phi) = \frac{25}{0.75 \times \dfrac{1000 \times 30}{\pi \times 20}} = 0.0697 \text{ min}$$

(ii) Time required for taper turning from 30 mm φ to 18 φ can be calculated as follows:

$$\text{Length of cut CD} = \sqrt{ED^2 + EC^2}$$

$$ED = \frac{30-18}{2} = 6 \text{ mm}$$

$$EC = 80 \text{ mm}$$

$$CD = \sqrt{6^2 + 80^2} = 80.22 \text{ mm}$$

$$\text{Average length of cut} = \frac{CD}{2} = 40.11 \text{ mm}$$

$$\text{Number of cuts required} = \frac{EF}{2.5}, \text{ because one cut is 2.5 mm deep}$$

$$\sin\alpha = \frac{EF}{EC} = \frac{ED}{CD}$$

$$EF = EC \times \frac{ED}{CD} = \frac{80 \times 6}{80.22} = 5.98$$

$$\text{Number of cuts} = \frac{EF}{2.5} = \frac{5.98}{2.5} = 3 \text{ cuts}$$

$$\text{Average diameter, D} = \frac{18 + 30}{2} = 24 \text{ mm}$$

$$T_m = \frac{L}{f \times \dfrac{1000 \times V}{\pi \times D}} = \frac{40.11}{0.5 \times \dfrac{1000 \times 30}{3.14 \times 24}} = 0.2 \text{ min}$$

$$\text{Total time required for these cuts} = 0.2 \times 3 = 0.6 \text{ min.}$$

Example 5.62

Find the time required to turn 25 mm dia bar to the dimension shown in figure. Cutting speed shall be 13.5 m/min. and feed 1.6 cuts per mm. All cuts shall be 3.125 mm deep.

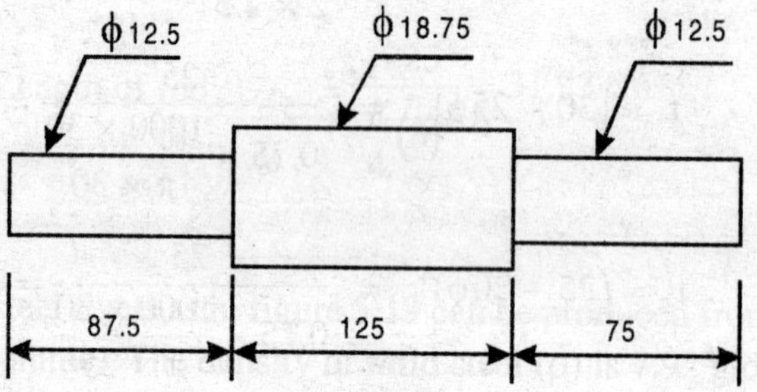

Fig. 5.55

Solution

(*a*) Turning from 25 to 18.75 mm (1st cut)

$$N = \frac{1000 \times 13.5}{\pi \times 25} = 172 \text{ rpm}$$

$$\text{Time taken} = \frac{(\text{Length of the job + Approach + Over – run}) \times \text{Number of cuts/mm}}{N}$$

$$= \frac{(287.5 + 3.125 + 3.125) \times 1.6}{172} = 2.73 \text{ min}$$

(*b*) Turning from 18.75 to 12.5 mm (2nd cut)

$$N = \frac{1000 \times 13.5}{\pi \times 18.75} = 229$$

$$T_2 = \frac{(87.5 + 3.125) \times 1.6}{229}$$

$$T_2 = 0.634 \text{ min}$$

$$\text{Total time} = 2.73 + 0.634 + 0.546 = 3.91 \text{ min.}$$

Example 5.63

A ms shaft is to be turned out of a 15 mm ϕ and 75 mm long ms bar as shown in figure. The following operations are to be done on the shaft:

(i) Facing 15 mm ϕ (both ends).

(ii) Turning to 12.5 mm ϕ.

(iii) Turning to 10 mm ϕ, a portion of the length 9.25 mm.

(iv) Chamfering on the 10 mm ϕ end 3 mm × 45°.

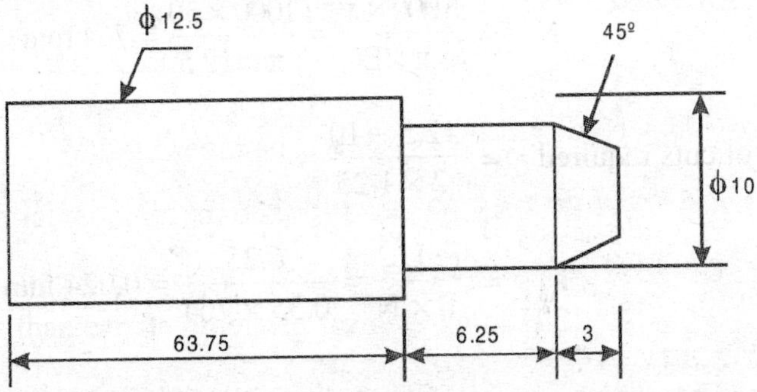

Fig. 5.56

Take, 'f' for facing 0.125 mm/rev;

'f' for turning 0.35 mm/rev

'f' for chamfering 0.25 mm/rev

Depth of cut = 1.25 mm

Solution

Total length of shaft = 63.75 + 6.25 + 3 = 73 mm

(i) Facing

$$D = 15 \text{ mm}, N = \frac{1000 \times V}{\pi \times D} = \frac{1000 \times 30}{\pi \times 15} = 640 \text{ rpm}$$

$$L = \frac{D}{2} + \text{Over} - \text{run} = \frac{15}{2} + 5 = 12.5 \text{ mm}$$

$$\text{No. of cuts required on each end face} = \frac{75 - 73}{2 \times 1.25} = 1$$

$$\text{Time for facing 2 ends} = \frac{L}{f \times N} \times 2$$

$$= \frac{12.5 \times 2}{.125 \times 640} = 0.3125 \text{ min}$$

(ii) Turning to 12.5 mm diameter from 15 mm

$$N = \frac{1000 \times V}{\pi \times D} = \frac{1000 \times 30}{\pi \times 15} = 640 \text{ rpm}$$

$$\text{Number of cuts required} = \frac{15 - 12.5}{2 \times 1.25} = 1$$

$$\therefore \quad T_m = \frac{L}{f \times N} = \frac{73}{0.35 \times 700} = 0.3 \text{ min}$$

(iii) Turning from 12.5 to 10 mm ϕ

$$N = \frac{1000 \times V}{\pi \times D} = \frac{1000 \times 30}{\pi \times 12.5} = 764 \text{ rpm}$$

$$\text{Number of cuts required} = \frac{12.5 - 10}{2 \times 1.25} = 1$$

$$T_m = \frac{L}{f \times N} = \frac{6.25}{0.35 \times 764} = 0.024 \text{ min}$$

(iv) Chamfering

$$\text{Length of work} = \frac{3}{\cos 45^\circ} = 4.24 \text{ mm}$$

$$N = \frac{100 \times 30}{\pi \times 10} = 960 \text{ rpm}$$

Maximum depth of cut in chamfering = $3 \sin 45^\circ = 2.121$ mm

$$\text{Number of cut} = \frac{2.121}{1.25} = 2$$

$$T_m = \frac{L}{f \times N} \times N$$

$$= \frac{4.24}{0.25 \times 960} \times 2 = 0.035 \text{ min}$$

$$\text{Total time} = 0.3125 + 0.3 + 0.024 + 0.035$$

$$= 0.6715 \text{ min}$$

Machining time calculations

Turning

Example 5.64

Determine the machining time to turn the dimensions given in figure. The material is brass, the cutting speed with H.S.S tool being 80 m/min and the feed is 0.8 mm.rev.

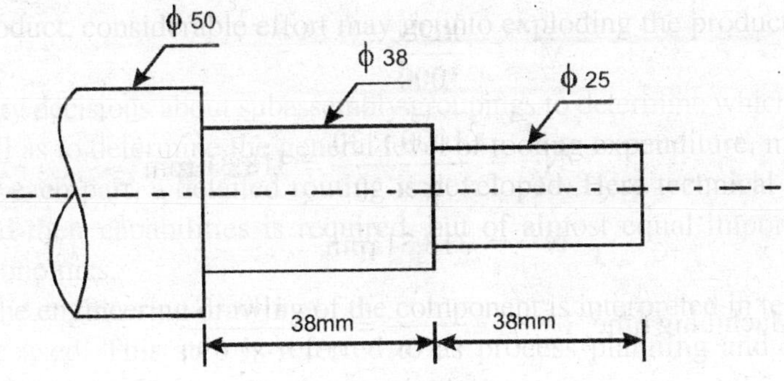

Fig. 5.57

Solution

(i) **First find the time to turn 38 mm diameter by 76 mm length of cut. Using the formula,**

$$V = \frac{\pi DN}{60}$$

$$80 = \frac{\pi \times 50 \times N}{1000}$$

$$N = 509.3 \text{ rpm}$$

$$T_{m_1} = \frac{L}{f \times N}$$

$$= \frac{76}{0.8 \times 509.3} = 0.187 \text{ min}$$

(ii) **Next to turn 25 mm diameter by 38 mm length**

$$V = \frac{\pi DN}{1000}$$

$$80 = \frac{\pi \times 38 \times N}{1000}$$

$$N = 670.13 \text{ rpm}$$

$$T_{m_2} = \frac{L}{f \times N} = \frac{38}{0.8 \times 670.13}$$

$$\boxed{T_{m_2} = 0.071 \text{ min}}$$

$$\text{Total time } T_m = 0.187 + 0.071$$

$$T_m = 0.258 \text{ min.}$$

Example 5.65

Estimate the machine time to turn a M.S. bar of 30 mm diameter down to 25 mm for a length of 100 mm in a single cut. Assume cutting speed as 30 m/min and feed as 0.4 mm/rev.

Solution

$$V = \frac{\pi DN}{1000}$$

$$N = \frac{1000 \times 30}{\pi \times 30} = 318.31 \text{ rpm}$$

$$N = 318.31 \text{ rpm}$$

$$\text{Machining time, } T_m = \frac{L}{f \times N} = \frac{100}{0.4 \times 318.31}$$

$$\boxed{T_m = 0.785 \text{ min}}$$

Example 5.66

The shaft shown in figure is to be manufactured by turning out of 85 mm steel rod. Find out the minimum time if the job is to be turned at 300 rpm with feed 0.5 mm/rev and depth of cut 3 mm.

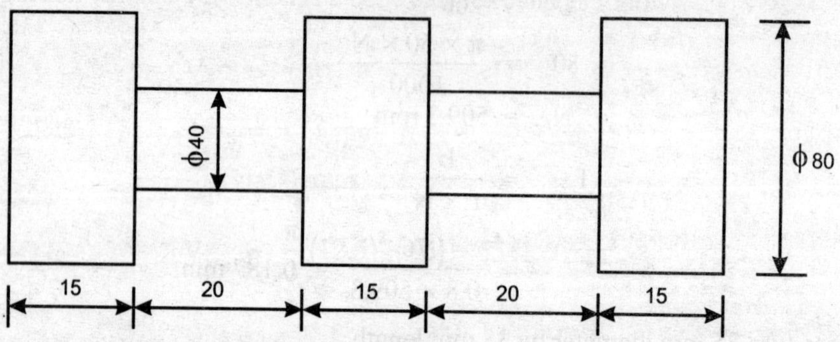

Fig. 5.58

Solution

The shaft is turned in stages from 85 mm φ to the required dimensions

$$\text{Machining time, } T_m = \frac{L}{f \times N}$$

Time for first cut to reduce from 85 to 80 mm

$$= \frac{85}{0.5 \times 300} = 0.567 \text{ min}$$

Now to reduce from 80 to 40 mm diameter with 3 mm cut,

$$\text{Number of cuts} = \frac{80 - 40}{2 \times 3} = 6.67 \text{ say 7 cuts}$$

$$\text{Time for 7 cuts} = 7 \times 2 \times \frac{20}{0.5 \times 300} = 1.867 \text{ min}$$

$$\text{Total time required for m/cing the shaft} = 0.567 + 1.867 = 2.434 \text{ min}$$

Example 5.67

Find the time required to face both ends of a component shown in figure in one cut. Assume speed of rotation of the job as 100 rpm and cross feed as 0.8 mm/rev.

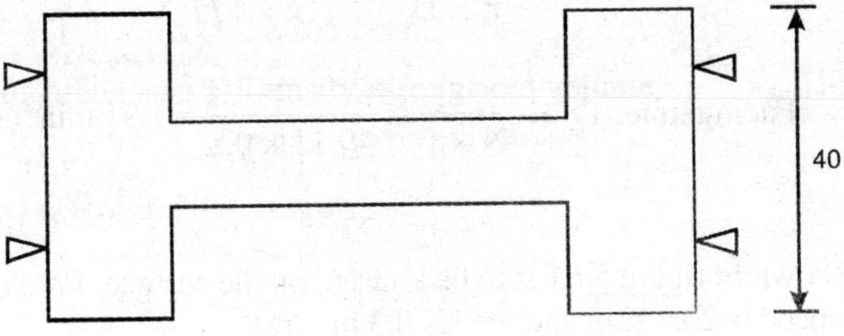

Fig. 5.59

Solution

$$\text{Time for facing} = \frac{L}{f \times N}$$

$$L = \frac{D}{2} = 20 \text{ min}$$

$$T_m = \frac{20}{0.3 \times 100}$$

$$T_m = 0.666 \text{ min}$$

$$\text{Time for facing both ends} = 2 \times 0.666 = 1.333 \text{ min.}$$

Example 5.68

Calculate the machining time to face on a lathe a C.I. flange shown in figure cutting speed and feed for the H.S.S. tool is 27 m/min and 0.8 mm/rev. respectively.

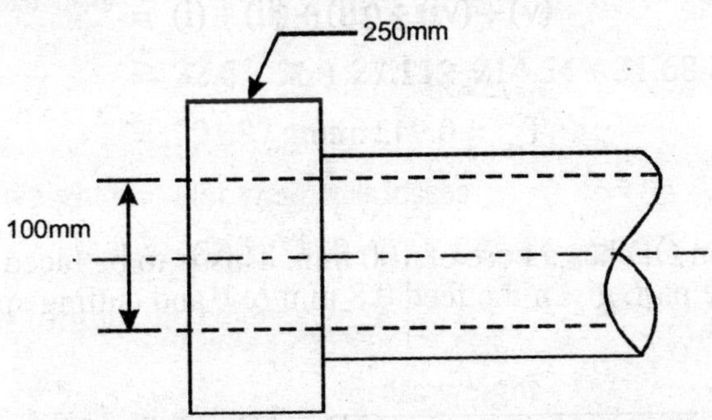

Fig. 5.60

Solution

$$\text{Length of cut, } L = \frac{250 - 100}{2} = 75 \text{ mm}$$

$$\text{Average diameter, } D_{avg} = \frac{250 + 100}{2} = 175 \text{ mm}$$

$$\text{Average rpm, } N = \frac{1000 \times V}{\pi \times D_{avg}} = \frac{1000 \times 27}{\pi \times 175} = 49.11 \text{ rpm}$$

$$\text{Facing time, } T_m = \frac{L}{N \times f} = \frac{75}{49.11 \times 0.8} = 1.91 \text{ min}.$$

Example 5.69

A component as shown in figure 5.61 is to be knurled on the surface. Find the time required for knurling it, if cutting speed is 20m/min and feed is 0.3 mm/rev.

Fig. 5.61

Solution

$$\text{RPM } N = \frac{1000 \times V}{\pi \times D} = \frac{1000 \times 20}{\pi \times 30} = 212.2 \text{ rpm}$$

$$T_m = \frac{L}{N \times f}$$

$$= \frac{60}{212.2 \times 0.3} = 0.942 \text{ min}$$

$$= 212.2 \times 0.3$$

$$T_m = 0.942 \text{ min.}$$

Example 5.70

A CI flange of 300 mm OD has a bore of 100 mm. This is to be faced on a lathe. Calculate the machining time to face the part, given the feed 0.8 mm/rev. and cutting speed of 80 m/min.

Solution

$$\text{Machining length } = L = \frac{\text{O.D} - \text{I.D}}{2} = \frac{300 - 100}{2} = 100 \text{ mm}$$

$$\text{Average work diameter, } D_{avg} = \frac{300 + 100}{2} = 200 \text{ mm}$$

$$V = \frac{\pi \times D_{avg} \times N}{1000}$$

$$30 = \frac{\pi \times 200 \times N}{1000}$$

$$= N = 47.75 \text{ rpm}$$

$$T_m = \frac{L}{N \times f} = \frac{100}{47.75 \times 0.8}$$

$$T_m = 2.62 \text{ minute.}$$

Example 5.71

Find the time required to drill 4 holes in a cast iron flange each of 2 cm depth, if the hole diameter is 2 cm. Assume cutting speed as 21.9 m/min. and feed as 0.02 cm/rev.

Solution

Depth of hole = 2 cm = 20 mm

Diameter of hole = 2 cm = 20 mm

Cutting speed = 21.9 m/min

Feed = 0.02 cm/rev, Depth hole $= l + 0.3\text{ d}$

Number of holes = 4 $= 2 + 0.3\ (2) = 2.6$

(i) $$N = \frac{1000\ V}{\pi \times D} = \frac{1000 \times 21.9}{3.14 \times 20} = 350 \text{ rpm}$$

(ii) $$T_m = \frac{\text{Depth of hole}}{\text{Feed} \times \text{rpm}} = \frac{2.6}{0.02 \times 350} = 0.3714 \text{ min}$$

(iii) Time for drilling four holes $= 0.3714 \times 4 = 1.486$ min.

Example 5.72

A 9 cm thick laminated plate consists of a 7 cm thick brass and a 2 cm thick mild steel plate. A 20 mm diameter hole is to be drilled through the plate. Estimate the total time taken for drilling if,

Cutting speed for brass = 44 m/min

Cutting speed for mild steel = 30 m/min

Feed of 20 mm drill for brass = 0.26 mm/rev

Depth of cut $= l + 0.3\text{ d} = 7 + 0.3\ (2) = 7.6$ cm

$= l + 0.3\text{ d} = 2 + 0.3\ (2) = 2.6$

Feed of 20 mm drill for mild steel = 0.25 mm/rev

Solution

(i) $$N = \frac{1000 \times V}{\pi \times D} = \frac{1000 \times 30}{\pi \times 2} = 477 \text{ rpm}$$

(ii) T_1 = Time taken to drill through brass plate

$$= \frac{\text{Depth of cut}}{\text{rpm} \times \text{Feed}} = \frac{7.6}{477 \times 0.026} = 0.612 \text{ min}$$

(iii) T_2 = Time taken to drill through ms plate

$$= \frac{2.6}{477 \times 0.025} = 0.218 \text{ min}$$

(iv) Total time taken for drill = $T_1 + T_2 = 0.83$ min.

Example 5.73

Calculate the drilling time for drilling screw holes in the flanges.

Details of flanges

Cutting of speed for drilling g = 22 m/min

Feed of drill = 0.2 mm/rev

Setting time = 8 min

Auxiliary time per hole 1 min

Delay time 12% of machining and auxiliary time.

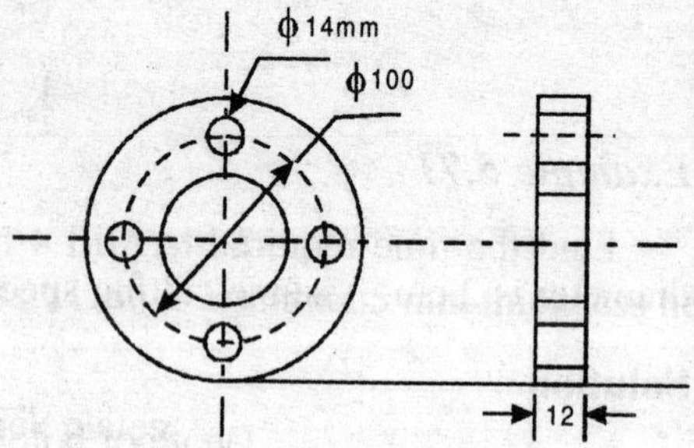

Fig. 5.62

Solution

(a) Machining time for drilling of hole

$$L = l + 0.3\,d = 12 + 0.3 \times 14 = 16.2 \text{ mm}$$

$$N = \frac{1000 \times V}{\pi \times D} = \frac{1000 \times 22}{\pi \times 14} = 500 \text{ rpm}$$

$$T_m = \frac{L}{f \times N} = \frac{16.2}{0.2 \times 500} = 0.162 \text{ min}$$

(b) Operation time for drilling of 24 holes

Machining time 0.162 min × 24 = 3.888 min

Auxiliary time 1 min × 24 = 24 min

27.888 min

Delay time

12% of machining and auxiliary = 3.35 min

Time i.e., (12% of 27.888) = 31.238 min

Setting time = 8 min

39.238 min

Drilling

Example 5.74

How long will it take a 12.7 mm to drill a hole 50 mm deep in brass? Take cutting speed as 75 m/min and feed as 0.175 mm/rev. Take A = 0.8 D for through hole.

Solution

$$N = \frac{1000 \times V}{\pi \times D} = \frac{1000 \times 75}{\pi \times 12.7} = 1880 \text{ rpm}$$

$$\text{Machining length, } L = A + t + A = t + 2A$$
$$= 50 + (2 \times 0.5 \times 12.7) = 62.7 \text{ mm}$$

$$\text{Drilling time} = \frac{L}{f \times N} = \frac{62.7}{0.175 \times 1880} = 0.191 \text{ min.}$$

Example 5.75

Find the time required to drill 6 holes in a casted flange of each of 10 mm depth, if the hole diameter is 15 mm. Assume cutting speed as 20 m/min and feed as 0.2 mm/rev.

Solution

$$\text{Length of drill travel } L = A + t + A = t + 2A$$
$$= 10 + (2 \times 0.5 \times 15) = 25 \text{ mm}$$

$$N = \frac{1000 \times V}{\pi \times D} = \frac{1000 \times 20}{\pi \times 15} = 425 \text{ rpm}$$

$$\text{Time for drilling 6 holes} = 6 \times \frac{L}{f \times N} = 6 \times \frac{25}{0.2 \times 425} = 1.76 \text{ min}$$

Example 5.76

Calculate the time required for drilling a component as shown in figure. Assume the cutting speed as 22 m/min and feed as 0.2 mm/rev.

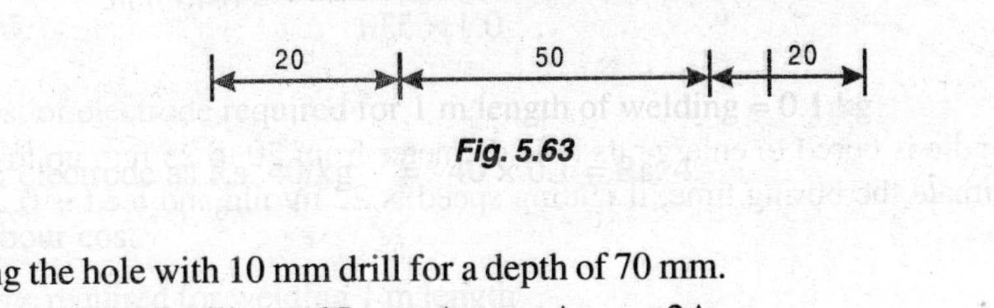

Fig. 5.63

Solution

1. Drilling the hole with 10 mm drill for a depth of 70 mm.

$$\text{Length of drill travel } L = A + t + A = t + 2A$$
$$\text{For blind hole } A = 0.29\,D$$
$$L = 70 + (2 \times 0.29 \times 10)$$
$$L = 15.8 \text{ mm}$$

$$N = \frac{1000 \times V}{\pi \times D_1} = \frac{1000 \times 22}{\pi \times 10} = 700 \text{ rpm}$$

$$T_{m_1} = \frac{L}{f \times N} = \frac{75.8}{0.2 \times 700} = 0.54 \text{ min}$$

Example 5.77

Drilling the hole with 20 mm drill up to 20 mm depth.

Solution

$$\text{Length of drill travel } L = t + 2A = 20 + (2 \times 0.29 \times 30) = 31.6 \text{ mm}$$

$$N = \frac{1000 \times V}{\pi \times D_2} = \frac{1000 \times 22}{\pi \times 20} = 350 \text{ rpm}$$

$$T_{m_2} = \frac{31.6}{0.2 \times 350} = 0.45 \text{ min}$$

$$\text{Total drilling time} = 0.54 \times 0.45 = 0.99 \text{ min.}$$

Example 5.78

A 15 mm hole is to be drilled in a C.I block with a feed of 0.4 mm/rev. The thickness of the block is 70 mm and tool, speed is 25 m/min. Determine (i) rpm, (ii) Machining time.

Solution

(a)
$$N = \frac{1000 \times V}{\pi \times D} = \frac{1000 \times 25}{\pi \times 15} = 530 \text{ rpm}$$

$$\text{Approach} = 0.5\,D = 0.15 \times 15 = 7.5 \text{ mm}$$

(b)
$$T_m = \frac{L}{f \times N} = \frac{2A + t}{f \times N}$$

$$= \frac{(2 \times 0.5 \times 15) + 40}{0.4 \times 530} = 0.40 \text{ min}$$

Example 5.79

A hollow spindle is bored to enlarge its hole diameter from 20 to 25 mm up to 100 mm depth in single cut. Estimate the boring time, if cutting speed is 22 m/min and feed is 0.2 mm/rev.

Solution

$$N = \frac{1000 \times V}{\pi \times D} = \frac{1000 \times 22}{\pi \times 20} = 350 \text{ rpm}$$

$$T_m = \frac{L}{f \times N} = \frac{100}{0.2 \times 350} = 1.43 \text{ min}$$

Milling

Example 5.80

Find the time required to face a job 20 cm long and 10 cm wide with the help of milling cutter of 10 f, having 8 teeth and revolving at 80 rpm. The feed per tooth should not exceed 0.125 mm. Assume that the width of cutter is sufficient to mill to whole of job at a time.

Solution

$$\text{Length} = \text{Length + Approach + Over travel}$$

$$= l + A + \frac{1}{2}\left(D - \sqrt{D^2 - b^2}\right)$$

$$= 200 + 20 + \frac{1}{2}\left(100 - \sqrt{100^2 - 100^2}\right) = 270 \text{ mm}$$

$$T_m = \frac{L}{f \times N \times T}$$

$$= \frac{270}{0.125 \times 8 \times 80} = 3.38 \text{ min.}$$

Example 5.81

A keyway has to be cut in spindle whose dimensions are 40 cm long 4 cm diameter with a 1 cm width. The cutter diameter is 10 cm. If the cutter is revolving at 120 rpm, what time will be required to cut one cm deep keyway at a feed of (i) 6 cm/min, (ii) 0.05 cm/rev of cutter?

Solution

$$\text{Table travel} = \sqrt{d(D-d)} + 0.5 = \sqrt{1(10-1)} + 0.5 = 3.5 \text{ cm}$$

$$\text{Total table movement} = 40 + 35 = 43.5 \text{ cm}$$

(i) Time required for cutting slot $= \dfrac{43.5}{6}$ min $= 7.25$ min

(ii) $$\text{Time required} = \frac{\text{Total table travel}}{N \times \text{Feed}}$$

$$= \frac{43.5}{120 \times .05} = 7.25 \text{ min.}$$

Example 5.82

What is the feed per tooth of a 32 tooth milling cutter of 37.5 cm diameter having a spindle speed of 75 rpm the table feed is 28.75 cm/min? Also find the time to face mill a C.I. Casting 1.2 m long and $26\frac{2}{3}$ cm wide.

Solution

$$\text{Table feed} = \text{Feed per tooth} \times \text{Number of teeth} \times N$$

$$\text{Feed/tooth} = \frac{\text{Table feed}}{\text{Number of teeth} \times N} = \frac{28.75}{32 \times 75} = 0.0119 \text{ cm}$$

$$\text{Added table travel for face milling} = \frac{1}{2}\left(D - \sqrt{D^2 - W^2}\right)$$

Where D = Diameter of cutter; W = Width of the job

$$\therefore \quad \text{Added table travel} = \frac{1}{3}\left(37.5 - \sqrt{(37.5^2 - 26.66^2)}\right)$$

$$= \frac{1}{2}\left(37.5 - \sqrt{1520 - 720}\right)$$

$$= \frac{1}{2}\left(37.5 - \sqrt{800}\right) = 4.6 \text{ cm}$$

$$\text{Total table travel} = 120 + 4.6 = 124.6 \text{ cm}$$

Taking 0.625 cm as over run at the finishing end

$$\text{Total travel of table} = 124.6 + 0.625 = 125.25 \text{ cm}$$

$$\text{Total time} = \frac{\text{Total length of cut}}{\text{Feed / tooth} \times \text{No. of teeth} \times N}$$

$$= \frac{125.25}{0.0195 \times 32 \times 75}$$

$$T_m = 2.74 \text{ min}$$

Example 5.83

A 3 cm deep slot is to be milled with a 8 cm diameter cutter. The length of the slot is 30 cm. What will be the total table travel to complete the cut? If the cutting speed is 20 m/min and feed per tooth is 0.2 mm, estimate the milling time. The cutter has 24 teeth and one cut is sufficient for the slot.

Solution

$$\text{Table travel} = \sqrt{d(D-d)} + 0.5 = \sqrt{3(8-3)} + 0.5$$

$$= \sqrt{15} + 0.5 = (3.873 + 0.5) = 4.373 \text{ cm}$$

$$\text{Total table travel} = 30 + 4.373 = 34.373 \text{ cm}$$

$$\text{Now feed/tooth} = 0.2 \text{ mm}$$

$$\text{Number of teeth} = 24$$

$$\therefore \quad \text{Feed/rev} = 0.2 \times 24 = 4.8 \text{ mm/rev}$$

$$V = 20 \text{ m/min}$$

$$N = \frac{1000 \times V}{\pi D} = \frac{1000 \times 20}{\pi \times 80} = 80 \text{ rpm } (D = 80 \text{ mm})$$

$$T_m = \frac{34.373}{\frac{4.8}{10} \times 80} = 0.8951 \text{ min}$$

Example 5.84

A 300 × 50 mm CI piece is to be face milled with a carbide cutter. The cutting speed and feed are 50 m/min and 50 mm/min. If the cutter dia is 80 mm and it has 12 cutting teeth, determine

(i) Cutter rpm

(ii) Feed/tooth

(iii) Milling time.

Solution

(i)

$$\text{Cutter rpm} = \frac{V \times 1000}{\pi \times D}$$

$$= \frac{50 \times 100}{\pi \times 80} = 200 \text{ rpm}$$

(ii)

$$\text{Feed/tooth} = \frac{\text{Feed/min}}{N \times \text{No. of teeth}} = \frac{50}{200 \times 12} = 0.02 \text{ mm/tooth}$$

(iii) For face milling

$$\text{Over travel} = \frac{1}{2}\left(D - \sqrt{D^2 - W^2}\right)$$

$$= \frac{1}{2}\left(80 - \sqrt{80^2 - 50^2}\right) = 8.8 \text{ mm}$$

$$\text{Total cutter travel} = 300 + 8.8 = 309 \text{ mm}$$

$$\text{Time for milling} = \frac{\text{Total cutter travel}}{\text{Feed/min}} = \frac{309}{50}$$

$$T_m = 6.18 \text{ min}$$

Example 5.85

A T-slot is to be cut in a C.I slab as shown in figure. Estimate the machining time. Take cutting speed 25 m/min feed us .25 mm/rev. Diameter of cutter for channel milling is 80 mm.

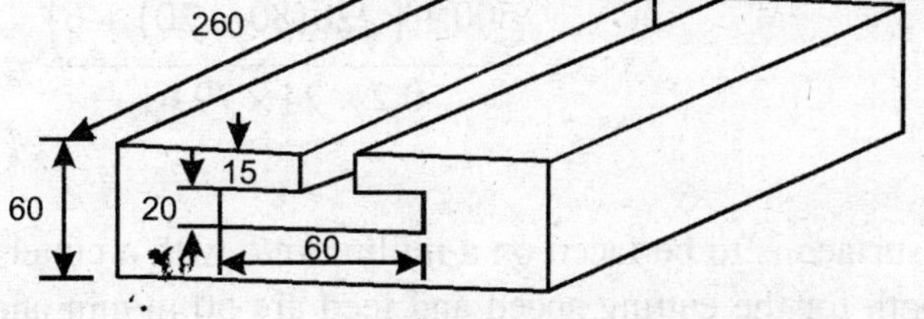

Fig. 5.64

Solution

Step 1

Cut a 20 mm wide and 35 mm deep channel along the length.

$$N = \frac{25 \times 1000}{\pi \times 80} = 100 \text{ rpm}$$

$$\text{Over travel} = \sqrt{Dd - d^2} = \sqrt{80 \times 35 - 35^2} = 40 \text{ mm}$$

$$\text{Total tool travel} = 260 + 40 = 300 \text{ mm}$$

$$\text{Time for cutting slot} = \frac{\text{Length of cut}}{\text{Feed/min}} = \frac{300}{0.25 \times 100} = 12 \text{ min}$$

Step 2

Cut T-slot of dimensions 60 × 20 with a T-slot cutter

$$N = \frac{25 \times 1000}{\pi \times 60} = 133 \text{ rpm}$$

$$\text{Over travel} = \frac{60}{2} = 30 \text{ mm}$$

$$\text{Total tool/table travel} = 260 + 30 = 290 \text{ mm}$$

$$\text{Time taken} = \frac{290}{0.25 \times 133} = 8.7 \text{ min}$$

$$\text{Total time to cut the T-slot} = 12 + 8.7 = 20.7 \text{ min.}$$

Example 5.86

A 20 mm deep slot is to be milled with a 80 mm cutter. The length of the slot is 50 cm. The cutter has 24 teeth and one cut is sufficient to cut the slot. If cutting speed is 20 m/min and feed/tooth 0.2 mm. Calculate the time review for milling the slot.

Solution

$$N = \frac{1000 \times V}{\pi \times D} = \frac{1000 \times 20}{\pi \times 80} = 79 \text{ rpm}$$

$$T = \frac{L + \sqrt{d(D-d)} + 6}{(f \times n) \times N}$$

$$= \frac{500 + \left(\sqrt{20(80-20)} + 6\right)}{0.2 \times 24 \times 79.61} = 1 = 1.414 \text{ min}.$$

Example 5.87

A 20 × 5 cm CI surface is to be faced on a milling m/c with a cutter having a diameter of 10 cm and having 16 tooth for the cutting speed and feed are 50 m/min and 5 cm/min respectively, determine the milling time, rpm, and feed/tooth.

Solution

$$N = \frac{1000 \times V}{\pi \times D} = \frac{1000 \times 50}{\pi \times 100} = 160 \text{ rpm}$$

$$\text{Feed/min} = f_t = n \times N = f_t \times 16 \times 160$$

$$\text{Feed/tooth } f_t = \frac{50}{16 \times 160} = 0.0196 \text{ mm}$$

$$\text{Milling time T} = \frac{L + \frac{1}{2}\left[D - \sqrt{D^2 - W^2}\right] + 7}{(f_t \times n) \times N}$$

$$= \frac{200 + \frac{1}{2}\left[100 - \sqrt{100^2 - 50^2}\right] + 7}{0.0196 \times 16 \times 160}$$

$$\boxed{T = 4.27 \text{ min}}$$

Example 5.88

A keyway has to be cut in a spindle whose dimensions are 500 mm/long, 50 mm diameter with a 10 mm width. The cutter diameter is 100 mm. If the cutter is revolving at 100 rpm. What time will be required to cut 8 mm deep keyway at a feed of 50 mm per min, 0.5 mm per rev. of cutter?

Solution

$$\text{Depth of cut d} = 8 \text{ mm}$$

$$\text{Cutter diameter D} = 100 \text{ mm}$$

$$\text{Here } d < d/2$$

$$\text{Added table travel} = 2\sqrt{D \times d - d^2} = 2\sqrt{100 \times 8 - 8^2}$$

$$\text{Total table travel} = 500 + 54.26 = 554.26 \text{ mm}$$

$$T_m = \frac{\text{Total table travel}}{\text{Feed / min}} = \frac{554.26}{50} = 11.09 \text{ min}$$

$$\text{Feed} = 0.5 \text{ mm/rev}$$

$$T_m = \frac{\text{Total table travel}}{\frac{\text{Feed}}{\text{rev}} \times \text{rpm}} = \frac{554.26}{0.5 \times 100} = 11.09 \text{ min}$$

Example 5.89

A 20 mm deep slot is to be milled with a 75 mm diameter cutter. The length of the slot is 400 mm. What will be the total travel to complete the cut? If the cutting speed is 20 rpm and feed/tooth is 0.2 mm, calculate the millling time. The cutter has 24 teeth and one cut is sufficient for the slot.

Solution

$$\text{Depth of cut d} = 20 \text{ mm}$$

$$\text{Cutter diameter D} = 75 \text{ mm. Here } d < \frac{D}{2}$$

$$\text{Total table travel} = \text{Length of job + Added – Table travel}$$

$$= 400 + 2\sqrt{D \times d - d^2}$$

$$= 400 + 2\sqrt{75 \times 20 - 400} = 466.33 \text{ mm}$$

$$N = \frac{1000 \times V}{\pi D} = \frac{1000 \times 20}{\pi \times 72} = 85 \text{ rpm}$$

$$T_m = \frac{\text{Total table travel}}{\frac{\text{Feed}}{\text{Tooth}} \times \text{No. of teeth} \times \text{rpm}}$$

$$= \frac{466.33}{0.2 \times 24 \times 85} = 1.14 \text{ min.}$$

Example 5.90

A slot 20 mm deep is to be cut through a work piece 30 mm long with the help of HSS side and face cutter whose diameter is 150 mm and that has 12 teeth. The cutting speed is 50 m/min and feed is 0.25 mm/tooth. Determine: (a) Table feed in mm/min, (b) Total cutter travel (c) Time required to m/c the slot.

Solution

(i) $$N = \frac{1000 \times V}{\pi \times D} = \frac{100 \times 50}{\pi \times 150} = 106 \text{ rpm}$$

(ii) $$\text{Table feed} = \frac{\text{Feed}}{\text{Tooth}} \times \text{No. of tooth} \times \text{rpm}$$

$$= 0.25 \times 12 \times 106 = 318 \text{ mm/min}$$

(iii) $$\text{Total cutter travel} = \text{Length of job + Added table travel}$$

$$= 300 + 2\sqrt{D \times d - d^2}$$

$$= 300 + 2\sqrt{150 \times 20 - 20^2} = 351 \text{ mm}$$

(iv) $$T_m = \frac{\text{Total table travel}}{\text{Feed/min}} = \frac{351}{318} = 1.1 \text{ min}$$

$$\boxed{T_m = 1.1 \text{ min}}$$

Example 5.91

A 50 mm diameter plain milling cutter having 8 teeth is used to face mill a stock of brass 200 mm long and 30 mm wide. The spindle speed is 1500 rpm and the feed is 0.125 mm/tooth/rev. Find cutting time.

Solution

$$\text{Cutter diameter D} = 50 \text{ mm; Width of job W} = 30 \text{ mm}$$

$$\text{Approach} = \frac{1}{2}\left[D - \sqrt{D^2 - W^2}\right]$$

$$= \frac{1}{2}\left[50 - \sqrt{50^2 - 30^2}\right] = 5 \text{ mm}$$

$$\text{Assume overrun} = 7 \text{ mm}$$

$$\therefore \quad \text{Total table} = 200 + 5 + 7 = 212 \text{ mm}$$

$$T_m = \frac{\text{Total table travel}}{\frac{\text{Feed}}{\text{Tooth}} \times \text{No. of teeth} \times \text{rpm}}$$

$$= \frac{212}{0.125 \times 8 \times 1500} = 0.141 \text{ min}$$

$$\boxed{T_m = 0.141 \text{ min}}$$

Example 5.92

Find the time required to shape a slot 300 mm long, 10 mm wide and 5 mm deep in a CI block. Given that cutting speed is 10 m/min, feed 1 mm/stroke and maximum depth of cut as 2.5 mm. Assume K = 0.25.

Solution

$$\text{Number of cuts required} = \frac{\text{Total depth of cut required}}{\text{Maximum depth per cut}} = \frac{5}{2.5} = 2$$

$$T_s = \frac{(L + 50)(B + 25)(1 + K)}{1000 \times V \times f}$$

$$= \frac{(300 + 50)(10 + 25)(1 + 0.25)}{1000 \times 10 \times 1} = 1.53 \text{ min}$$

$$\text{For 2 cuts } T_s = 1.53 \times 2 = 3.06 \text{ min}$$

Example 5.93

A CI rectangular block of 10 cm × 3.0 cm is required to be shaped to reduce its thickness from 1.8 to 1.3 cm in two cuts. Calculate the time required for shaping, if cutting speed is 20 m/min feed 0.2 mm/stroke and the cutting time 3/5 of total time.

Solution

$$\text{Number of cuts required} = 2 \text{ (given)}$$

$$T_s = \frac{(L + 50)(B + 25)(1 + K)}{1000 \times v \times f}$$

$$\text{Assume } K = 1/4 = 0.25$$

$$T_s = \frac{(100 + 50)(30 + 25)(1 + 0.25)}{1000 \times 20 \times 0.2} = 2.58 \text{ min}$$

$$\text{Time for 2 cuts} = 2 \times 2.58 = 5.156 \text{ min.}$$

Example 5.94

It is required to plane job on a shaping m/c. Length of job is 400 mm and width 150 mm. Find out the time required for shaping. Take V = 10 m/min, f = 1 mm.

Solution

$$\text{Assume } K = 0.25 \text{ mm}$$

$$T_s = \frac{(L + 50)(B + 25)(1 + K)}{1000 \times v \times f}$$

$$= \frac{(400 + 50)(150 + 25)(1 + 0.25)}{1000 \times 10 \times 1} = 9.8 \text{ min.}$$

Example 5.95

Find the time required on a shaper to a m/c a plate 600 × 1200 mm, if the cutting speed is 15 m/min. The ratio of return stroke time to cutting time is 2 : 3. The clearance at each end is 25 mm along the length and 15 mm on width. Find cuts are required, one roughing cut with cross feed of 2 mm per stroke and one finishing cut with feed of 1 mm/stroke.

Solution

$$\text{Length of stroke } L = \text{Length of plate + Clearance on both sides}$$

$$= 1200 + 2 \times 25 = 1250 \text{ mm}$$

$$\text{Cross travel of table} = \text{Width of job + Clearance}$$

$$= 600 + 2 \times 15 = 630 \text{ mm}$$

$$K = 2/3 = 0.67$$

$$\text{Time for one stroke} = \frac{L(1 + K)}{1000 \times V} = \frac{1250\,(1 + 0.67)}{1000 \times 15}$$

Number of strokes for roughing cut

$$= \frac{\text{Cross travel of table}}{\text{Feed/Stroke}}$$

$$= \frac{630}{1} = 630$$

$$\text{Total number of strokes requires} = 630 + 315 = 945$$

$$\text{Total m/c time} = 945 \times 0.139 \text{ min} = 131 \text{ min.}$$

Example 5.96

Calculate the time taken for shaping a CI blocking, long and 25 cm wide in a single cut. Feed is taken to be 0.8 mm/stroke and cutting speed 10 m/min.

Solution

$$\text{Assume } K = 0.25$$

$$T_m = \frac{(L+50)(B+25)(1+K)}{1000 \times v \times f}$$

$$= \frac{(400+50)(25+25)(1+0.25)}{1000 \times 10 \times 0.8} = 3.5 \text{ min.}$$

Example 5.97

Find the time required on the shaper to complete the cut on a plate 600 × 930 mm if the cutting speed is 6m/min. The return time to cutting time ratio is 1 : 4 and feed is 2 mm.

Solution

$$K = 1/4 = 0.25$$

$$T_m = \frac{(L+50)(B+25)(1+K)}{1000 \times 6 \times 2} = 63.8 \text{ min.}$$

Example 5.98

A planer has a cutting speed of 10 m/min and a return speed of 15 m/min. A casting 1 m long and 50 cm wide is to be machined and two cuts are required, one roughing with a depth of cut 5 mm and a feed of 1.25 mm, the other finishing with a depth of act of 1.25 mm, and a few of 0.375 mm. Estimate the planing time.

Solution

$$\text{Cutting speed} = 10 \text{ m/min}$$

$$\text{Return speed} = 15 \text{ m/min}$$

$$\text{Shaper ratio } K = \frac{10}{15} = \frac{2}{3} = 0.66$$

$$T_m = \frac{(L+250)(B+50)(1+0.66)}{1000 \times v \times f}$$

$$= \frac{(1000+250)(1500+50)(1+0.66)}{1000 \times 10 \times 0.375}$$

$$= 304.33 \text{ min.}$$

Example 5.99

Find the time required for planing a piece of ms 75 cm long and 30 cm wide on a planing m/c. The cutting speed of the tool is 12 rpm and feed is 0.0782 cm.

Solution

$$\text{Assume } K = 0.6$$

$$T_s = \frac{(L + 250)(B + 50)(1 + K)}{1000 \times v \times f}$$

$$= \frac{(750 + 250)(300 + 50)(1 + 0.6)}{1000 \times 12 \times 0.782} = 59.67 \text{ min.}$$

Example 5.100

On a planing machine the time taken on the cutting stroke on a job 3 m long is 12 sec. and the time taken on the return stroke is 4 sec. Calculate the time it will take to plane a surface 3 m long and 1.5 m wide if the feed is 6.23 mm/cutting stroke.

Solution

Time taken on the cutting stroke = 12 sec

Time taken on the return stroke = 4 sec

Total time = 12 + 4 = 16 sec

Width to be moved by the tool = Width of job + Tool clearance

= 150 + 5 = 155 cm

$$\text{Number of forward strokes} = \frac{155 \times 10}{6.25} = 248$$

$$\therefore \text{ Total time required} = 248 \times \frac{16}{60} = 66 \text{ min.}$$

Example 5.101

Estimate the planing time for a casting 1.25 m long and 1/2 wide which is machined on a planes having cutting speed of 12 m/min and a return speed of 30 m/min. Two cuts are required; one roughing with a depth of 3.125 mm and a feed of 0.1 mm per rev and other finishing with a depth of 0.125 mm, and using of few of 0.125 mm.

Solution

Length of stroke = Length of casting + Approach + Over run

= 1.25 + 0.05 + 0.025 = 1.325 m

Cross fed = Width of casting + Approach + Over runs

$= 0.5 + 0.00625 + 0.00625$

= 0.5125 m = 51.28 cm

$$\text{Time for one cutting stroke} = \frac{1.325}{12} = 0.1104 \text{ min}$$

$$\text{Time for returns stroke} = \frac{1.325}{30} = 0.0441 \text{ min}$$

$$\text{Time for one complete stroke} = 0.1104 + 0.0441 = 0.1545 \text{ min}$$

$$\text{Number of strokes (roughing)} = \frac{\text{Travel}}{\text{Feed}} = \frac{57.25}{\frac{0.1}{10}} = 5125$$

$$\text{Number of strokes (finishing)} = \frac{\text{travel}}{\text{Feed}} = \frac{51.25}{\frac{61.25}{10}} = 4100$$

$$\text{Cutting time for roughing} = 5125 \times 0.154 = 792 \text{ min}$$

$$\text{Cutting time for finishing} = 4100 \times 0.1545 = 633 \text{ min}$$

$$\text{Total cutting time} = 792 + 633 = 1425 \text{ min}$$

$$= \frac{1425}{60} = 23.75 \text{ hrs.}$$

Example 5.102

A work piece 144 × 68 cm requires one cut. The cutting speed is 1050 cm per min. and return speed in the ratio of 2:1. The feed is 1.5 mm/stroke. How long will the w/p take to get planed?

Solution

$$\text{Number of cutting strokes required} = \frac{\text{Width of job}}{\text{Feed/Stroke}} = \frac{68}{1.5/10} = 453$$

$$\text{Time taken in one stroke} = \frac{\text{Length of work}}{\text{Speed}}$$

$$= \frac{144}{1050} = 0.137 \text{ min}$$

$$\text{Cutting time} = 453 \times 0.137 = 62 \text{ min}$$

$$\text{Total time} = 62 + \frac{62}{2} = 93 \text{ min.}$$

Example 5.103

A CI part is to be planed in one cut on a planing machine. It takes 15 sec. in cutting stroke and 5 sec. in return stroke, calculate the time required to plane a width of 75 cm. Feed may be assumed as 1 mm/stroke.

Solution

$$\text{Total time for one complete stroke} = 15 + 5 = 20 \text{ sec}$$

$$\text{Distance to be covered by fool} = B + b$$
$$= 75 + 5 = 80 \text{ cm}$$

$$\text{Number of strokes needed} = \frac{\text{Distance covered}}{\text{Feed/Stroke}} = \frac{80}{0.1} = 800$$

$$\text{Time for one cut} = \text{Number of strokes} \times \text{Time for one stroke}$$

$$= 800 \times \frac{20}{60 \times 60} = 4.44 \text{ hrs.}$$

Shaping

Example 5.104

Find the time required on the shaper to complete one cut on a plate 600 × 900 mm, if the cutting speed is 6 m/min. The return time to cutting time ratio is 1 : 4 and the feed is 2 mm/stroke. The clearance at each end is 25 mm.

$$T_m = \frac{(L + 50)(B + 25)(1 + K)}{1000 \times v \times f}$$

$$K = \frac{\text{Return time}}{\text{Cutting time}} = \frac{1}{4} = 0.25$$

$$T_m = \frac{(900 + 50)(600 + 25)(1 + 0.25)}{1000 \times 6 \times 2}$$

$$\boxed{T_m = 61.85 \text{ min}}$$

Example 5.105

Calculate the time taken for shaping a CI block 500 mm long and 300 mm wide in a single cut. Feed is taken to be 1 mm/stroke and cutting speed is 10 m/min.

Solution

Since K is not given, assume $K = 0.6$

$$T_m = \frac{(L + 50)(B + 25)(1 + K)}{1000 \times v \times f}$$

$$= \frac{(500 + 50)(300 + 25)(1 + 0.6)}{1000 \times 10 \times 0.1}$$

$$T_m = 28.6 \text{ min}$$

Example 5.106

A CI block of size 300 mm × 100 mm is required to be shaped to reduce the thickness from 20 mm to 18 mm in one cut. Determine the time required for shaping. If cutting speed is 20 m/min and feed is 0.2 mm/stroke and the cutting time ratio is 3/5.

Solution

$$K = 3/5 = 0.6$$

$$T_m = \frac{(L + 50)(B + 25)(1 + K)}{1000 \times v \times f}$$

$$= \frac{(300 + 50)(100 + 25)(1 + 0.6)}{1000 \times 20 \times 0.2}$$

$$\boxed{T_m = 17.5 \text{ min}}$$

Example 5.107

Find out the time required for shaping a block of 350 × 150 mm size in two cuts. Assume feed as 0.6 mm/stroke and cutting speed as 15 mpm.

Solution

$$\text{Assume } K = 0.6$$

$$T_m = \frac{(L + 50)(B + 25)(1 + K)}{1000 \times v \times f}$$

$$= \frac{(350 + 50)(150 + 25)(1 + 0.6)}{1000 \times 15 \times 0.6}$$

$$\boxed{T_m = 12.4 \text{ min}}$$

Example 5.108

Calculate the time taken for shaping a CI block 400 mm long and 250 mm wide in a single cut. Feed is to be taken to be 0.8 mm/stroke and cutting speed is 10 mpm.

Solution

$$\text{Assume } K = 0.6$$

$$T_m = \frac{(L + 50)(B + 25)(1 + K)}{1000 \times v \times f}$$

$$= \frac{(400 + 50)(250 + 25)(1 + 0.6)}{1000 \times 10 \times 0.6}$$

$$\boxed{T_m = 24.75 \text{ min}}$$

Planing

Example 5.109

Find the time required for planing a piece of m.s. 900 mm long and 500 mm wide on a planing machine. The cutting speed of the tool is 20 mpm and feed 0.8 mm/stroke.

Solution

$$\text{Assume } K = 0.75$$

$$T_m = \frac{(L + 250)(B + 25)(1 + K)}{1000 \times v \times f}$$

$$= \frac{(900 + 250)(500 + 50)(1 + 0.75)}{1000 \times 20 \times 0.8}$$

$$\boxed{T_m = 69.18 \text{ min}}$$

Example 5.110

On a planing machine, the time taken on cutting stroke for a job 3 m long is 15 sec and the time taken for U turn is 5 sec. Calculate the time to plane a surface 3 m × 1.5 m if feed is 6 mm/stroke.

Solution

$$\text{Cutting stroke time} = 15 \text{ sec}$$

$$\text{Return stroke time} = 5 \text{ sec}$$

$$\text{Time for one cycle} = 20 \text{ sec}$$

$$= 20/60 \text{ min}$$

$$\text{Width of work B} = 1500 \text{ mm}$$

$$\text{Tool travel length } (B + 25) = 1500 + 25 = 1525 \text{ mm}$$

$$\text{Feed} = 6 \text{ mm/stroke}$$

$$\text{Number of cutting stroke} = \frac{1525}{6}$$

$$\text{Total machining time, } T_m = \frac{1525}{6} \times \frac{20}{60} = 84.78 \text{ min.}$$

Example 5.111

Find the time required for planing a piece of ms 750 mm long and 300 mm wide on a planing machine. The cutting speed of the tool is 12 mpm and feed 0.8 mm.

Solution

$$\text{Assume } K = 0.7$$

$$T_m = \frac{(L + 250)(B + 25)(1 + K)}{1000 \times v \times f}$$

$$= \frac{(750 + 250)(300 + 50)(1 + 0.7)}{1000 \times 12 \times 0.8} = 61.98 \text{ min.}$$

Example 5.112

On a planing machine the time taken in cutting stroke for a job 4 m long in 15 sec and the time taken on return stroke is 5 sec. Calculate the time it will taken to plane a surface 4 m long and 2.5 m wide, if feed is 6 mm/cutting stroke.

Solution

$$\text{Cutting stroke time} = 15 \text{ sec}$$

$$\text{Return stroke time} = 5 \text{ sec}$$

$$\text{Time for one cycle} = 20 \text{ sec}$$

$$= \frac{20}{60} \text{ min}$$

$$\text{Width of work B} = 2500 \text{ mm}$$

$$\text{Tool travel length (B + 25)} = 2500 + 25$$

$$\text{Feed} = 6 \text{ mm/stroke}$$

$$\text{Number of cutting stroke} = \frac{2525}{6}$$

$$\text{Total machinery time } T_m = \frac{2525}{6} \times \frac{20}{60}$$

$$= 140.27 \text{ min.}$$

Example 5.113

A shaft of st 42, ϕ 40, 400 mm long is to be grounded. It is supplied with a grinding size of ϕ 40.3. Calculate the machining time where grinding wheel is 40 mm wide, feed per cycle 20 mm. No. of cuts = 15.

Solution

(i) $$N = \frac{1000 \times V}{\pi \times d} = \frac{1000 \times 12}{\pi \times 40} = 95 \text{ rpm}$$

(ii) Number of cuts = 15

(iii) $$T_m = \frac{2 \times L \times i}{f \times N} = \frac{2 \times 400 \times 15}{95 \times 20} = 6.31 \text{ min.}$$

Example 5.114

Find the time required for doing rough grinding of a 16 cm sling step 1 shaft to reduce its diameter from 4.2 to 4 cm in a grinding wheel of 2 cm face width. Assume cutting speed as 16.5 m/min and depth of cut as 0.25 mm.

Solution

$$\text{total stock to be removed} = \frac{4.2 - 4}{2} = 0.1 \text{ cm}$$

but depth of cut is 0.025 cm

$$\therefore \quad \text{Number of cuts required} = \frac{0.1}{0.025} = 4$$

$$\text{Time/cut} = \frac{L}{f \times N}$$

$$\text{Feed f} = W/2 = 2/2 = 1 \text{ cm}$$

$$N = \frac{1000 \times S}{\pi \times D} = \frac{1000 \times 16.5}{\pi \times 42} = 125 \text{ rpm}$$

$$L = l + 0.5 = 16 + 0.5 = 16.5 \text{ cm}$$

$$T_m = \frac{16.5}{1 \times 125}$$

$$\text{Total time for 4 cuts} = \frac{16.5}{1 \times 125} \times 4 = 0.528 \text{ min.}$$

Example 5.115

The top of a CI table of size 40 × 90 cm is to be grounded by a wheel having 2 cm face width. If the feed is ¼th of the width of the wheel, and the table moves 9 m is one minute, find out the time required for grinding in two cuts.

Solution

$$\text{Time required/stroke} = \frac{\text{Length of table}}{\text{Speed of table}} = \frac{90}{9 \times 100} = \frac{1}{10} \text{ min}$$

$$\text{Feed} = 0.5 \text{ cm}$$

$$\text{Number of strokes required} = \frac{\text{Width of table}}{\text{Feed}}$$

$$= \frac{40}{0.5} = 80$$

$$\text{Time required/cut} = \text{Time/stroke} \times \text{Number of strokes}$$

$$= \frac{1}{10} \times 8 = 8 \text{ min}$$

$$\therefore \quad \text{total time required for 2 cuts} = 2 \times 8 = 16 \text{ min.}$$

REVIEW QUESTIONS

1. From the following data, calculate the

   (a) Total cost.

   (b) Selling price for an electric motor.

Material cost of motor = Rs.6000

Manufacturing wages = Rs.4000

Factory overhead, to the manufacturing

Wages = 100%

Non manufacturing overheads = 15%

Profit on the total cost = 13%

2. From the records of an oil milk, the following data are available.

(*a*) Raw material:

Opening stock = Rs.1, 60,000

Closing stock = Rs.1,10,000

Total purchase during the year = Rs.2,10,1000

(*b*) Finishing good:

Opening stock = Rs.25,000

Closing stock = Rs.35,000

Sales = Rs.7,00,000

(*c*) Direct wages = Rs.1,10,000

(*d*) Factory expenses = Rs.1,20,000

(*e*) Non-manufacturing expenses = Rs.95,000

Find out what price should be quoted for product involving an expenditure of Rs.40,000 in material and Rs.50,000 wages. Factory expenses to labour cost is 100%.

3. Estimate the weight and lost of the mild steel casting shown in figure 1. Assume density of steel as 7.85 gm/cm^3 and the steel cost as per Rs.11/ kg.

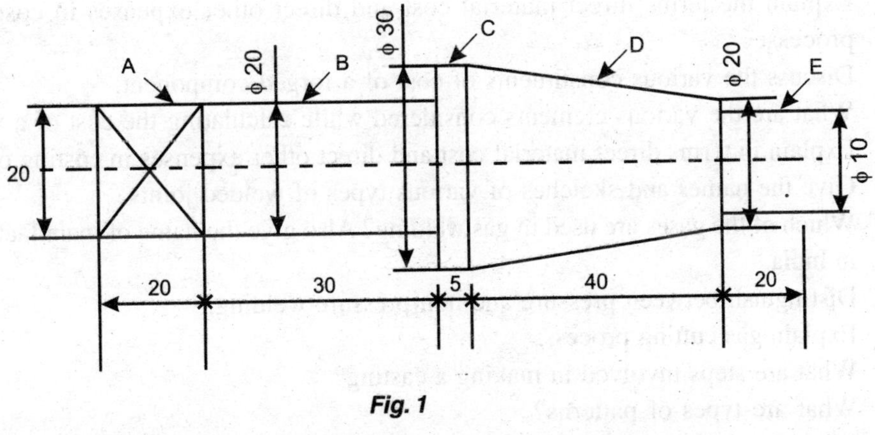

Fig. 1

4. Find the volume, weight and cost of material require for making a mild steel shaft figure 2. Assume that mild steel costs Rs.12/kg.

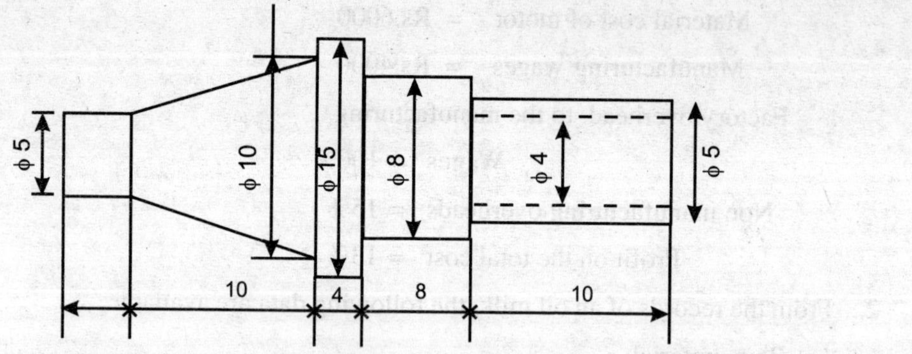

Fig. 2

5. Figure 3 shows a level gear blank made up of mild steel. Find the weight and cost of material required for it. Assume the density as 7.85 gm/cm^3 and its cost as Rs.12/kg.

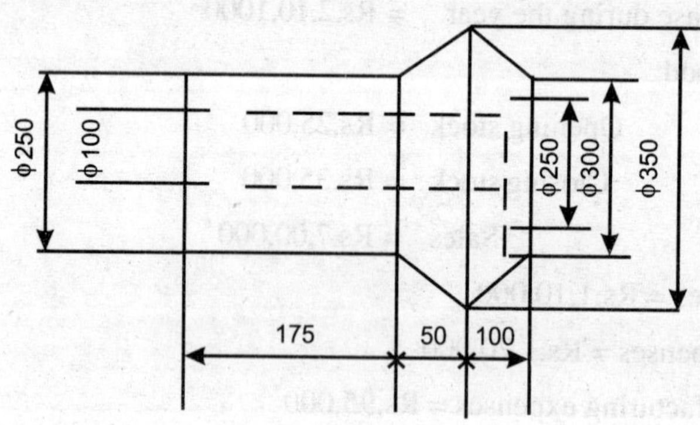

Fig. 3

6. Explain briefly forging processes.
7. What are the losses in forging shop?
8. What are the elements while calculating the cost of a forging processes?
9. Explain the terms direct material cost and direct other expenses in costing of forging processes.
10. Discuss the various constituents of cost of a forged component.
11. What are the various elements considered while calculating the cost of a welded joints?
12. Explain in terms direct material cost and direct other expenses in costing of welded joint.
13. Give the names and sketches of various types of welded joints.
14. Which of the gases are used in gas welding? Also give the name of manufacturing concerns in India.
15. Distinguish between pressure and non-pressure welding.
16. Explain gas cutting process.
17. What are steps involved in making a casting?
18. What are types of patterns?
19. What are pattern materials used in casting processes?
20. Write short notes on the following:

(*i*) Pattern allowance.
(*ii*) Shrinkage allowance.
(*iii*) Draft allowance.
(*iv*) Distortion allowance.
(*v*) Shake or rapping allowance.

21. What are the various losses considered while calculating for a casting?

22. Find the cost of drop forging a shaft figure from 20 mm diameter bar. The material cost is Rs.10.00 per metre, cost of forging Rs.1200 per square metre of surface area to be forged and overhead expenses 10% of the forging cost. Take scale loss 6%, shear loss 5%, sprue loss 7% and other losses as usual figure (4).

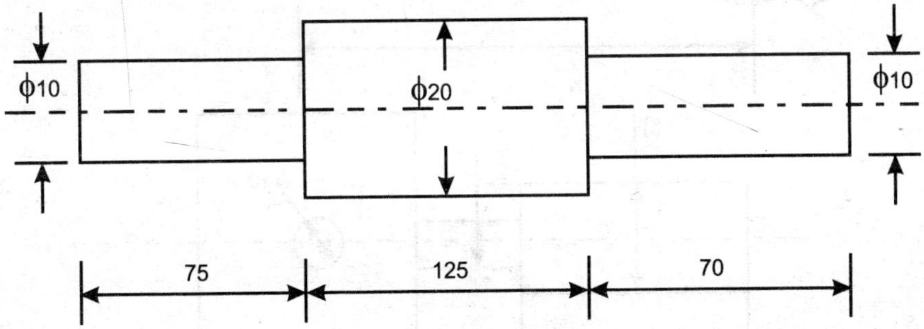

Fig. 4

(**Ans.** Volume of forging 50.98 cm^3. Total losses 50.2 cm^3. Cost of material Rs.3.17).

23. Estimate the length of 20 mm diameter rod to be used for making a key of given dimensions as in figure. Take scale loss as 5% of the total volume figure (5).

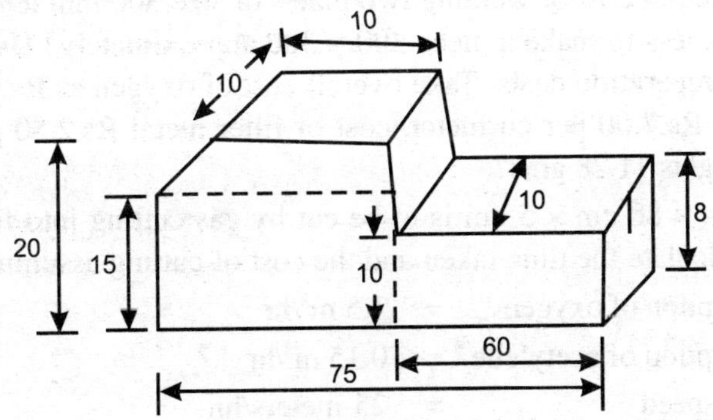

Fig. 5

24. Estimate the cost of manufacturing high carbon steel spanner (figure 6) to be made by die forging.

(*i*) Batch size	:	Rs.500 pieces
(*ii*) Die cost per batch	:	Rs.300
(*iii*) Stock cutting charges	:	Rs.5 per batch
(*iv*) Set-up and machine operation cost	:	Rs.75 per batch

(v) Labour charges : Rs.30 per batch

(vi) Density of steel : Rs.8.5 gm/cc

(vii) Cost of high carbon steel : Rs.10 per kg

Assume suitable allowances for calculating the weight of the component.

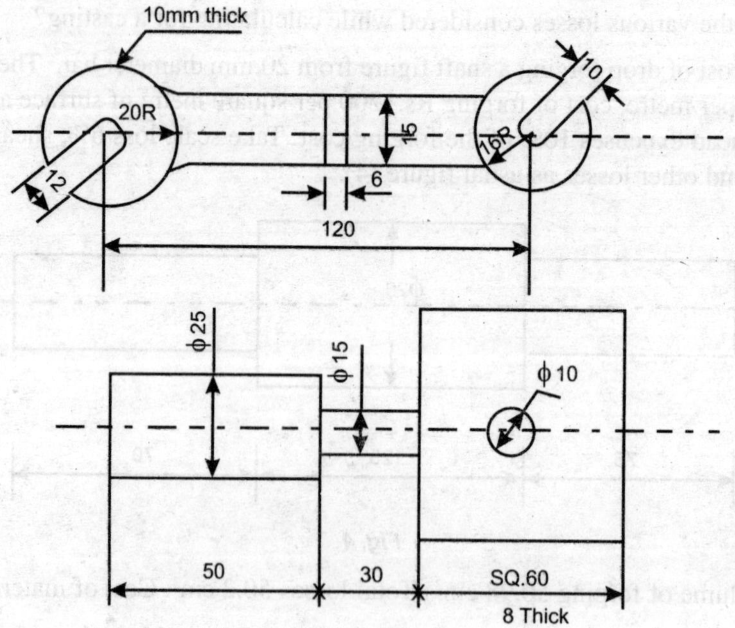

Fig. 6

25. What is the material cost of welding two plates of size 300 mm length and 150 mm width and 8 mm thickness to make a piece 300 × 300 approximately? Use right ward technique with no edge preparation costs. Take overall cost of oxygen as Rs.0.70 per cu meter, cost of acetylene at Rs.7.00 per cu meter, cost of filler metal Rs.2.50 per kg and 1 cu-cm of filler metal weights 11.28 gms?

26. A plate 100 cm × 80 cm × 5 cm is to be cut by gas cutting into four pieces 50 cm × 40 cm × 5 cm. Calculate the time taken and the cost of cutting assuming following data.

(i) Consumption of oxygen = 1.5 m³/hr

(ii) Consumption of acetylene = 0.15 m³/hr

(iii) Cutting speed = 25 meters/hr.

27. Estimate the total cost of 20 cast iron flanged pipe castings as in figure. Assume the following data:

Cost of CI = 70 paise/kg

Cost of scrap = 25 paise/kg

Process scrap = 2% of net weight of casting

Moulding and pouring charges = Rs.1.00/piece

Casting removal and cleaning charges = Rs.0.20/piecc

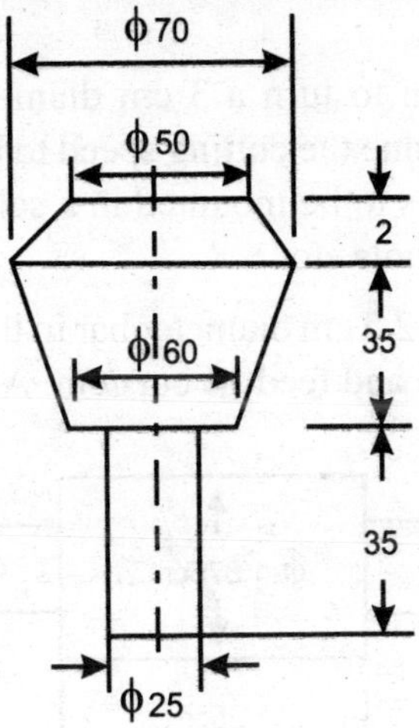

Fig. 7

28. The figure shows a finished gear blank. 2 mm machining allowance in the pattern is to be added on each side. Find selling price with the help of following data:
    Cost of CI = Rs.5/kg
    Melting charges = 15% of material cost
    Administrative overheads = 15% of material cost
    Profit = 20% of total cost
    Moulding charges = Rs.2 each mould.

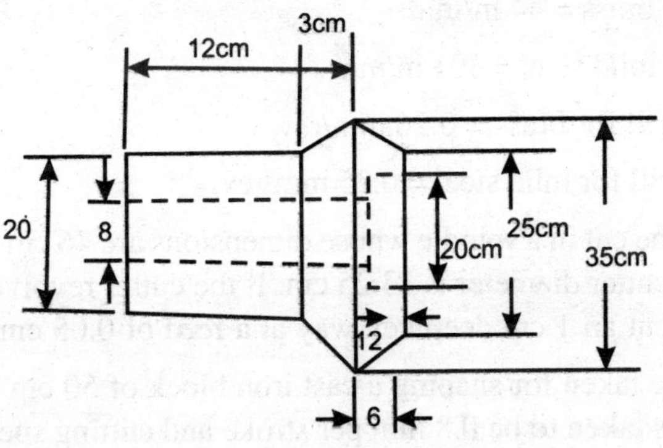

Fig. 8

29. What do you understand by the following terms:
    (*a*) rpm.
    (*b*) Feed.
    (*c*) Length of cut.
30. Write short notes on
    (*a*) Set-up time.
    (*b*) Operation time.
    (*c*) Tear down time.

31. Define cutting speed.

32. Estimate the total time taken to turn a 3 cm diameter ms stock 15 cm long to 2.8 cm diameter in a single cut. Assume the cutting speed to be 20 m per minute and the feed to be 0.2 mm/revolution. The job is to be mounted in a self centering S jaw chuck. Neglect the time taken for setting up of tools etc.

33. Find the time required to turn 2.5 cm diameter bar to the dimensions shown in figure cutting speed shall be 13.5 m/minute and feed 16 cuts/cm. All cuts shall be 3.125 mm deep.

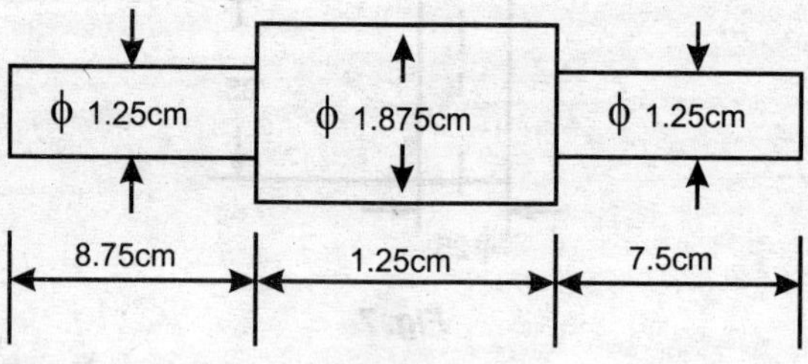

Fig. 9

34. Find the time required to drill 4 holes in a CI flange each of 2 cm depth. If the hole diameter is 2 cm. Assume cutting speed as 21.9 m/min. and feed as 0.02 cm/rev.

35. A 9 cm thick laminated plate consists of a 7 cm thick brass and a 2 cm thick mild steel plate. A 20 mm diameter hole is to be drilled through the plate. Estimate the total time taken for drilling if

    Cutting speed for brass = 44 m/min

    Cutting speed for mild steel = 301 m/min

    Feed of 20 mm drill for brass = 0.26 mm/rev

    Feed of 20 mm drill for mild steel = 0.25 mm/rev.

36. A keyway has to be cut in a spindle whose dimensions are 46 cm length, 5 cm diameter and 1 cm width. The cutter diameter is 13.25 cm. If the cutter revolves at 120 rpm. What is the time required to cut an 1 cm deep key way at a feed of 0.05 cm/rev of cutter?

37. Calculate the time taken for shaping a cast iron block of 50 cm long and 30 cm wide in a single cut. Feed is taken to be 0.8 mm per stroke and cutting speed 11 m/mm.

38. Find the time required for planing a piece of mild steel 75 cm long and 30 cm wide on a planing machine. The cutting speed of the tool is 12 m/min and feed 0.0782 cm/stroke.

39. Find the time required for doing rough grinding of a 16 cm long steel shaft to reduce its diameter from 4.2 to 4 cm in a grinding wheel of 2 cm face width. Assume cutting speed as 16.5 m/min and depth of cut as 0.25 mm.

INDEX

A

B

C

D

E